AIKIDO
AND THE
DYNAMIC SPHERE

An Illustrated Introduction

by A. Westbrook and O. Ratti

Illustrations by O. Ratti

TUTTLE PUBLISHING
Boston • Rutland, Vermont • Tokyo

Published by Tuttle Publishing, an imprint of Periplus Editions (HK) Ltd., with editorial offices at 153 Milk Street, Boston, Massachusetts 02109.

Copyright © 1970 Charles E. Tuttle Publishing Co., Inc.

Library of Congress Catalog Card Number: 69-16181

ISBN: 0-8048-0004-9 (hardcover)
ISBN: 0-8048-3284-6 (paperback)

Distributed by:

North America
Tuttle Publishing
Distribution Center
Airport Industrial Park
364 Innovation Drive
North Clarendon, VT 05759-9436
Tel: (802) 773-8930
Fax: (802) 773-6993
Email: info@tuttlepublishing.com
Web site: www.tuttlepublishing.com

Japan
Tuttle Publishing
Yaekari Building, 3rd Floor
5-4-12 Ōsaki, Shinagawa-ku, Tokyo
Japan 141-0032
Tel: (03) 5437-0171
Fax: (03) 5437-0755
Email: tuttle-sales@gol.com

Asia Pacific
Berkeley Books Pte Ltd
130 Joo Seng Road
#06-01/03 Olivine Building
Singapore 368357
Tel: (65) 6280-3320
Fax: (65) 6280-6290
Email: inquiries@periplus.com.sg

Indonesia
PT Java Books Indonesia
Jl. Kelapa Gading Kirana
Blok A14 No. 17
Jakarta 14240 Indonesia
Email: cs@javabooks.co.id

First published 1970
First paperback edition 2001
Fiftieth printing, 2004 (hardcover)
Eighth printing, 2005 (paperback)

Printed in the United States of America

To Master Morihei Uyeshiba
who did not believe his
aikido was for any particular
individual, elite or nation
—but for the whole human family.

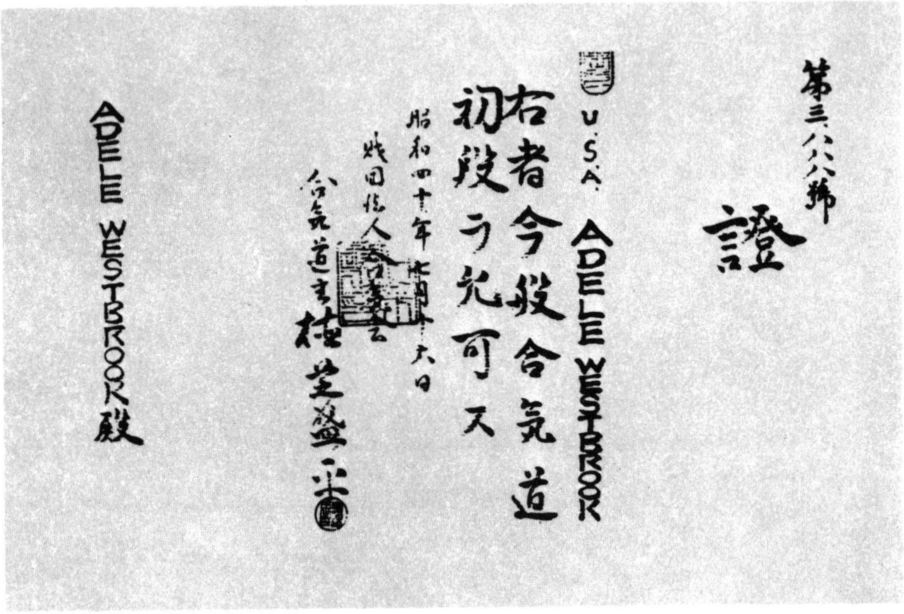
第三八八八號

證

U.S.A. ADELE WESTBROOK

右者今般合気道
初段ヲ允可ス

昭和四十年七月廿六日

財団法人合気会

合気道主 植芝盛平

ADELE WESTBROOK殿

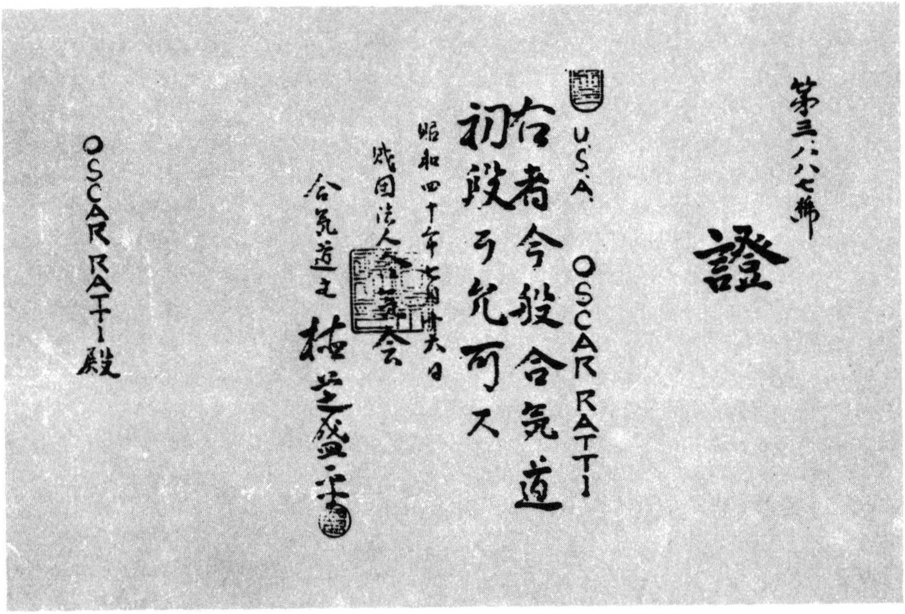
第三八八七號

證

U.S.A. OSCAR RATTI

右者今般合気道
初段ヲ允可ス

昭和四十年七月廿六日

財団法人合気会

合気道主 植芝盛平

OSCAR RATTI殿

Table of Contents

ACKNOWLEDGMENTS 9

PREFACE 11

LIST OF CHARTS 13

I **WHAT IS AIKIDO?** 17
Defense in Aikido · The "Centre" and "Ki" · The Strategy of Neutralization · The Potential of Aikido

II **THE FOUNDATIONS OF AIKIDO** 29
The Founder · Main Sources of Formation and Inspiration · The Martial Arts · The "Ethics" of Defense

III **ORGANIZATION** 35
The Hierarchy · Promotion · The Uniform · The Practice Hall · The Mat · Etiquette and Classes

IV **THE PRACTICE OF AIKIDO** 45
The Theory of Attack · Physical Factors · Dynamic Factors · Technical Factors · The Unified Power of Attack

V **THE THEORY OF DEFENSE** 61
The Process of Defense and Its Factors · The Inner Factors: the Role of the Mind · The Principle of Centralization · The Principle of Extension · The Principle of Leading Control · The Principle of Sphericity · Circuits of Neutralization · Spirals and Semi-Spirals of Neutralization · The Dynamic Sphere · Fusion and Special Exercises

VI **THE PHYSICAL PREPARATION** 113
Preliminary Exercises: Suppleness · Basic Exercises: Coordination · Rolls and Somersaults

VII **THE POSTURE AND MOTION OF DEFENSE** 143
Stages and Unity of the Aikido Process of Defense · The Posture · The Motion

VIII **THE BASIC TECHNIQUES OF NEUTRALIZATION** 159
General Recommendations · Immobilizations · Projections · Combinations

IX **ADVANCED PRACTICE** 323
"Mat" or Kneeling Aikido · The Stave Exercises · The Techniques of Neutralization Applied Against an Armed Attack · The Techniques of Neutralization Applied Against a Multiple Attack · Free Style

X **CONCLUSION** 359

GLOSSARY 365

SELECTED BIBLIOGRAPHY 371

INDEX 373

Acknowledgments

THE SOURCES of direct and indirect assistance to the authors in the process of collecting the material for *Aikido and the Dynamic Sphere* are too many to be acknowledged individually here. In the former category, for example, are all those instructors and advanced students of the art, scattered throughout the world, under whose personal guidance the authors explored the practical dimensions of this Discipline of Coordination, or with whom they practiced and corresponded for years. In particular, however, they wish to express their personal gratitude to Yasuo Ohara, who introduced them to aikido for the first time in New York in 1962; to Edi Hagihara, Barry Bernstein, and Virginia Mayhew, who helped them overcome many difficulties during their "apprenticeship" period; to Walter N. Dobson, Motokage Kawamukai, and Yoshimitsu Yamada, who clarified many problems of technical application and style; to Koichi Tohei, chief instructor at Hombu Dojo in Tokyo who—in April, 1965—conferred upon them the rank of black belt, 1st degree; and to Kisshomaru Uyeshiba, son of the founder of aikido, who instructed them during his brief visit to New York in 1966.

The authors are not listing individually, by name and rank—but do remain deeply indebted to—all those other instructors and advanced students in the United States (from the East Coast to the West Coast, and Hawaii), in Japan, France, Italy, and Belgium who illustrated and explained their particular methods and technical interpretations of aikido, either personally or in lengthy correspondence.

Styles of performance are as many and as unique as the individuals who practice an art—aikido being no exception. Each and every one to which the authors were exposed offered them an opportunity to view various aspects of the practice in a new light and to re-examine their own basic premises.

The sources of indirect assistance, invaluable moral support and encouragement include in particular Dr. Elizabeth Richards and Mr. Charles G. Partington; Edward M. Kinney, Edward O'Brien, Anthony Foddai, and Edvi Illes Gedeon.

Finally, the authors wish to express their heartfelt gratitude to all those aikido practitioners with whom they were privileged to practice in the United States, France, and Italy, and to those students at all levels of development who willingly cooperated in the testing and refining of the authors' theories on the *tatami* in *dojo* all over the world.

Last, but certainly not least, we wish to express our appreciation to the members of the Editorial and Design departments of the Charles E. Tuttle Company for their patient and painstaking efforts on behalf of *Aikido and the Dynamic Sphere.*

Preface

IN ORDER to be consistent and have any significance whatsoever, a book—any book—must have a purpose and a system for achieving that purpose. The primary purpose of *Aikido and the Dynamic Sphere* is to widen and deepen knowledge of this Discipline of Coordination. In the authors' estimation, the art of aikido contains valuable directives for helping man in his struggle against the age-old predicament represented by that dispersive (and dispersed) condition of physio-functional and psychological lack of coordination which can undermine the very foundation of his character, personality, and—eventually—his entire well-being. This art also contains an ethical message, a reason why, as well as a means of harmonizing that character and that personality in the sphere of superior development and of coordinating it with the everyday conduct of man—in his individual niche, in his society, in his world.

Such a purpose, however, because of its very depth and extension, is extremely difficult (if not impossible) to achieve in a single book. Aikido, in fact, rests upon cultural foundations drawn from the life of Japan in particular, and Asia in general. Its theory is complex and its practice extremely varied—both replete with unexplored possibilities. At best, then, what we have systematically gathered together here can serve only as an introduction to the subject.

Aikido consists of, and may be systematically approached as, theory and practice. Volumes could be devoted entirely to either, and anthologies to both (the Bibliography found at the end of this book indicates a very bare beginning). We were forced to consider whether *Aikido and the Dynamic Sphere* should concentrate primarily on the former—the history, philosophy, ethical motivations of the art, etc.—or should deal more specifically with its practice, i.e., its techniques, exercises, and strategies.

We decided finally in favor of the second possibility, and have consequently gone very deeply into the practice of aikido, taking great pains to demonstrate through examination of concrete conduct of actual techniques, exercises, and strategies, what their theoretical motivations are (or should be), hoping that the image of an action or the action itself may prove to be worth the proverbial "thousand words."

As to the system adopted, we would propose that there are two equally valid ways of approaching any experience—both with their positive and negative aspects. In the East, the general tendency historically has been that of approaching it as a totality, as an indivisible entity whose hidden laws must be felt intuitively and followed absolutely if the desired result is to be obtained. There is, of course, a tacit acceptance of order and therefore, implicitly, a system of some sort; but the emphasis is upon leaping into the experience with both feet—as into a pond—and sinking or swimming as the case may be.

In the West, analysis plus the ability to project abstractions have been largely responsible for the advances (and the horrors) of Western civilization. However, in the West, the pervading theme is beginning to be: "We have progressed from primitive and unself-conscious participation to analytical thinking and an appreciation of awareness on the individual level—now, finally, let us move onward toward synthesis and unity on a higher and more truly humane level."

In the East, on the other hand, they began with the idea of unity accepted a priori—an acceptance which was to be largely responsible for the wonders and the tragedies of their civilization. But with the coming of industrialization, Asia of necessity began to respond to the analytical resonances buried just beneath the surface of that word. In Asia too, however, it is only a matter of time before there will be a move toward blending the original and largely unexamined totality with the newly acquired tradition of analysis—gravitating, as in the West, toward a higher and more consciously constructed unity.

In this book, we, being Westerners, have analyzed and systematized the practice of aikido, always keeping in mind the ultimate unity of the art and hoping that the method we have devised will help to introduce other Westerners to this marvelous Discipline of Coordination.

And, as we—although steeped in Western ways—learned aikido by studying with many Japanese instructors, so we hope that it may prove enlightening for readers in the Orient to catch a glimpse of their art as seen through Western eyes.

List of Charts and Tables

CHARTS

CHAPTER 2   PAGE

1   Main Sources of Formation and Inspiration   30
2   Major Armed Martial Arts   31
3   Major Unarmed Martial Arts   32
4   Major Schools of Martial Arts   33
5   The Ethics of Defense in Combat   34

CHAPTER 3

6   Categories and Ranks of the Aikido Hierarchy   36
7   Hombu Dojo Grading System   37
8   Requirements for Promotion—New York   38
9   The Uniform   39
10 The Practice Hall   40

CHAPTER 4

11 The Practice of Aikido   47
12 "Uncontrolled" Neutralizations Affecting the Physical Factors of an
    Attack   50
13 "Controlled" Neutralizations Affecting the Functional Factors of an
    Attack   52
14 Motion, Resistance, Control   53
15 Guiding the Motion of Convergence   54
16 Directions of Aggressive Convergence   55
17 Basic Holds   56
18 Basic Blows   57
19 Basic Combinations   57
20 Aggressive Coordination of Power   59
21 Inner and Outer Limits of Power   60

CHAPTER 5

22 The Theory of Defense   61
23 The Process of Defense and Its Factors   62
24 The Process of Defense: Stages and Qualities   63
25 The Process of Defense   65
26 Aggressive Solicitation   66

13

27 The Process of Defense: Stages and Factors   66
28 The Inner Factors: the Role of the Mind   68
29 Centralization   71
30 Coordination   79
31 Types of "ki"   85
32 The Power of UPA   88
33 The Points of Control of UPA   88

TABLES

1 The Basic Techniques of Neutralization   161
2 Examples of Basic Techniques of Neutralization Illustrated   162

Aikido and the Dynamic Sphere

CHAPTER I

What is Aikido?

EMERGING from a long period of obscurity in the East—during which time it was familiar only to relatively restricted circles—aikido has been called one of the most subtle and sophisticated of the martial arts, and—at its higher levels—an effective discipline for the development, integration, and utilization of all man's powers, physical and mental (spiritual).

What may appear at first glance to be a unique method for efficiently defending yourself against any form or type of attack will reveal itself under careful scrutiny to be not only an effective method of self-defense derived from Japanese Bujutsu (warrior arts); in addition—and this is the element which interests many who are strangers to the traditional *dojo,* or practice hall—it is a Discipline of Coordination, a way of strengthening the mind and body, of fusing the individual's physical and mental powers so that he or she will emerge as a more fully integrated human being. The word, in fact, means, "method or way [*do*] for the Coordination or Harmony [*ai*] of Mental Energy or Spirit [*ki*]."

17

The particular martial art method developed by Master Morihei Uyeshiba in Japan which he referred to as "aikido" combines practical self-defense movements taken from sword and spear fighting, jujutsu, *aikijutsu* and other ancient, more esoteric forms of the martial arts—with an emphasis from the very first moment of practice upon a characteristic centralization of thought and action, and the extension of mental energy or *ki* that makes this such an intriguing art.

It is a unique method of self-defense equally adaptable to and effective against a single attacker or several. The practice section of this book (Chapters IV–IX) is devoted to explanations and illustrations of the particular methods employed to achieve these often spectacular results—and to achieve them, moreover, in a manner which makes aikido practice possible for people of all ages and both sexes.

But why do we say that aikido is unique? Almost every martial art can claim to be an efficient means of self-defense and many can be safely practiced by old and young alike. How does aikido differ from all the others?

The difference lies in the essential motivations and characteristic effects which identify its practice, and the early as well as continuing emphasis placed upon them.

These include the following:

1. Aikido, purely in its practical application, is an art of self-defense. It is entirely reflexive, and related ethically to defense against an unprovoked attack. There is no attack in aikido. When the techniques are applied by aikidoists who have achieved a certain degree of mastery in the art, they will leave no serious injury in their wake.

2. There is the constant reference to the *hara,* or a man's "Centre" (i.e., center of gravity), as the point of concentration of energy; there is the predominance of references to *ki,* or "Inner Energy," as the particular form of energy to be employed. Finally, there is the interesting possibility of expanding these concepts and their relevance to areas outside the comparatively restricted world of the martial arts.

3. There is the characteristic strategy (i.e., movements, displacements, techniques) peculiar to the art, and the emphasis upon circularity or "sphericity" in the application of that strategy.

We will enlarge upon these three categories in some detail in the pages that follow, as well as upon the application of aikido training programs in the interest of physical fitness.

Defense in Aikido

As a self-defense art, aikido recognizes that one individual attacked by another has the right (and, of course, usually the instinctive urge) to defend himself against that aggression.

But *how* will he defend himself? This will depend upon the degree of his personal development. If he is still on a primitive level—mentally and/or physically—he may react wildly (often ineffectively); from the depths of his lack of preparation, he may clumsily inflict whatever damage he can upon his aggressor. Or, if skilled in one of the more deadly of the self-defense arts, he may cold-bloodedly proceed to seriously injure if not actually kill his attacker.

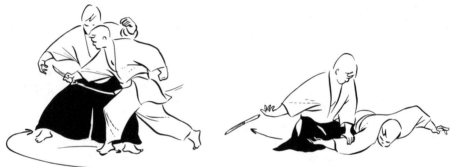

Using aikido properly however, an unjust and violent aggression can be neutralized swiftly and cleanly with demonstrable control over all the aspects of attack and defense—so that effective self-defense becomes possible without the necessity for inflicting serious injury upon an aggressor.

In other words, aikido says that you should and must defend yourself, and supplies you with an extensive practice that will enable you to do so with optimum efficiency. But aikido also says that you must be responsible for not inflicting unnecessary damage upon your attacker. He is still operating on a lower level. You aspire to a superior level where your proven ability, well-earned self-confidence, and refinement of technique, will allow you to defend yourself without resorting to the brutal methods so often taught as legitimate means of self-defense.

This definitely more difficult and therefore more sophisticated concept of self-defense, and the correlative control which must be developed in order to concretely achieve such aims in the practice of combat, becomes the testing ground for a developed aikido personality and the evidence of its existence. It is, therefore, in the very meaning attributed to the word "defense" that aikido differs from the other martial arts. This difference is graphically examined in the sections of this book concerned with the ethics of the art (Chapter II and Chapter X).

The "Centre" and "Ki"

Westward from the Orient have come many tales of strange forms of power —of strength like that of "massed wind or water" sweeping everything away before it. This power has been called by many names, but the one that appears most often in these accounts, especially in Japan, is *ki* and the seat of that power is said to be the *hara*, or Centre.

Almost all of the martial arts at some point in their development mention this power and the various means by which it may be developed. It is held to be "Intrinsic Energy" or "Inner Energy" and possessed by everyone although developed consciously by only a few.

The seat of this energy, the *hara*, or Centre, is a point approximately two inches below the navel. This corresponds roughly to the physical balance point of a man's anatomy which we in the West call his center of gravity.

In aikido, the emphasis upon this balance point and this Inner Energy (as differentiated from purely physical, muscular energy) is the very core and lodestone of the method.

We are faced with certain difficulties in attempting to explain and define this power according to generally accepted Western terminology. It is mental as opposed to physical and yet more than mental in the restricted, Occidental sense of "mental power"—although Western psychology does speak of "will power," the "will to live," etc., all aspects of attitudes and mental impulses which, while unsubstantial, can nevertheless produce concrete physical results.

By far the most serious obstacle to any discussion of the particular strength referred to in aikido as *ki* is the strict division which Western terminology usually makes between what is mental and what is physical—between the mind and the body. But of what use is the mind and its reasoning, directing powers without the body to act and carry out its decisions? And of what use is the body without any over-all conscious control and direction? The mind and the body are not separate entities; the mind is part of and contained within the body. The closer unity of mind and body—the fusion of these two functions (direction and action)—seems to come closest to an acceptable Western explanation of the strange strength which aikidoists call *ki*. It can be demonstrated quite convincingly by reference to the phenomenon called the "unbendable arm"—as well as to many others.

What do we mean, exactly, by this "fusion" of mind and body? Well, if you have ever tried unsuccessfully to open a tiny baby's tightly closed fist, you will have encountered an example of this fusion. The baby is relaxed and obviously not straining to resist you—he may not even seem to be aware of you —but that little fist remains closed. Since a baby responds instinctively to its environment, there is hardly any separation between perception and reaction, or between the mental and the physical. But as we grow older and develop our rational powers, we find, especially in Western cultures, a widening of the gap between the mind and the body, a noticeable hesitation between decision and action. It is as if the mind is to review, decide, and then leave the body to carry out the physical activity, depending solely upon the muscle power which can be generated.

But if this gap can be bridged, the result will be a closer unity of mind and body, with the strength, decision, and direction of the mind flowing directly and without interruption through all the channels and into all the recesses of the body.

Then as we note in the section on "Operational Principles" (Chapter V), since the force generated by the use of the body as a whole will be greater than that obtainable by employing any of its parts separately (i.e., arms, legs, etc.), so will the force resulting from the use of the mind and body as a totality be greater than that realizable by their separate employment.

Many scholars and practitioners of the martial arts, as well as monks and medical men have spoken of and demonstrated this Inner Energy and the ofttimes almost unbelievable results of its development and use.

One frequently mentioned method of developing this Inner Energy is by the regular practice of deep or abdominal breathing, since *ki* is held to be closely connected with breathing and has indeed even been called the "breath of life." (A method similar to that recommended by Mr. Tohei for breathing practice is included in Chapter V.)

Every beginner who steps on the mat in an aikido *dojo* soon encounters examples of Inner Energy. The most common among them is the exercise known as the "unbendable arm": he is told to extend his arm in front of him slightly inclined so that it describes a shallow half-circle extending forward, with his fingers outstretched. Then he is told to relax, not to tense his muscles, and to concentrate upon a point beyond his extended fingertips—perhaps the wall in front of him, or the other side of that wall. Someone will then try to bend his arm. If he has grasped the idea of "mental extension" and does not resist muscularly, his arm will not bend. The authors have seen this concrete demonstration of the extension of mental or Inner Energy many times, and the result is always the same: regardless of how slight or lacking in muscle power an individual may be, the extended arm cannot be bent.

The "unbendable arm" is, however, more than just a static example of mental projection. It is a basic concept related to the practice of aikido, and thus to motion on the mat. In fact, Mr. Tohei says that if a student does not keep his unbendable arm, he will not be able to perform the techniques properly. A note explaining this in detail is to be found immediately preceding the illustrations and explanations of the techniques (Chapter VIII).

There are many other methods of exercising and testing this mental "extension" or "projection" and these are outlined in detail in the section on Basic Exercises.

It might be possible to link the idea of the *hara*, or Centre, more closely to what Westerners know as a man's center of gravity—the spot where his weight reaches its concentration and balance, achieving equilibrium between the central and upper anatomy above and the supporting architecture of his hips and legs below. Mr. Tohei especially warns again and again that you cannot "keep one point" or stay centralized (and thus be able to extend and utilize your *ki*, or Inner Energy) unless you keep your balance.

It might also be possible to approximate and expand upon the idea of Inner Energy in terms of recent developments in the field of psychology in the West, but this might lead us too far afield, and unfortunately research undertaken in this general area in the West has not been extensive enough or concentrated enough to provide us with exact parallels. We will, however, discuss the Centre and *ki* in more detail in other sections of this book, drawing heavily upon Eastern sources (Chapter V).

The Strategy of Neutralization

Although certain general movements and technical applications evident in the art have been drawn from sword and spear fighting as well as from various ancient schools of jujutsu and *aikijutsu,* they have been expanded and developed with certain unique additions and modifications made so that the strategy characteristic of aikido today (i.e., the movements, displacements, and techniques) cannot easily be confused with any other method or art.

The strategic methodology of aikido consists, more precisely, of dynamic movements of evasion, extension, and centralization, which are the foundation for more technical actions of neutralization in the form of the now-famous techniques of immobilization and/or projection; their number in combination is almost unlimited.

The general principles ruling the application of both these stages of the strategy: the dynamic or preparatory, and the technical or conclusive are many, but those of circularity (sphericity), control and extension of power predominate in an absolute sense.

In aikido the purpose of this practical training is to replace certain instinctive responses (such as clashing directly into or against another person's

force) with other, more subtle and refined instinctive responses (such as evading a direct attack almost as soon as it is launched and then directing or guiding it away from you).

Of course, before undertaking any program such as aikido training, the rational intellectual faculties will be used to review the program and study its elements. Thus a man will decide, after due consideration, whether or not to pursue the program any further. But once the decision has been taken and aikido training commences, then the immediate practical end in view is to obliterate certain inherent or acquired responses and replace them with others more selective and less primitive.

For make no mistake—when events overtake you suddenly—(as they may if you are unexpectedly attacked) it will not be possible to pause, consider, decide, and then act. You must react instinctively. But how will you react, and what kind of instinctive responses will you exhibit?

This will depend almost entirely upon the diligence with which you have applied yourself to your aikido training because, as is true of any and all arts, no proficiency in the practical performance of movements or techniques is possible without continuous, programmed practice of the various movements, etc. This training is undertaken in the same spirit in which one attempts to learn to ski, to type, or to play the piano. The ideal, as indicated above, is to go beyond technique so that after repeated exposure to aikido training methods your experiences actually become part of you. They are programmed into your psyche so thoroughly that you no longer think of them as separate movements or techniques. And of course no one ever learned to play the piano by discussing composers and their compositions, but only by a physical application to a mentally prepared program. If you are interested in a fusion of the strength of mind and body, you must remember that one cannot function at optimum efficiency unless both parts are kept in good working order.

The Potential of Aikido

Aikido training functions on many levels, since the ultimate aim for the individual is his development and integration physically, mentally, and thus functionally.

It has been noted previously that the practice of aikido is characterized by a particular sphericity of action and smooth extension of power. A high degree of coordination is the main result: fluid, supple, functional movements which are free from any form of rigidity, whether physical (muscular contraction and/or over-development) or mental (tension).

In the first sense, and for this reason —over and above its proven efficiency as a superior art of self-defense —aikido has attracted athletes of all persuasions who have found it a method for improving their coordination, reflexes, timing, and general physical well-being. This includes swimmers, skiers, dancers, etc., who find the exercises and movements to be an excellent form of conditioning. (Of special interest to them is the concept of extension which is so fundamental to their respective sports or arts.)

Even women, children, and older people find the combination of mental and physical activity to be stimulating and of such a nature that it can be safely adapted to the needs of the individual in actual training.

Among the concrete results of regular practice of aikido exercises will be a noticeable improvement in your general health, with special emphasis upon respiration and circulation. The practice of abdominal breathing will obviously influence the development of the former, while the regular exercise of the joints and the body as a whole will promote the latter. The improvement in respiration and circulation in turn, will allow the blood to bring fresh material more rapidly and regularly to all the organs of the body, while at the same time helping to keep veins and arteries free from clogging materials and fatty deposits which might otherwise build up.

In the second sense, as a practice centered upon the reduction, elimination and/or sublimation of mental tensions, aikido provides proven outlets for any accumulation of such "mental debris" through the practice of the arts—the exercises and techniques. The usually relaxed, good-humored atmosphere of an aikido *dojo* is, in fact, a striking contrast to the ofttimes intense, rigidly controlled atmosphere typical of the practice of so many other martial arts. The authors' personal experiences include relief of insomnia and the disappearance of a serious ulcer condition which had developed prior to beginning aikido practice.

Of course, any regular physical activity will greatly improve one's general physical condition, but physical fitness as an end in itself can become boring and eventually be reduced to a tiresome routine which most people will abandon sooner or later.

The possibilities of aikido training, however, are so varied and demand such application of both mental and physical powers that one can continue practicing the art indefinitely without ever feeling that he has learned everything aikido could teach him, nor accomplished all that he could.

CHAPTER II

The Foundations of Aikido

The Founder

AIKIDO was founded by Master Morihei Uyeshiba. He developed and synthesized it from various other martial arts which he learned as a young man. His practical experience in these arts is one of the richest and most thorough of any *sensei* (teacher). Many of the arts and techniques which are found in aikido date back, in fact, more than 700 years to the time of the Genji and Heike regimes. A number of the masters under whom Master Uyeshiba studied died without revealing their arts to any other disciple.

The records of Master Uyeshiba's studies include, among others:
1. jujutsu—Kito School, under Master Tokusaburo Tojawa (1901)
2. fencing—Yagyu School, under Master Masakatsu Nakai (1903)
3. jujutsu—Daito School, under Master Sakaku Takeda (1911–1916)
4. jujutsu—Shinkage School (1922)
5. spear fighting—(1924)

He also pursued religious and philosophical studies: Zen, under Priest Mitsujo Fujimoto of the Shingon School of Buddhism at the Jizo-ji (1890–1893). In later years (1918–1926), he became deeply involved with the religious school of Omoto-kyo, founded by the Rev. Wanisaburo Deguchi, to the extent of participating actively in the promotion of the sect in Korea, China, and Manchuria.

Master Uyeshiba himself marks 1925 as the year in which his thus far unsatisfied search for a deeper meaning to be attributed to the martial arts came to an end, or rather to the threshold of a new dimension which was to be explored further by him and by his followers. It was in this year that he succeeded in blending the highest ethics of mankind with the practice of the martial arts: he developed that practice into a particular, truly defensive art in accordance with the highest dictates of those ethics.

In 1927 his *dojo,* or practice hall, was moved to metropolitan Tokyo. His method aroused interest in the highest circles. He taught until World War II emptied his *dojo* of its most promising pupils.

There was a temporary ban on any instruction in military arts (1945), but with renewed stability Japan once more assumed a position of prominence in Asia and in the community of nations, and this ban was lifted. Since then, aikido has expanded until today it is being taught all over the world.

Main Sources of Formation and Inspiration

In the chart which follows, you will find an outline of the main sources of formation and inspiration tapped by Master Uyeshiba in developing the art of aikido.

1. MAIN SOURCES OF FORMATION AND INSPIRATION

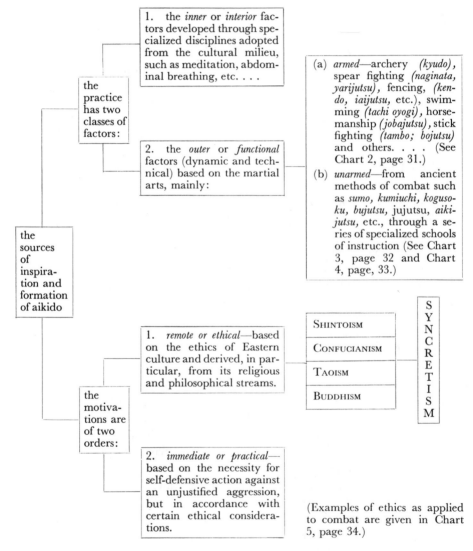

the sources of inspiration and formation of aikido

the practice has two classes of factors:

1. the *inner* or *interior* factors developed through specialized disciplines adopted from the cultural milieu, such as meditation, abdominal breathing, etc. . . .

2. the *outer* or *functional* factors (dynamic and technical) based on the martial arts, mainly:

(a) *armed*—archery *(kyudo)*, spear fighting *(naginata, yarijutsu)*, fencing, *(kendo, iaijutsu,* etc.), swimming *(tachi oyogi)*, horsemanship *(jobajutsu)*, stick fighting *(tambo; bojutsu)* and others. . . . (See Chart 2, page 31.)

(b) *unarmed*—from ancient methods of combat such as *sumo, kumiuchi, koguso-ku, bujutsu,* jujutsu, *aiki-jutsu*, etc., through a series of specialized schools of instruction (See Chart 3, page 32 and Chart 4, page, 33.)

the motivations are of two orders:

1. *remote or ethical*—based on the ethics of Eastern culture and derived, in particular, from its religious and philosophical streams.

SHINTOISM
CONFUCIANISM
TAOISM
BUDDHISM

S Y N C R E T I S M

2. *immediate or practical*—based on the necessity for self-defensive action against an unjustified aggression, but in accordance with certain ethical considerations.

(Examples of ethics as applied to combat are given in Chart 5, page 34.)

The Martial Arts

Since the martial arts of Japan played such an important role in the formation of the techniques, or "forms," of aikido, we have included in the following charts examples of the most important of those armed and unarmed arts and their major schools.

2. MAJOR ARMED MARTIAL ARTS

archery—*kyudo*

swimming—*tachi oyogi*

spear fighting—*yarijutsu*

stick fighting—*jo* or *bojutsu*

fencing—*kenjutsu*

complex—*tantojutsu*

horsemanship—*jobajutsu*

others—*ninjutsu*, etc. . . . .

3. MAJOR UNARMED MARTIAL ARTS

sumo ⟶ kumiuchi
kogusoku

ancient *bujutsu*   *tendori, tegiki, koshi mawari,*
yawara, torite, hakuda,
kempo, wajutsu, shubaku, etc.

jujutsu   judo

kempo   (Shaolin)   karate

aikijutsu   aikido

4. MAJOR SCHOOLS OF MARTIAL ARTS

takenouchi-ryu

sekiguchi-ryu

kyushin (yoshin)-ryu

kito-ryu

shinkage-ryu

tenjin shinyo-ryu

daito-ryu

yagyu-ryu

others

The "Ethics" of Defense

But as indicated in Chart 1, page 30, self-defense according to Master Uyeshiba's method must always comply with certain ethical imperatives. These are many and complex, but for our purposes we have devised Chart 5, page 34. It briefly illustrates the basic differences in various forms of self-defense.

In this chart, each panel represents an ethical level of combat. The level rises as we proceed from Panel A through Panel D.

In Panel A, the man on the left, without provocation and on his own initiative, attacks the other man and kills him. Ethically, this is the lowest of the four levels—unprovoked aggression in the form of a direct attack.

In Panel B, the man on the left has not directly attacked the other man, but he has provoked the other man to attack him. It may have been an obvious provocation, such as an insulting remark or the more subtle provocation of a contemptuous attitude. In either case, when the other man is invited to attack and does so, he is killed. While the first man is not guilty of launching the actual attack, he is responsible for inciting the other man to attack. There is only a shade of difference ethically between Panel A and Panel B.

In Panel C, the man on the left neither attacks nor provokes the other man to attack. But, when attacked he defends himself in a subjective manner, i.e., he takes care of only "number one," and the other man is killed or at least seriously injured. Ethically, this is a more defensible action than the other two. The man still standing was in no way responsible for the attack, neither directly nor indirectly. His manner of defense, however, while protecting him from possible harm, resulted in the destruction of another man. As you can see, the result in all three Panels—A, B, and C—is identical: a man is killed.

In Panel D, we have the ultimate in ethical self-defense. Neither attacking nor provoking an attack, the man on the left defends himself in such a way, with such skill and control that the attacker is not killed. In this case he is not even seriously injured.

This last and highest level is the goal of all aikido self-defense arts. It requires skill: the result of intensive practice of the technical means of defense devised by the founder, Master Uyeshiba. But it requires more than that. It requires an ethical intention. A man must sincerely desire to defend himself without hurting others. He must be well on the way toward integration of mind and body, of physical means and ethical motives.

He will often have practiced various other disciplines. Breathing exercises and meditation are common means employed in the East to further this integration (these and other disciplines also being employed in the West).

As we have seen then, at this ethical level aikido emerges as a Discipline of Coordination, where a man develops his own coordination of mind and body while helping his partner or partners to develop theirs as well.

The practice of the art of aikido then becomes a harmonious interaction between two or more people, fulfilling Master Uyeshiba's intention via translation of the highest ethics of the East (and West as well) into vital and active modes of conduct.

5. THE ETHICS OF DEFENSE IN COMBAT

Panel A

Panel B

Panel C

Panel D

CHAPTER III

Organization

The Hierarchy

THE HIERARCHICAL structure of aikido follows substantially the ranking system adopted by almost all the other major martial arts. The students of the art are divided into two categories: one including students of *kyu* rank, and the other including students of *dan* rank.

The category of *kyu* rank embraces students of aikido who have not yet attained the status of *dan,* and thus have not yet received their black belt. According to their degree of experience, as illustrated in Chart 6, page 36, they are subdivided into ranks which usually begin with the rank of 6th *kyu* (the lowest) and progress upward to the rank of 1st *kyu*. In some aikido clubs, all students below the rank of 1st *dan (shodan)* wear white belts over their uniforms regardless of their *kyu* standing. In other clubs, however, various colored belts are used to denote the various *kyu* ranks, as in the other martial arts.

The category of *dan* ranking embraces those students of aikido who have been awarded their black belts. According to their experience and proficiency, they are also subdivided into ranks which progress upward from 1st *dan (shodan)* to 9th *dan (kudan)* and above.

The founder of the art and his son, according to Japanese custom, are above the ranking system. The students who hold *dan* rank, from 1st *dan* upward, wear the black belt over their uniforms *(gi)* and under the divided skirt or trousers *(hakama)* inherited from the samurai who wore it while practicing the martial arts. There are some clubs, however, where all students, regardless of category or rank, wear this *hakama,* as do students of Japanese archery *(kyudo)*, Japanese fencing (kendo), etc. . . .

6. CATEGORIES AND RANKS OF THE AIKIDO HIERARCHY

the *kyu* category and its ranks:	rank of 6th *kyu (rokkyu)*	(white belt)
	rank of 5th *kyu (gokyu)*	
	rank of 4th *kyu (yonkyu)*	(white or blue belt)
	rank of 3rd *kyu (sankyu)*	
	rank of 2nd *kyu (nikyu)*	(white or brown belt)
	rank of 1st *kyu (ikkyu)*	
the *dan* category and its ranks:	rank of 1st *dan (shodan)*	(black belt and *hakama*)
	rank of 2nd *dan (nidan)*	
	rank of 3rd *dan (sandan)*	
	rank of 4th *dan (yodan)*	
	rank of 5th *dan (godan)*	
	rank of 6th *dan (rokudan)*	
	rank of 7th *dan (shichidan)*	
	ranks of 8th *dan (hachidan)*, 9th *dan (kudan)*, etc. . . .	

Promotion

There are three basic methods of conferring class or rank:

1) examination—for each *kyu* class and for each *dan* rank, there are certain precise requirements pertaining to hours practiced, techniques mastered, etc., which must be fulfilled. However, these requirements may differ according to the *dojo*. Following are two tables: one listing the requirements for promotion up to and including the rank of *shodan* as posted for examinations in New York in the spring of 1965; the other outlining the requirements at Hombu Dojo in Tokyo in October, 1964.

2) honorary—for contributions to the introduction and promotion of aikido.

3) combination of examination and honorary—one supplementing the other.

7. HOMBU DOJO GRADING SYSTEM
(As of October, 1964)

EXAM. FOR GRADE OF:	PREREQUISITE FOR EXAM:	BASIC TECHNIQUES*	OPTIONAL TECHNIQUES*
5th *kyu*	40 hours practice	standing: *katate tori shiho nage, shomen uchi irimi nage, shomen uchi ikkyo.* sitting: *kokyu ho*	None
4th *kyu*	40 hours practice after obtaining 5th *kyu*	add *shomen uchi nikyo* to above	*yokomen uchi shiho nage, kata tori ikkyo,* and *nikyo*
3rd *kyu*	30 hours practice after obtaining 4th *kyu*	add *shomen uchi sankyo* and *yonkyo* to above	*shomen uchi kote gaeshi, munetsuki kote gaeshi, sankyo* and *yonkyo katate tori, yokomen uchi ikkyo* to *yonkyo*
2nd *kyu*	60 hours practice after obtaining 3rd *kyu*	same as above	add: *hammi hantachi* (*uke* standing, *nage* sitting) *jiyu waza* (free style), *ushiro waza* (rear techniques)
1st *kyu*	60 hours practice after obtaining 2nd *kyu*	same as above	same as above
shodan (1st grade black belt)		same as above	same as above
nidan (2nd grade)	1 year after *shodan*	same as above plus *tanto dori* (knife technique)	same as above plus *futari gakari* (two-man attack)
sandan (3rd grade)	2 years after *nidan*	same as above plus *tachi dori* (sword technique)	same as above

* *irimi (omote)* and *tenkan (ura)* when applicable.

8. REQUIREMENTS FOR PROMOTION — NEW YORK

(Spring, 1965)

rank	techniques required:	English equivalents in authors' system: (att. = attack; imm. = immobilization; proj. = projection)	time of previous practice required:
5th *kyu*	1. *katate tori shiho nage* 2. *shomen uchi ikkyo* 3. *shomen uchi kokyu nage* 4. *mune tsuki kote gaeshi* 5. *kokyu ho*	att. no. 1 neutralized by imm. no. 6 att. no. 13 ,, ,, imm. no. 1 att. no. 13 ,, ,, proj. no. 1 att. no. 15 ,, ,, imm. no. 7 sitting extension (Chapter V)	60 hours
4th *kyu*	the techniques shown above plus: 1. *yokomen uchi shiho nage* 2. *shomen uchi nikyo* 3. *shomen uchi kote gaeshi* 4. *mune tsuki kaiten nage* 5. *ushiro tekubi tori ikkyo*	att. no. 14 neutralized by imm. no. 6 att. no. 13 ,, ,, imm. no. 2 att. no. 13 ,, ,, imm. no. 7 att. no. 15 ,, ,, proj. no. 3 att. no. 7 ,, ,, imm. no. 1	60 hours (*)
3rd *kyu*	the techniques shown above plus: 1. *yokomen uchi kokyu nage* (2) 2. *shomen uchi sankyo* 3. *shomen uchi kaiten nage* 4. *kata tori kokyu nage* 5. *ushiro tekubi tori kote gaeshi*	att. no. 14 neutralized by proj. no. 18 att. no. 13 ,, ,, imm. no. 3 att. no. 13 ,, ,, proj. no. 3 att. no. 5 ,, ,, proj. no. 1 att. no. 7 ,, ,, imm. no. 7	60 hours (*)
2nd *kyu*	the techniques shown above plus: 1. *yokomen uchi kokyu nage* 2. *shomen uchi yonkyo* 3. *yokomen uchi ikkyo* 4. *katate tori ryote mochi kokyu nage* 5. *ushiro kata tori ikkyo*	att. no. 14 neutralized by proj. no. 2 att. no. 13 ,, ,, imm. no. 4 att. no. 14 ,, ,, imm. no. 1 att. no. 4 ,, ,, proj. no. 1 att. no. 9 ,, ,, imm. no. 1	60 hours (*)
1st *kyu*	the techniques shown above plus: 1. *yokomen uchi nikyo and sankyo* 2. *suwari waza:* *shomen uchi ikkyo* *shomen uchi kokyu nage* *hammi hantachi shiho nage* 3. free style against one	att. no. 14 neutralized by imm. 2 and 3 mat or kneeling aikido: att. no. 13 neutralized by imm. no. 1 att. no. 13 ,, ,, proj. no. 1 att. no. 1 ,, ,, imm. no. 6 (with *uke* standing) free style *(randori)*	90 hours (*)
1st *dan* (shodan)	the techniques shown above plus: 1. free style against four 2. free style against knife	free style *(randori)* free style against armed attack	150 hours (*)

(*) In each case, the number of hours indicated are additional hours—i.e. they are the total number of hours required for that rank, in addition to the total number of hours completed for the previous rank.

The Uniform

As shown in the illustrations, the uniform worn by aikido students does not differ substantially from the uniform adopted by other martial arts such as judo or karate. This uniform, worn by everyone, consists of a jacket and pants with an appropriate belt (white, black, or colored—according to rank and/or the custom of the individual *dojo*).

In connection with the tying of the belt, the procedure is the same as that adopted by most martial arts, with the exception that in aikido it is purposely worn low on the hips in order to create a physical point of reference for that concentration on the *hara* which is typical of aikido.

Students of aikido who have attained *dan* ranking (black belt) wear the divided skirt called a *hakama*—usually black. This article, which is also used in the martial arts of kendo and *kyudo*, was worn by the samurai. The securing of the *hakama*—also low on the hips—increases that aforesaid feeling of centralization and adds a certain plastic beauty to the performance of aikido on the mat.

9. THE UNIFORM

jacket

belt

pants

hakama

zori

tying pants

attaching belt

student in complete *gi* (below black belt, or *shodan* rank)

student in complete *gi* and *hakama* (black belt, or *shodan* rank, and above)

The Practice Hall

The place where aikido students gather together with their instructor for the purpose of practicing the art is called a *dojo*. The name is adopted, according to the doctrine of the martial arts, from Buddhist lore relating to the hall in which monks practice the disciplines of meditation, concentration, breathing, etc.

Usually, a *dojo* will consist of:

1. an area for an office where files, records, registration, and progress records, correspondence, information notices, etc., are kept. In this area will often be found:
    (a) the name board *(nafuda kake)* containing the names of the members, arranged according to rank;
    (b) a bulletin board.
2. an area with seating accommodations for visitors, spectators, press, general public, etc., usually located on the sides of the mat—the upper *(joseki)* or the lower *(shimoseki)* (see Chart 10).
3. an area for the dressing rooms, lockers, and showers.
4. an area for the mat.

10. THE PRACTICE HALL

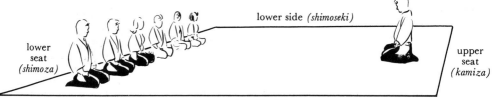

lower side *(shimoseki)*

lower seat *(shimoza)*

upper seat *(kamiza)*

upper side *(joseki)*

The Mat

The area where aikido is actually taught and practiced consists of a smooth and elastic surface, not so hard as to damage the human body due to lack of necessary shock-absorbing resiliency for the falls or somersaults, not so soft as to injure feet or hamper that fluid and rapid movement which is so basic in aikido.

In Japan, this area is covered by a number of traditional *tatami* which are mats made of canvas-covered or uncovered rice-straw padding *(toko)*, grass matting, or rush matting *(i-omote)*. Each measures approximately 3 feet in width, 6 feet in length, and is about 2 1/2 inches in thickness. A number of these *tatami*, when placed together, will provide the smoothest of surfaces possible. Often they will be mounted on an undersurface of wooden planks suspended upon steel springs which will increase the already high natural elasticity.

In Western countries where these *tatami* are not so easily available, the required smooth and elastic surface is usually provided in the form of wrestling mats, foam-rubber mats, etc. They are covered by a single piece of canvas. The whole is often supported by a flexible wooden platform, raised on planks from the non-yielding concrete or flat wood floor. This area is usually rectangular or square, and its sides have particular names related to their specific function in the field of *dojo* etiquette.

The predominant side—which acts as the central part of the *dojo* and its main area of orientation—is called upper seat, or *kamiza (joza)*. It is reserved for instructors, honored guests, and *dojo* officers during special meetings. It is usually identified by the traditional display of Master Uyeshiba's picture or by an appropriately framed sample of calligraphy *(gaku)* of philosophical content hanging centered on the wall behind that selected side. In Japan, this upper seat is identified by a raised dais, with typical emblems on display (swords, the ceremonial drum, painted scrolls, etc.). Opposite the *kamiza* is the side called lower seat, or *shimoza*. It is the meeting place for all the students, and the side from which they will face their instructor. They will usually line up or sit down by order of rank, with the advanced students on the upper side, or *joseki,* i.e., on the left side of the *kamiza*. This area is also used by instructors in place of the *kamiza,* when the latter is pre-empted for ceremonies, visiting dignitaries, etc. On the right side of the *kamiza* is the area of the mat called the lower side, or *shimoseki,* which is used by students facing their instructors on the *joseki*.

Etiquette and Classes

The behavior of the aikido student in the *dojo* is prompted by deep respect for the place, for the people in it, for the purpose of the practice hall. In general, this behavior conforms to the norms of "good manners" adopted by civilized people in their social encounters.

In particular, however, the student follows certain precise rules of conduct once he steps on the *tatami*—a form of ceremony which has been adapted from the martial customs of Japan and is adhered to by the practitioners of most Japanese martial arts today.

Ritsurei

When he steps on the mat, for example, the student bows slightly in the direction of the *kamiza*. This bow follows the rules established for standing salutation *(ritsurei)*. It is executed in the normal, natural posture *(shizen hontai)* in which the student stands with the chest bent forward at an angle of approximately 30 degrees, his fingertips lightly touching the front of his thighs near the knees. It is usually considered bad form to bend the head so low that a person in front of the student can see the nape of his neck.

The student will wait for the instructor and employ his time profitably by performing light calisthenics or the basic exercises, if these are not performed during the instructor's class. He may also sit down, relax, and perform the special exercises for the development of the Inner Factors of the art. As the time approaches for the beginning of the class, the student will sit in *seiza* in line with the other students, and in the customary place.

Seiza

The sitting position is called *seiza* and it is achieved by withdrawing the left foot half a pace, placing the left knee on the mat with toes bent, but with the body and head kept erect. The right foot is then withdrawn and placed close to the left, with the big toes crossing or touching each other. The hips, of course, have been lowered so that the body weight will settle on the inside of your heels.

The hands should be placed lightly on your thighs, palms downward, with the fingers either turned inward slightly or curled into a half-fist. The distance maintained between the knees should be approximately that which could be occupied by two fists.

The variations in this posture will affect only the positions of the legs and feet. It is permissible, therefore, to keep the feet crossed, or rest one on each side—as shown in the illustration—or sitting always with the spine kept straight, but with the legs crossed in front of you, adopt the style popular in India.

One rises from the *seiza* position by reversing the above process. The student will raise his hips, bending his toes, with their tips on the mat. He will raise his right knee first and place his right foot near the left knee. Then he will raise the left knee and place his left foot alongside the right one. The entire movement is performed smoothly and quickly.

The instructor usually sits in front of the class, and—turning his back so that he and the students are facing in the same direction (that of the *kamiza*) —he will signal, usually by clapping his hands. At the signal, the whole class will perform the ceremonial bow from the sitting position.

Zarei

The ceremonial bow in the style of *zarei* starts from the *seiza* posture. The palms of the hands are placed on the *tatami* at a distance of about 6 inches in front of your knees, the fingers pointing inward. The chest is bent forward, as in *ritsurei,* at an angle of 30 degrees, with the elbows slightly apart. The head should not bend so as to touch the mat, but should be kept in line with the trunk of the body, and the hips should not be raised from the mat, but should maintain their contact with the heels.

The instructor will then turn, face his students and repeat the *zarei,* which is returned by them. The instructor will usually then rise and begin the basic exercise, or—if these have already been performed under the supervision of advanced students—he will proceed to illustrate and explain the defensive strategy employed in aikido.

Usually, an instructor will show a technique of neutralization applied against a specified form of attack, while the students remain seated in *seiza.* At his signal, they will bow to him, stand up, and select a partner (both per-

forming an introductory *ritsurei*) and practice the technique with that partner. When the instructor claps his hands, they will sit down again.

At the end of the class, the instructor will clap his hands and then sit down in *seiza* facing the *kamiza*. He and his students will bow in *zarei* toward the upper seat, after which he will turn and bow again to his students, who will reciprocate. The class is thus dismissed, with a "thank you" from the students.

CHAPTER IV

The Practice of Aikido

As WE HAVE said, aikido can be many things to many people, depending upon the degree of their personal development. It can be an efficient art of self-defense, aimed at neutralizing any possible form of attack; at its higher levels it can become a Discipline of Coordination, a continuing, ever expanding method whereby a man works toward that fusion of mind and body discussed earlier. It can become, finally, a philosophy of integration, of a harmonious blending of man with man—of men with their environment. All of these aims can be achieved through its practice.

And this practice consists of a distinctive series of movements, embodied in the techniques of neutralization—each capable of deflecting or redirecting any attempted attack, whether launched by a single man or several. This, of course, is in accordance with the first outline of aikido, i.e., an effective means of self-defense derived from a sophisticated blending and adaptation (with judicious additions) of many martial art systems, based upon ethical considerations contained in Eastern religious and philosophical thought.

As indicated in Chart 11, page 47, however, the practice is not based solely upon a thorough knowledge and mastery of the aikido techniques of neutralization themselves, but also upon an equally thorough familiarity with all types and forms of possible attack—in accordance with the ancient Japanese axiom that "The very first requisite for defense is to know the enemy."*

Eventually, through a better understanding of the interrelation of cause-effect, action-reaction, solicitation-response, on the practical self-defense level

---

* *Journal of World History* by Shozan Sakuma, III-3, UNESCO, Switzerland, 1957.

(resulting from regular practice of the art), the student will begin to develop a deeper understanding of the relationship and interdependence of these factors in his life as a whole, beyond the comparatively limited domain of the *dojo*.

The practice then is the way along which a man can proceed from the basic, utilitarian consideration of learning an efficient means of self-defense which will follow certain ethical guide lines, to the "high country" where the art becomes a Discipline of Coordination aimed at the harmonizing of opposites or alternates—not an art bent on or resulting in destruction, individual or wholesale.

The practice of the art, then, is based upon a series of carefully programmed movements and actions, strategically linked, which are or can be actual responses to various forms of aggression or attack. The dramatic and vital effectiveness of this strategic activity, in fact, is perhaps the most immediately impressive element of the art, as anyone who has witnessed a demonstration by skilled aikido practitioners can testify.

However, the strategic activity has been particularly and pointedly structured; i.e., aikido is an art of reactivity, all of its movements, all the techniques are based upon individual responses to various forms of attack. The first factor which must be analyzed then, in any study of the practice of the art, is the attack—that attempted dynamic intrusion which will be neutralized by one or more aikido techniques.

This is because the attack itself contains the very elements which an aikido defensive strategy will utilize physically, functionally, and of course psychologically in neutralizing that attempted aggression.

Because of this close interrelation between the attack and the defense, between the aggressor and the defender, we will outline here a brief theory of attack followed by a theory of defense which will explore the ways and means of guiding any form of attempted violence into a harmless Circuit of Neutralization—always in a manner typical of, and in accordance with, the ethical principles of the art.

11. THE PRACTICE OF AIKIDO

THEORY OF THE ATTACK: FACTORS

INNER	OUTER		
MENTAL	PHYSICAL	FUNCTIONAL	
		DYNAMIC	TECHNICAL
THE MIND, its aggressive intention and total commitment	THE BODY, as the physical weapon of attack	motion of attack	technique of attack

All these factors of the attack are fused together against you in the Unified Power of Attack (UPA).

THEORY OF THE DEFENSE: FACTORS

INNER	OUTER		
MENTAL	PHYSICAL	FUNCTIONAL	
		DYNAMIC	TECHNICAL
THE MIND, as a Centre of inner stability of control (*hara*) and of power (*ki*).	THE BODY, as the instrument of defense.	the motion of evasion, centralization, and extension	the techniques of neutraliza-tion—conclud-ing the process of defense

All these factors of defense are fused together in a single, fluid, and powerful defense.

The functional fusion of both attack and defense, used as practice or an exercise, develops that coordination which is the basis of the art of aikido.

The Theory of Attack

Very few martial arts have analyzed the various forms of physical aggression—the attack, and its possible strategies and basic forms—as thoroughly and accurately as aikido.

An attack is defined here as an unjustified, unprovoked attempt to destroy or injure another person, or even interfere with his freedom of action. There may be a single man attacking or several men—aikido techniques in particular, and strategies in general, can be adapted to either eventuality. In this book, we will be mainly outlining techniques applied defensively against an attack launched by a single man (singular attack) since there are numerous basic techniques which should be explained and illustrated here and so many combinations, some of which must also be discussed. We will, however, also include a few examples of defense against multiple attack (plural attack).

Many different elements are blended together to produce an attack. Multiple factors, some apparent and some so subtle as to escape the notice of all but the most discerning spectator, are fused in the act to actually give shape and recognizable form to an aggression.

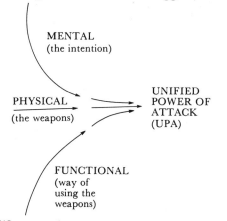

MENTAL
(the intention)

PHYSICAL
(the weapons)

UNIFIED
POWER OF
ATTACK
(UPA)

FUNCTIONAL
(way of
using the
weapons)

We must, however, examine these elements separately before we can consider their fusion in a unified and coherent form of attack. Generally, these factors fall into two classes: Inner Factors (mental/psychological) and Outer Factors (physical/functional).

The psychological factors of any attack provide the background and setting for the attempted aggression. These include the "will to harm," the total or partial commitment to the inflicting of pain and/or injury. This intention may be conveyed by a threatening attitude or gesture; it may, on the other hand, only be revealed at the moment when a person actually launches his attack. In many cases, the threatening glance or gesture is sufficient to literally frighten the intended victim into submission, and to paralyze his will and/or reflexes so that he is utterly unable to defend himself efficiently.

Physical Factors

The physical factors of an attack are represented by the parts of a man's body that he can use as natural weapons in an unarmed attack. In addition, of course, are those deadly extensions of his aggressive instinct: a sword, stave, a knife, a gun.

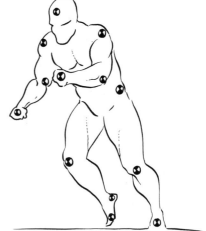

(NOTE: In this book, we will be dealing mainly with aikido techniques of neutralization against unarmed forms of aggression, although we will include several examples of defense against armed attacks. The field of defense against unarmed attacks, however, is so vast that we cannot even cover it adequately in this book, but must content ourselves with outlining the basic techniques of neutralization and some forms of the advanced practice.)

In most utilitarian methods of self-defense, the prime targets of any defense are the physical factors—the attacker's body (Chart 12, page 50). In aikido, however, the strategy of defense is centered mainly upon the functional factors of an attack; i.e., the way in which those physical weapons are being employed.

In fact, the more a person concentrates his defensive actions upon those physical factors, the less controlled, or *aiki,* his strategy is considered to be, since he should be neutralizing the aggressive action. Any aikido strategy of defense, in fact, is qualified and classified according to:

1. the theory of physical injury which, in obedience to the ethical principles of the art, requires that the student respect the "natural" integrity of his opponent's anatomy; and

2. the theory of physical pain which assigns only a subsidiary and temporary importance to the inflicting of pain in the process of neutralizing an attack, and further refines self-defense in a particularly *aiki* manner.

12. "UNCONTROLLED" NEUTRALIZATIONS AFFECTING
THE PHYSICAL FACTORS OF AN ATTACK

involving
the entire
anatomy

involving
particular
elements

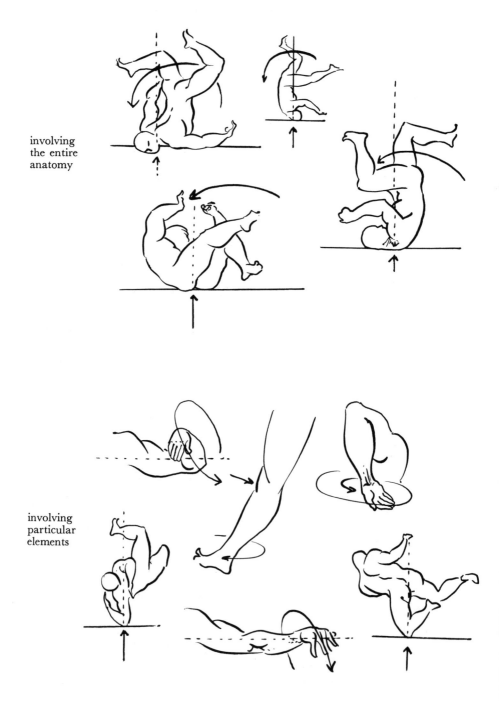

The theory of physical injury is based upon the obvious structural limitations of a man's body. An arm can be twisted only so far before it will break. So much pressure can be applied against a spine before it will crack. Inflicting serious injury on anyone—including an attacker—is considered "un-*aiki*" and an indication of lack of control and skill, since a superior strategy can accomplish the desired result, i.e., neutralization of any attack and efficient self-defense without resorting to such comparatively primitive means.

The theory of physical pain goes even one step further and insists that any pain felt during the application of an aikido technique—if that technique is being applied properly—should be momentary only. In fact, the best teachers continually admonish their students never to apply pressure against the joints, but merely to exaggerate the normal extension, as indicated below. Any pain felt is transitory and only intended to facilitate the completion of a particular technique of neutralization. The practicality of this strategy is obvious: pain acts as a warning signal and causes a man either to stiffen against the pain or attempt to elude it in some way. Such a stiffening or attempt to escape on the part of an attacker the moment you applied the severe pressure of a "static" strategy would make the application of a particular technique more difficult. In aikido at its best, almost before the attacker realizes what has happened, his attack has been neutralized, quickly and cleanly.

Even in the ancient martial arts, merely defending oneself well was not as admired as was the ability to defend oneself with the same efficiency, but with such control and power that the opponent/attacker was left substantially unharmed, even if greatly chagrined. These arts were qualified as "extremely difficult," "highly sophisticated," "esoteric," and eventually came to be linked not so much to the martial reality of particular combat encounters as to religion, philosophy, or the higher spheres of man's existence.

But most martial arts were—and most have remained—highly practical and subjective. The aim was to achieve as close to perfection as possible in the particular method or methods being studied, and even if not actually attacking, nevertheless to destroy the enemy as quickly as possible with a well-prepared counterattack.

In aikido, however, through the skilled employment of its carefully structured techniques of neutralization, it is not only possible, it is actually imperative, to exercise such control over the entire process of attack and defense that both will merge into one smooth exercise of circular dispersion of an aggressive motion/action into nothingness. And, as we have noted, this dispersion is to be achieved by acting upon the "functionality" of the natural weapons a man employs, i.e., the way in which he uses hands, arms, legs, and body to attack (Chart 13, page 52). Therefore, in any aikido strategy, of the three classes of factors of any attack—psychological, physical, functional—the last will be the most important.

13. "CONTROLLED" NEUTRALIZATIONS AFFECTING
THE FUNCTIONAL FACTORS OF AN ATTACK

involving
the entire
anatomy

involving
particular
elements

Dynamic Factors

In any attack there will be two stages: first, the dynamic stage of generic motion toward you, around you, etc.; second, the technical stage which consists of the particular form the attack will assume—punch, kick, slap, etc. The dynamic stage involves what we call a motion of convergence, i.e., the attacker must close the distance between himself and his intended target— you, and the particular part of your body he intends to push, hit, or kick. Even if he is comparatively close to you, he still must take a step or lean forward, twist or turn, in order to be in position to attack.

A defensive aikido strategy begins the moment a would-be attacker takes a step toward you or turns aggressively in your direction. His initial motion (movement) in itself contains the factors you will use to neutralize the action of attack which will spring with explosive force from that motion of convergence. The most important dynamic factor to be reckoned with in developing your defense will be the dynamic momentum generated by your attacker's initial motion—its speed and its direction.

The dynamic momentum of convergence is represented by the amount of force generated by the motion of convergence. The human body in motion tends to become extremely easy to maneuver and its vertical stability greatly reduced by any dynamic inertia. If you push a man standing still, bracing himself, you will meet a definite resistance. The same push, however, or even a lesser one (in approximately the same direction) if that man is in motion, can send him flying.

This dynamic momentum is closely related to the speed of the initial motion of convergence. As shown in Chart 14, the faster a man moves, the less control he has over his movements and the easier it is to unbalance him. Conversely, the more slowly he moves, the more control he has and the harder it will be to unbalance him.

14. MOTION, RESISTANCE, CONTROL		
SPEED	COEFFICIENT OF VERTICAL STABILITY	COEFFICIENT OF VERTICAL MOBILITY
low	high (strong)	low
high	low	high
fast	very low	very high

The factor of direction must be added to the dynamic momentum and to the speed of the aggressive motion of convergence, because it is of the utmost importance that you never meet that dynamic momentum head on—never clash with or oppose it directly and frontally. You might enlarge upon that dynamic momentum frontally with a maneuver which would extend your opponent's attack beyond the point where he can maintain his balance, but usually you will guide his motion of convergence from the side, curving it slightly and adding a certain amount of your own force (dynamic force) to his already exaggerated movement, thus depriving him of control over his motion and bringing him into a condition of unbalance and decentralized, dispersed power (Chart 15).

There are two main types of convergence an attacker may employ: straight (frontal and direct); and circular (spiral closing in upon you). Both can actually be used in your own strategy of defense—in fact will become its foundation; i.e., his motion will provide you with those factors you need to gain control over your attacker's movements through their "amplification" and then lead him into one of the aikido Circuits of Neutralization (Chart 16, page 55).

15. GUIDING THE MOTION OF CONVERGENCE

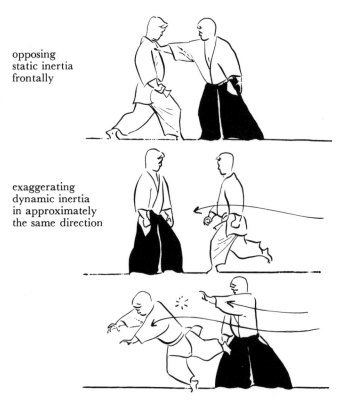

opposing
static inertia
frontally

exaggerating
dynamic inertia
in approximately
the same direction

16. DIRECTIONS OF AGGRESSIVE CONVERGENCE

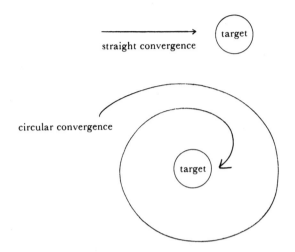

Technical Factors

The second stage of any aggression—if it is allowed to develop that far—is qualified as "technical" because it deals with the specific way in which a man may attack you. Specific actions of attack are generally classified in aikido practice within three groups: unarmed attacks; armed attacks; and combinations of armed and unarmed attacks.

Unarmed Attacks

Aikido has subdivided the unarmed forms of attack into three main divisions: twelve attacks consisting primarily of a hold (Chart 17, page 56); three attacks employing blows (Chart 18, page 57); and a series of combinations resulting from the use of a blow and a hold (Chart 19, page 57).

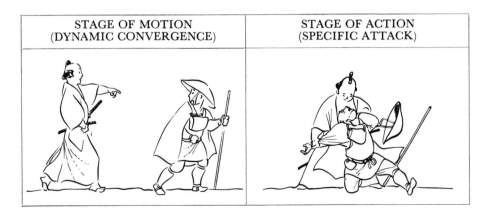

STAGE OF MOTION (DYNAMIC CONVERGENCE)	STAGE OF ACTION (SPECIFIC ATTACK)

The first group consists mainly of a hold, i.e., grasping, strangling, immobilizing, etc., whose primary purpose is to paralyze or delay your defensive reaction for the length of time necessary to completely subdue you. They are considered preliminary steps toward further more drastic attacks: a blow, perhaps a definitive choke, which will put you at the absolute mercy of an attacker. These holds are further classified as either "frontal" or "dorsal," i.e., from behind. The system of identification adopted by the authors, with Japanese names and English equivalents, is included in the chart which follows.

17. BASIC HOLDS

FRONTAL		DORSAL	
attack no. 1 (*katate tori*—one-hand hold, same side)		attack no. 7 (*ushiro tekubi tori*—wrist hold from behind)	
attack no. 2 *katate tori*—one-hand hold, opposite side)		attack no. 8 (*ushiro hiji tori*—elbow hold from behind)	
attack no. 3 (*katate tori ryote mochi*—two-hand hold, on one hand)		attack no. 9 (*ushiro kata tori*—shoulder hold from behind)	
attack no 4. (*katate tori ryote mochi*—two-hand hold on two hands)		attack no. 10 *ushiro kubi shime*—strangulation from behind)	
attack no. 5 (*kata tori*—one-hand hold on shoulder)		attack no. 11 (*ushiro tori*—high arm hold from behind)	
attack no. 6 (*ryokata tori*—two-hand hold on shoulders)		attack no. 12 (*ushiro tori*—low arm hold from behind)	

The second group of unarmed attacks includes a direct punch or blow, a chopping cut with the knife-edge of the hand, a variety of jabs, or thrusts, etc. These attacks are further subdivided into two main classes: the first involves blows aimed at your upper body (the head, the throat, the chest) whether directly from the front or circularly from the side; the second class includes those blows aimed at the center—or lower parts of your body. Chart 18, illustrates these blows (giving their respective numbers as well as their Japanese and English names).

18. BASIC BLOWS		
H I G H	attack no. 13 (*shomen uchi:* straight blow to the head, punch, jab, etc.)	
	attack no. 14 (*yokomen uchi:* circular blow to the head, hook, etc.)	
L O W	attack no. 15 *mune tsuki:* blow to the abdomen)	

Finally, Chart 19 shows a few examples of the third group of attacks which combine a hold with a blow. Numbers and descriptions are also given.

19. BASIC COMBINATIONS				
attack no. 16 (hold with hold)		Frontal		Dorsal
attack no. 17 (hold with blow)		Frontal		Dorsal
attack no. 18 (blow with blow)		Frontal		Dorsal

Armed Attacks

The armed attacks included in this second group are divided into two classes. The first class includes ancient forms of aggression inherited from the martial past of Japan and its arts of combat. The techniques of neutralization developed by most ancient martial arts were geared to the neutralization of attacks in which weapons (the sword and the spear in particular) played a determinant role. Aikido techniques of defense are often employed against attacks using a *bokken* or *jo* (stick or stave) because the coordination required to control a strategy of defense against such an impressive physical extension of an attacker's personality is of the highest degree. These forms are to be found in the advanced practice of aikido.

The second class includes modern techniques of armed aggression employing firearms, knives, etc. The practice of forms of defense against such attacks is also understandably rather advanced and complex, and really necessitates a book in itself. In this introductory study of aikido, limitations of space and the vast field which must be covered permit us to give only a few examples of such defensive neutralizations.

The Unified Power of Attack

In conclusion, the importance of the factors of attack—the aggressive intention, the motion of convergence, and the specific attack—can be expressed in a single concept: the "Unified Power of the Attack" (UPA). All of these factors will be fused into that singular, intense, and dangerous stream of aggression which results when a man attacks totally, without reservation. The aikido doctrine refers to this aggressive concentration of all a man's powers, factors, and features in an attack as "aggressive *ki*" or "your opponent's *ki*," etc.

This aggressive coordination of power has definite limits of concentration within which its dangerous potentiality will be at its maximum. Outside those limits, a man's capacity to do damage will decrease considerably, until his aggressive coordination vanishes completely, leaving him highly vulnerable and his motion/action comparatively easy to maneuver. The examples in the charts which follow (Charts 20 and 21) illustrate this more fully.

20. AGGRESSIVE COORDINATION OF POWER

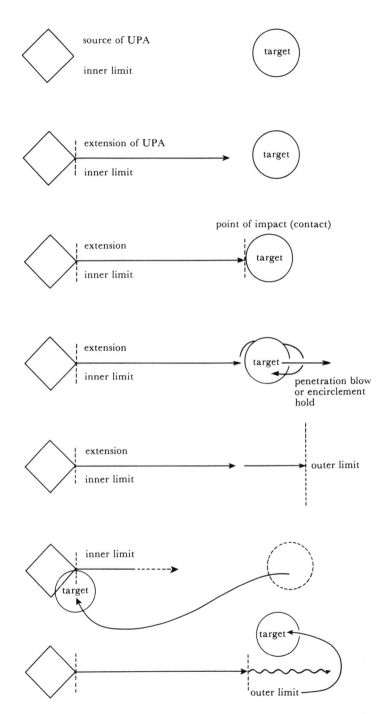

21. INNER AND OUTER LIMITS OF POWER

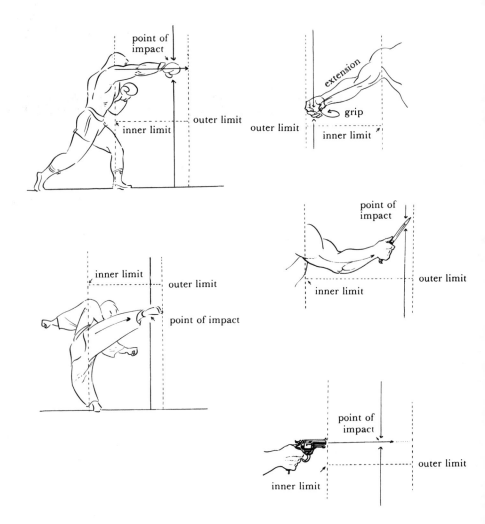

CHAPTER

The Theory of Defense

	INNER FACTORS OF DEFENSE: —centralization —extension —leading control —sphericity	22. THE THEORY OF DEFENSE
THE PROCESS OF AIKIDO DEFENSE AND ITS FACTORS:		—PHYSICAL: the body as the instrument of defense
	OUTER FACTORS OF DEFENSE:	—its basic posture;
		—FUNCTIONAL: the strategic way of using it in defense, through:
		—its motion of evasion and of centralization;
		—its techniques of neutralization: the basic immobilizations, the basic projections and their combinations

23. THE PROCESS OF DEFENSE AND ITS FACTORS

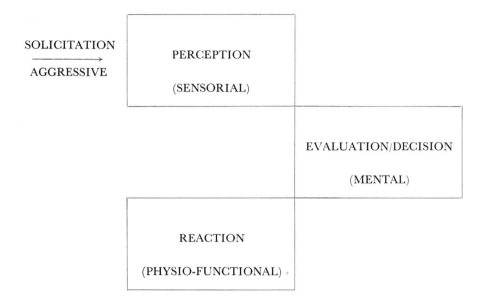

SOLICITATION
——————→
AGGRESSIVE

PERCEPTION

(SENSORIAL)

EVALUATION/DECISION

(MENTAL)

REACTION

(PHYSIO-FUNCTIONAL)

EVERY process of defense will consist of three stages: perception, evaluation-decision, and reaction. And the effectiveness of any defensive strategy will depend largely upon the time lapse between the first inkling that an attack may be imminent, and your defensive reaction. In aikido the strategic aim is to train and refine your faculties to such an extent that perception, evaluation-decision, and reaction will become almost simultaneous.

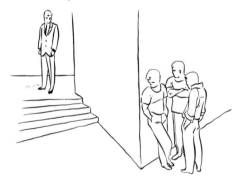

In the first stage of perception, on the most obvious sensorial level, we may see someone preparing to attack, or hear him as he approaches, or feel the actual, physical contact of a hold. On the subliminal, and more difficult to define sensorial level, we say that we "sense" something—without being conscious of seeing or hearing anything menacing, we nevertheless sense or know that something is wrong.

In the second stage, that of evaluation-decision, the various elements of an attack are analyzed: the amount of its dynamic momentum, the speed, the direction—and a decision is made concerning the most appropriate technique to apply.

The third and final stage is that of reaction. The decision "comes to life" via the motion/action of a specific aikido technique of neutralization.

As we have noted, however, these three stages—perception, evaluation-decision, and reaction—will be so closely identified and so nearly simultaneous in an advanced aikido strategy that they will appear as one. This of course is the immediate, strategic goal of your training.

Keeping this criterion in mind, any process of defense can accordingly be qualified as normal (positive) or abnormal (negative). The normal process of defense proceeds smoothly and culminates in the effective neutralization of an attack. The abnormal (or negative) process will be one which exhibits either faulty perception, poor judgment, or an insufficient reaction—and does not result in the desired neutralization.

In the normal process of any defense, perception will be both general and particular at one and the same time. In other words, if you are in a room,

		NORMAL (positive)	ABNORMAL (negative)
24. THE PROCESS OF DEFENSE: STAGES AND QUALITIES	I PERCEPTION	—general (awareness) particular (concentrated)	unaware dispersed
	II EVALUATION-DECISION	calm and precise	perturbed and confused
	III REACTION	—specific —immediate —powerful —consistent	—unrelated —anachronistic (too early or too late) —inadequate (too strong or too weak) —erratic

you will be aware of the entire room and its contents, while remaining alert to the motions/actions of the people within that room. This is only possible, of course, if all the powers of perception are "turned on" at all times.

On the basis of this positive state of perception, the second stage of a normal process of defense (evaluation-decision) will develop smoothly and as a natural consequence of that correct perception.

In the astoundingly swift process of defense which characterizes an efficient aikido strategy, this intermediate stage may be imperceptible, i.e., it may appear that reaction (third stage) follows perception (first stage). This, however, is not entirely correct.

What has happened, actually, is that intensive and specialized training has reduced the span of time between perception and evaluation-decision so that this stage of the process of defense has become unconscious, the body having been trained to react in a specialized way to a certain type of stimulus, to a certain type of attack. Reaction has thus become almost a conditioned reflex; and the response, almost simultaneous with the perception.

Here, of course, we are speaking of a process of defense which belongs to the highest levels of aikido. At the beginning of a student's practice this second stage of evaluation-decision will be noticeable in the form of a slight hesitation between the attack and the response. Even here, however, in the normal (positive) process of defense, a student will be working toward maintaining a calm, objective awareness of what is happening so that he will be able to take the proper action and successfully perform an appropriate aikido technique.

A positive defensive strategy is further qualified as being specific, immediate, consistent, and powerful.

It will be specific when you select the proper technique to neutralize a particular attack. All aikido techniques are tailored responses to certain motions and actions of attack. And some are more appropriate and easier to perform in response to certain types of attack. An attack from behind, for instance, will be neutralized by the application of a defensive technique particularly geared to that form of attack, not by attempting a technique more suitable to a frontal attack.

It will be immediate or instantaneous when your reaction is so swift that you apply a technique of neutralization while the attack is still developing, and at the higher levels of the practice even before an attack has been fully launched.

A positive reaction will be consistent or constant, i.e., it will become so much a part of your personality that an efficient defensive reaction will become the rule rather than the exception, when and if you should be attacked.

A positive reaction, finally, will be powerful when it contains sufficient centralized energy to control the entire process of defense from beginning to end. This control is evidenced by the fluid shifting from one defensive strategy to another if necessary, by efficient defense against an attack launched by one man or several men, and by the calm and controlled manner in which your defensive strategy will be developed and concluded.

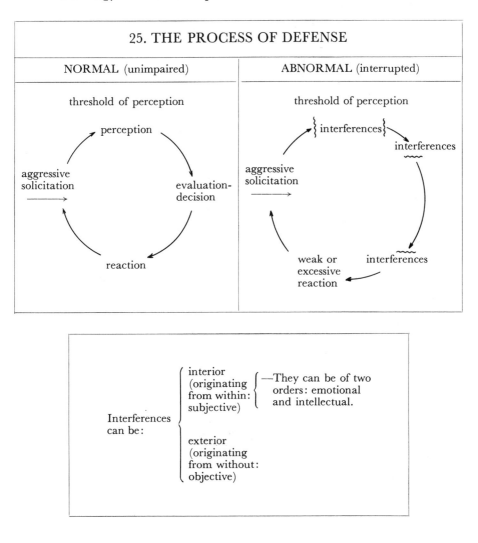

25. THE PROCESS OF DEFENSE

| NORMAL (unimpaired) | ABNORMAL (interrupted) |

26. AGGRESSIVE SOLICITATION

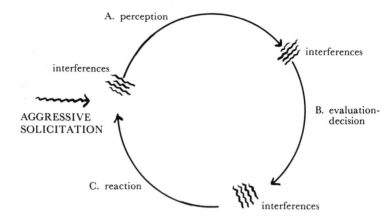

In the abnormal process of defense, as we have said, the perception may be faulty, the judgment poor, or the reaction insufficient. This may take a variety of forms: as far as your perceptions are concerned, you may not see an attack coming until it is too late, you may not hear someone as he comes up behind you, and, of course, you may not possess that peripheral awareness which would serve to alert you to an impending attack before it actually materialized. You may also be hypnotized by the very fact of the attack, or your attention may be captured by one element of the attack so that your assessment of its speed, direction, dynamic momentum, etc., may not be correct. This kind of poor judgment may be responsible for an ineffective reaction, for a hesitant or badly timed response to an attack. Or, even if your perceptions are adequate and your judgment correct, your reflexes may be poor, your muscles unresponsive through lack of regular physical exercise. Thus lack of proper physical conditioning may also make it impossible for you to respond effectively.

	STAGES	FACTORS
27. THE PROCESS OF DEFENSE: STAGES AND FACTORS	1. PERCEPTION	PHYSIO-PSYCHOLOGICAL
	2. EVALUATION-DECISION	MENTAL (INNER)
	3. REACTION	PHYSIO-FUNCTIONAL (OUTER)

In order to insure that the process of defense will be positive, i.e., specific, immediate, consistent, and powerful—the Inner and Outer Factors of that defense must conform to certain patterns.

The Inner Factors of defense in aikido are related to the role of your mind in combat; to the spiritual attitude and to the interior forces activating, controlling, and directing the defensive strategy of the art; to the energy employed in carrying it out; to the particular principles which rule any defense from beginning to end.

The Outer Factors of defense are related to the physical and functional dimension of combat, to the physical instrument or weapons employed (your body), and to the dynamic and technical ways of using your body under the directing and controlling power of the mind.

Of these two classes of factors, the former, i.e., the Inner Factors of defense, are considered within the doctrine of aikido to be of primary importance if you are to practice the art correctly and if your strategies are to be successful. As Mr. Tohei points out, ". . . the physical techniques can be easily learned within a short span, like other Martial Arts." But, in order to develop the keen powers of perception, the flexibility and the concentration of powers—which alone will insure the immediacy of your reaction and the maintenance of a properly calm and undaunted attitude—a stringent, continuous program of mental as well as physical application is required.

In aikido, it is considered meaningless and ultimately self-defeating to concentrate primarily and almost exclusively upon the Outer Factors of the art, and upon the physical development of the body or upon a skillful maneuvering of the various strategies of defense (both dynamically and technically), without at the same time developing an inner condition of calm and constant control. The body has its all too obvious limitations, but who can describe with certainty the limits of the mind and its possibilities of development? Moreover, who can deny that combat, in reality, begins in the mind?

In the best aikido *dojo,* you will be told over and over again that the domain of the mind is unlimited and ever expanding. To develop the imaginative and controlling powers of the mind, to coordinate them all with the

physical and functional capacities of the body means that the possibilities of the body will be enhanced and its general functionality will be improved, while the character and personality of the student will develop and mature. Without this inner development, the rest is an illusion.

The practice of the art provides ample material for the development of both the physical and functional aspects of your defensive personality. What is necessary, however, is to create a Centre of control, of direction and concentration which will make the fusion of mind and body possible.

From the very beginning of aikido practice, then, the emphasis is upon creating the proper mental condition for an effective defense.

28. THE INNER FACTORS: THE ROLE OF THE MIND

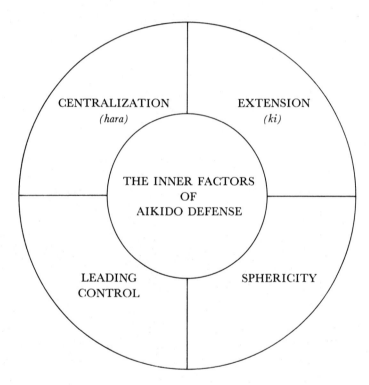

"The mind leads the body," Tohei Sensei proclaims again and again during his lessons, thus re-emphasizing the ancient axiom of almost every great civilization: "Spirit rules matter."

One of the elements which sets aikido apart from many other martial arts (in addition to the special forms and types of techniques of neutralization which Master Uyeshiba adapted and developed for his art) is the predominant role assigned, from the first moment you step on the mat, to the role of your mind and its functions of control, direction, and power.

In combat, the mind must control the process of defense from the moment an aggression is perceived to the moment when a reaction occurs, while channeling a particular type of totally coordinated energy in the appropriate direction.

In analyzing this process of control and the type of energy referred to above, four basic principles emerge. These are:

1. The principle of centralization
2. The principle of extension
3. The principle of leading control
4. The principle of sphericity

The Principle of Centralization

> "Be stably centralized, inwardly and outwardly, in the lower abdomen!"

As soon as you step on the mat in an orthodox aikido *dojo,* you will be encouraged to acquire and develop, through appropriate exercises, a feeling of stable centralization of your whole being in the lower abdomen. This is the area which corresponds to what Westerners know as a man's "center of gravity," or the spot where your weight reaches its maximum concentration and

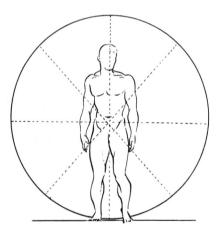

balance, achieving equilibrium between the central and upper anatomy above, and the supporting architecture of your legs below. This area, with its powerful pelvic structure, represents the balanced center of elevation which allows you to stand erect and maintain an upright posture continually and with comparative ease.

From that center of elevation and support, the sum total of your central and upper weight is channeled downward through your legs to the ground.

Known in Japan generally as *hara,* this Centre of unification and coordination is more specifically identified in aikido terminology as *seika no itten* ("one point," K. Tohei), and as *seika tanden* ("centrum," K. Uyeshiba). We refer to it simply as the "Centre."

We speak of centralization in the lower abdomen. This is one of the most basic techniques of aikido and must be mastered if any real progress is to be made, on the mat or off. However, it is a technique, a device, a form of training or discipline, not an end in itself. It has as its final aim the achievement of total coordination and harmony of mind and body, of man and men, of man and his environment (now expanded to include the whole universe). In sum, by following this discipline of initially conscious centralization in the lower abdomen, a point can be reached where centralization becomes automatic and unconscious, where you will not "think centralization"—you will be centralized.

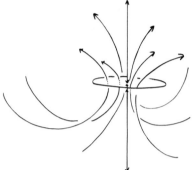

This Centre will be used as a unifying device in the difficult process of co-ordinating the whole range of your powers and possibilities. It will be used in establishing a stable platform of unification and independence from which you may operate in full control, relating to and coping with your reality, combat, or an aggressor.

Your training in becoming and ultimately in being centralized will involve your personality totally, both within and without. We will, therefore, speak of a subjective form of centralization—involving your personality alone ("Be centralized within! Keep One Point!"); and of an objective form of central-ization which will expand to include your external reality—("Be in the 'Centre' of the action, of the Technique!").

This interesting concept of centralization is well known in the Orient and amazingly comprehensive. Its dimensions range from the cosmic or universal where the Centre is identified with the idea of order, harmony, and total integration in the balance of opposites, to the human and personal, where it is seen as the balance point of your personality, the unified basis of your in-dividuality and particular character (see Chart 29, page 71).

Both the cosmic and the human dimensions of the concept, however, are closely identified, man being an integral part of creation. The true and all-encompassing Centre, according to Eastern philosophy, is the same for both the general and the particular, for the universe and for man. This is under-scored in many Japanese tales of the wise man who lives in harmony with him-self and with nature. Separation of man from that identity with the universe, alienation of man from man, and finally, a man's feeling of a split within himself are considered to be the result of paying too much attention to the surface differences, to the details of life. This completely ignores the under-lying identity of all life, the basic "oneness" of its essence.

29. CENTRALIZATION

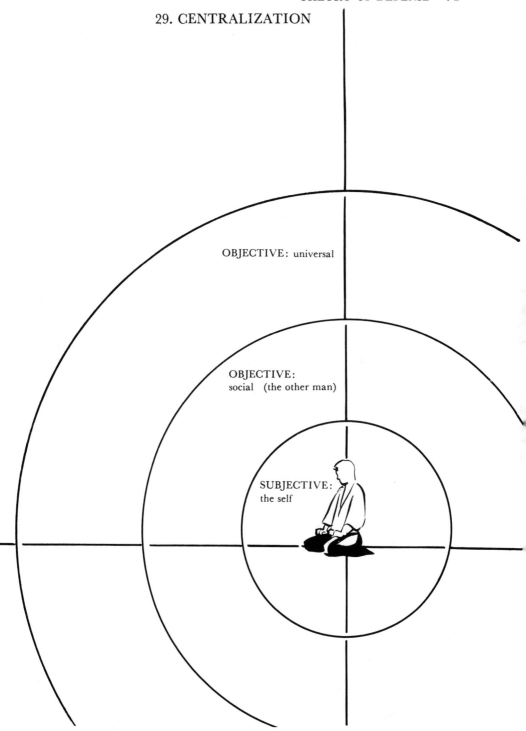

OBJECTIVE: universal

OBJECTIVE:
social   (the other man)

SUBJECTIVE:
the self

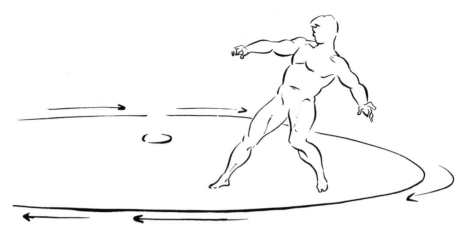

Man, even if unconsciously, seeks to find a Centre. In Western psychology we say that he is "goal-directed" or "goal-motivated." He is considered to be functioning properly only when he is working toward a specific goal or goals. If he has no goals, he has no "life" in the social sense of the word, since he is existing merely as all animals do, in response to certain basic life-preserving instincts (territory, food, sex, etc.), but not as man does, or should. In other words, it is not enough for man to ask "how"—he also seeks to know "why."

However, even if he is striving toward a goal (actually doing, moving), he may have selected the wrong goal for himself. Therefore, the problem is two-fold: first he must be provided with the instruction and guidance, with the "education" in the most comprehensive sense of the word, which will enable him to select the proper goals for himself; then he must be encouraged to strive toward that goal, an actual process of doing, of becoming. And even then he must maintain a certain objectivity, a certain balance or independent Centre so that he can pursue his goals without becoming totally immersed in them. One man may play many parts, but only if he remains flexible, only if he develops and maintains his Centre.

Asia has many schools of thought devoted solely to the search for and development of the Centre *(haragei)*. The concept, however, has been adopted by many other schools of thought and action (such as the martial arts) as a means of achieving other more practical ends.

In this sense it has been incorporated into almost all the arts of the Orient wherever performance and not merely contemplation is essential. In the martial arts it became a Centre of stability and power for the specific purpose of controlling the reality of combat.

In a comparatively specialized and necessarily limited book such as this, it is impossible to examine the general theory of the Centre in both the culture of Asia and in the martial arts, in great detail. We can only outline the applications of this concept to the art of aikido, hoping to enlarge upon both the Centre *(hara)* and intrinsic, inner, or total energy *(ki)* in another book.

Subjective Centralization

Centralization is intended to further the unification and coordination of all of your powers—mental, physical, and functional—so that yours will become a truly coordinated personality.

The effects of this "inner" centralization, according to the doctrine of aikido, will be evident. In the mental dimension, all of your powers of perception, of evaluation and decision, and of reaction will be heightened and sharpened as a result of this fusion. You will find yourself seeing, understanding, responding with extraordinary clarity and intensity.

This "clear vision" is possible because effective centralization acts as a screen between you and the often confusing, disturbing sequence of events accompanying any form of combat—just as a screened-in porch in the summertime allows you to sit outside and talk without continually interrupting yourself to shoo away the mosquitoes.

Centralization, therefore, means adopting a new point of reference, a new platform from which you can exercise a more objective form of control over events and over yourself.

But such objectivity—i.e., a clear understanding of the nature, extent, and complexity of a given problem, is impossible if your mind is obsessed by that problem, unable to consider it dispassionately. Objectivity requires as much impartiality as you can muster, and this will depend, in turn, upon the degree of mental independence you have achieved.

If you are not capable of maintaining this mental distance between yourself and events as they unfold—or even explode—around you, then the events will begin to dominate you and your control will disappear. Mr. Tohei often warns students not to pay undue attention to or become hypnotized by the weapons, face, or threatening posture of an opponent. These, as the ancient teachers of martial arts often wrote, ". . . are only appearances." What you must seek to develop then in your aikido training, is the ability to stay centralized and to be centralized, so that when and if a concrete attack should materialize you will be able to perceive it clearly, to decide and respond effectively, and to channel all of your powers toward the neutralization of the aggressive action in a total, decisive manner.

Clarity of vision, in turn, has two aspects: the first is awareness, which covers the entire field being perceived; the second is concentration, which is related to a specific event, person or persons within that field.

Awareness is the foundation of effective combat readiness. Episodes such as that of the fencing master mentioned in the Monk Takuan's letter as translated by Dr. Suzuki* indicate the intense and refined level of perception which the disciplined and experienced mind can attain.

In aikido practice this condition is best displayed when an advanced practitioner defends himself against four, five, or six attackers closing in upon him from every side. Whirling in their midst, the aikido practitioner seems to "sense" which one is about to attack at any given moment, even if that attacker is behind him. And this perception is blended so smoothly with his strategy of defense that his reactions will be coordinated with the various attacks considered as a whole. His control over the neutralization is as complete as the circumstances will permit.

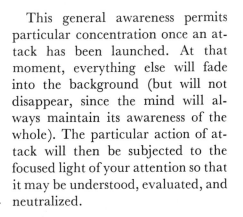

This general awareness permits particular concentration once an attack has been launched. At that moment, everything else will fade into the background (but will not disappear, since the mind will always maintain its awareness of the whole). The particular action of attack will then be subjected to the focused light of your attention so that it may be understood, evaluated, and neutralized.

* *Zen and Japanese Culture*, New York, 1959.

This inner centralization, when correctly understood and practiced, will produce certain noticeable effects in your body, i.e., the development of balanced stability and relaxed suppleness.

In aikido, balance means: vertical alignment of the body with the perpendicular axis of gravity (therefore, maintenance of a "normal" posture; Chapter VII), and a state of fluid poise between rest and motion (therefore, readiness to maintain or return to either state).

Again, we are brought back to your body's maximum balance point which is located in the lower abdomen, i.e., your center of gravity.

Maintaining your balance is of the utmost importance in aikido practice, whether you are simply standing still or in full motion. Even when whirling about on the mat as one man after another attacks, you must seek to maintain the correct posture, to keep your balance, so that your upper anatomy will be in vertical alignment with your center of gravity or Centre.

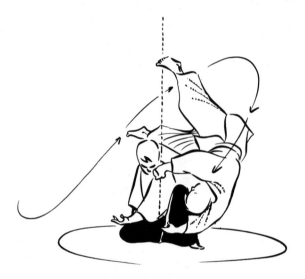

There will, of course, be moments when you will twist, turn, or bend your body as you lead a motion of attack around you and away from its intended target. But always, upon completion of such an evasion or leading motion, your trunk will be brought back into alignment with your Centre.

It is interesting to note how many Japanese practitioners of the art bend their knees deeply, keeping their trunks straight (but not rigid) when they wish to lead an attacker down, rather than bending over, pretzel fashion, which would leave them extremely vulnerable to even a slight push from behind.

This physical centralization is a "constant" of combat. There are even special exercises for its development (see Chapter VI). And, of course, even a cursory glance at the techniques of neutralization will reveal how important the maintenance of correct posture is to any defensive strategy.

Centralization in the lower abdomen, moreover, represents a sort of gravitational descent of your body's weight, draining the upper anatomy of excessive muscular stress and leaving it extremely supple and mobile (especially the muscles of the neck and shoulders which so often display the first signs of paralyzing rigidity).

In the area of "relaxed suppleness," the literature available on aikido always stresses the importance of relaxation; in fact, this is considered one of the basic requirements for an effective aikido performance.

As Mr. T. P. Leggett (Judo, 6th *dan*) has observed in *The Demonstration of Gentleness,* London, 1964, the word "relaxation" as commonly used and interpreted in the West may be misleading.

In aikido terminology, "relaxation" does not mean a collapsed, weak, or comatose condition, but rather a state of muscular pliability and smooth flexibility which permits an unimpaired reaction in any direction, at the first indication of an aggressive movement.

The authors, therefore, prefer to refer to this condition as one of "relaxed suppleness," with the intention of conveying the idea of softness without rigidity or abnormal muscular tension, while also suggesting resiliency, or a lively, smooth readiness to react when and if necessary.

For those who maintain that without tension there can be no reaction, and that tension therefore is the indication of preparedness, we refer to the example so frequently cited in works on the martial arts, of a cat's reactivity. If you have ever watched a cat curled up in a ball on the living room rug or stretched out lazily in the sun taking a nap, you will have noticed that it seems as limp as a piece of fluff: all of its muscles are relaxed, no tension is evident in any line of its body, and only an almost imperceptible rise and fall indicates its breathing.

Approach it as stealthily as you can in an attempt to catch it off guard, bend down ever so carefully, and—at the very moment when your outstretched hand is about to close upon the animal—there will be a flash of movement. The next instant that same cat will be on the other side of the room, calmly licking its paws.

Another example widely employed in aikido and in other martial arts (see the Chinese Classic, *Tao Te Ching,* quoted by Mr. Leggett in his book, *The Demonstration of Gentleness*) is that of the infant whose body is supple and full of life and whose grip—total, blending with the object held—is astoundingly strong and difficult to break, and yet not rigid or tense.

Finally, in relation to functionality, centralization will result in increased power and effectiveness, since in combat the Centre will operate as a unified source of motion and action—the power of both seeming to flow upward from the very earth, as from an inexhaustible well. It is immediately noticeable in aikido that movement is always from the hips involving your entire body and your entire personality in the action.

You will move about on the mat with a particular gliding step, searching for the appropriate centralized position. Once you have found it you will maneuver your attacker's body with ease, keeping him spinning orbitally around his own Centre. And this will apply even in the immobilizations— as you lead your attacker into one of the Circuits of Neutralization.

Objective Centralization

Your own Centre must become the center of your attacker's action as well. The Centre is not restricted in aikido, as we have indicated, to your personal dimension. If a man attacks you, he has lost his own point of independence and balance by the very irrationality of that act, and you must substitute your own Centre in an attempt to return the situation to normal. Thus he attacks, you evade; he plunges into a vacuum, you lead and guide him back around your own Centre and neutralize his attack.

In every technique of neutralization there is this constant, fluid centralization of the action around you, before you pin an opponent down in an immobilization beneath your Centre, or project him away from that Centre.

Your Centre may be located almost directly beneath him or at his side, but it is always the Centre of a dynamic circle along whose fringes your attacker will be forced to spin without any possibility of controlling his motions. This process is explained in detail in the section entitled "Principle of Sphericity."

30. COORDINATION

centralization	subjective	mental	independent control clear vision (general and specific, awareness and attention)
		physical	stable balance relaxed suppleness
		functional	extreme mobility and centralized power
	objective		centrality of defense correlated orbital centrifugality of its attack

The Principle of Extension

One of the most important and truly amazing features of aikido, the aspect which never ceases to astound even the practitioner, is represented by the essence, the spirit—the *ki* or centralized energy—which animates the application of all the techniques (when the art is being practiced properly), and characterizes aikido in a particular way.

Aikido begins, in fact, with the fundamental assumption that every human being possesses this *ki:* this vital force which when concentrated in a single unified stream can be extended and channeled into a practically irresistible action of defense, into a technique.

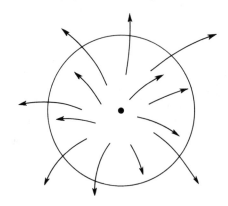

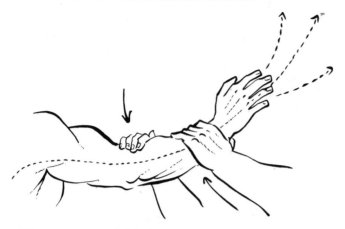

The presence of this *ki* and the way it can be extended is very often demonstrated in aikido *dojo* by a series of tests or practical demonstrations. Among these, the most popularly persuasive is that of the unbendable arm described in the introductory chapter. The idea of an unbendable arm is an example of what may be defined as static *ki*, or extension in the sense that what the student achieves is a powerful concentration of consciousness and energy within the Centre, in the interest of immovability.

But the real basis of aikido is "dynamic" *ki*, the same concentration and unified power in motion.

Here we are faced with the problem of defining just what type of energy or power we mean by *ki*. Is it mental, physical, or a combination of both? In the West we tend to measure strength in terms of muscle power, while in the East they often refer to the "power of the spirit" or "mind over matter." If, however, man is considered not as a divided being—mental vs. physical—but rather as an entity, a whole human being whose mental activity involves physical changes in the brain and whose physical activity can have long lasting, supra-physical results, then his energy, his power—when unified and coordinated—can also be considered to be a "total" type of strength. The universe throbs with energy; energized particles in various forms bombard our globe constantly. So man is "energized" and displays that energy in everything he does. If, however, he works toward becoming a truly integrated, unified human being with all of his powers coordinated and harmonized, then he will be truly able to "flow *ki*," or extend that energy.

It should be remembered, however, that *ki,* considered specifically as energy, is employed like the Centre and techniques to achieve certain aims, neutralize an aggression, promote harmony (according to Master Uyeshiba). Like any other force, it can be misapplied or negatively applied from a moral point of view. Therefore, "strong *ki*" does not necessarily mean a morally positive or "good *ki*," a distinction not too often made in the Orient where (like many of their counterparts in the West) quite a number of martial art scholars tend to see this form of "might" as being automatically "right." Ancient masters of the martial arts, however, who recognized that strong or well-developed *ki* without an ethical or moral foundation could be unleashed as a force for terrible destruction, were very discriminating when selecting students since they were well aware of the evil uses to which this tremendous power could be put.

This type of energy or power is referred to constantly in most works on the martial arts and is often called intrinsic or inner energy *(prana* in India, *ch'i* in China, *ki* in Japan). It is usually developed through conscious, disciplined programs; and once it has been concentrated in a total sense, it is "extended" in the desired direction. The expression "mental projection" is a frequently recurring one in the literature of the martial arts. (The authors, however, prefer to use "mental extension" to avoid any confusion between mental projection and the group of techniques of neutralization known as "projections.")

As is true of the concept of *hara,* or Centre, to which this intrinsic or total energy is closely linked (being its point of maximum concentration, storage, and extension), the concept of *ki* can be expanded to include the cosmos and the ever expanding energy of life in the universe as a whole, and then contracted to a consideration of the character, personality, and vitality of the individual man.

Here, too, the authors can only briefly outline its general dimensions, particularly as they relate to the practice of aikido, and treat the theory of *ki* in depth in their monography on the Centre and *ki*.

In Master Uyeshiba's martial art, this form of energy is considered to be the fundamental, all-pervasive force activating any strategy of defense. The statements of the highest instructors of the art, in this context, are unmistakably clear: "No *ki*—no aikido."

This intrinsic or total energy, present potentially in every human being in an uncoordinated and dispersed state, must be unified, accumulated, stabilized, and extended.

The task of developing *ki* in aikido is fulfilled through special exercises, among which abdominal breathing is one of the most important. This technique of deep breathing is found in the esoteric disciplines of Yoga and Zen, as well as in many other martial arts.

The exercise of abdominal breathing in aikido is usually linked to that of concentration of energies in the Centre.

Ki is accumulated, in fact, in the Centre, where its full coordination is achieved. The two concepts—that of the Centre and that of intrinsic, inner, or total energy—are thus really one:—the Centre, vitally active and ever expanding through this form of energy; the energy, fully coordinated and stabilized in the Centre (centralized energy). The entire body of the student seems to become a compact source of power, without undue emphasis upon individual parts of that body acting or performing on their own. In this context, *ki* can also be qualified as "global" energy, "total extension," or "full coordination of powers."

This totality of extension is particularly evident in every movement of aikido practitioners on the mat when the art is being practiced properly. In fact, many of the Japanese instructors with whom we have practiced have stressed the idea of moving from the hips or Centre and of being whole, i.e., not performing techniques by stretching out an arm, pulling, or pushing, but rather by moving with the whole body and involving it totally (under the mind's concentrated and controlling leadership) in the action.

Totality of extension is also the reason why in aikido practice the student is encouraged to think of his body as an extension of his mind, and his arms and legs as extensions of that body, not as separate entities.

This is not to say that your arms and legs will not have their functions, but rather that these functions will be integrated with, and subordinated to, the general unified movement of the body as a whole. Even apart from any esoteric considerations of *ki,* it seems logical to assume that the power efficiently generated by the body used as a single unit will be greater than that which could be generated by the use of the arms and legs alone.

In aikido practice, legs will carry your centralized anatomy from place to place; hands will grasp or guide an opponent, but only as extensions of and in accordance with the movement of the body as a whole. There is no pushing, pulling, or straining of individual limbs, but rather a whirling, unified movement with dominant emphasis upon hip motion.

In aikido practice, you will be trained to extend as well as move from the hips. Through the basic exercises, you will be encouraged to let your *ki* flow outward from the Centre, in the specific directions which identify the particular ways of neutralizing an aggression. Thus the extension of defensive energy becomes automatic and constant. An aggressive solicitation (an attack) triggers the appropriate defensive response flowing from the Centre of control and power, intended to neutralize that attack through the extension of centralized, "soft," and yet powerful energy.

And this concept of constant extension underlies the unbendable arm exercise. In his lessons, Mr. Tohei always insists that if you do not maintain this unbendable arm at all times (in other words, if you do not keep your extension constant), you will be unable to perform the techniques correctly.

This expression, so popular in aikido *dojo,* identifies both an exercise and an idea. In the first sense, it is related to an outpouring of your coordinated energy in a given direction through your extended arm as previously explained. In the second sense, it is related to the extension of energy from the Centre which must be constant and centrifugal, i.e., directed outward.

The unbendable arm, however, does not mean an absolutely straight, ramrod arm, but an arm slightly curved in the form of a half-circle. This will permit you to guide and direct your attacker's force without smashing directly into it. This is a particularly important point, since the notion of going "through" an obstacle is a rather alien one at the highest levels of the art. But whatever the degree of half-circle extension you maintain, your arm must not collapse in the face of an oncoming blow or any other form of attack.

This is the real meaning of unbendable arm, not that it juts out straight and rigid in front of you, but rather that the mental energy directing the half-circle extension of your arm will maintain that half-circle intact, protecting the rest of your body while you lead and guide your aggressor's attack into a Circuit of Neutralization.

Whether taking falls (the particular, circular aikido roll-out illustrated in Chapter VI), or reacting to an attack with a technique of immobilization or projection, you must maintain unbendable arm. If you do not, if you attempt to "grab" a blow or a punch in mid-air, you will be practicing incorrectly since it is obvious that you could not possibly hope to grab a blow directed toward you suddenly and with great force. So you must extend at all times—this is a mental and physical form of extension—just as the energy is total energy, so also must your extension be "total extension." And this warning should be kept in mind especially when you are performing those techniques which require an *irimi,* or "entering" movement, since it will be then that the tendency to try to grab will be very strong.

After the first movement and extension, you will usually secure a hold on your aggressor's arm, hand, etc., but this will only be *after* you have parried and led your opponent's motion through your extension, the outer perimeter of which is your unbendable arm.

As you progress in the art, as your reflexes become more keenly honed and your perceptions refined, the entering and/or evading motions as well as the initial extension will be briefer, and the hold will be secured with often blinding speed. But the basic mental and physical extension must be maintained constantly, even if the initial extension is barely perceptible when techniques are performed by an advanced practitioner of the art. For, if you should miscalculate the speed or exact angle of an attacker's motion, if you should be tripped, if more than one person attacks you, that mental and physical extension may very well mean the difference between defending yourself efficiently and being overcome.

Outward extension represents, on one side, comprehensive control over the outside reality through this "turning on" of mental, physical, and thus functional powers, which we may relate to that condition of independent awareness surveyed in the principle of centralization, in the mental dimension. It also implies impenetrability, the impossibility of an opponent reaching your Centre either by hitting it or capturing it in any way.

Aikido doctrine often refers to the image of a spring whose waters flowing outward are crystal clear. The moment the outward flow ceases, muddy, polluted waters will rush in. Impenetrability, therefore, is the active part of that Centre of independent control which we encountered on pages 69–79.

This centralized energy also appears to be of the all-pervading, force-field type, as compared with (or opposed to) the concentrated and sharp form of energy which cuts through an opposing target, smashing anything in its path—a form of energy cultivated in many other martial arts. In aikido however, as in certain ancient martial arts, the emphasis is upon the unified harmonized personality and therefore upon centralized energy.

The general doctrine of the martial arts also enlarges at great length upon the basic differences between the "hard" form of *ki* and the "soft" form. Hard *ki* appears to be sharp and concentrated to a dangerous point of fusion resembling the edge or point of a Japanese blade. As such, when used in combat (whether offensively or defensively), it will cut through the physical target against which it is being directed. It is predominantly straight (direct) although there are circular forms of hard *ki* (theory of the slashing extension).

The very concentration of this form of *ki* usually requires that a single anatomical weapon, i.e., arm, leg, hand, foot, elbow, etc., be employed to deliver the force of the concentrated energy.

31. TYPES OF "KI"

Soft *ki,* by contrast, appears to be evenly diffused, irradiating, and expanding like a huge globe to envelop the target completely or spin tangentially against it. Here again we have the image of "massed wind or water."

This form of energy does not cut through the target; it sweeps it away in a tangential, circular pattern that sends that target spinning in full centrifugal unbalance or extends and stretches it elastically in the desired direction. The diffusive nature of this soft *ki* implies necessarily a typically circular form of extension as well as the employment of the whole body to produce it.

In aikido, soft *ki* is the desired form, and according to Master Uyeshiba, it should be employed within the framework of the natural laws of creation. Aikido does not, in other words, advocate the employment of intrinsic or total energy in a way which breaks those laws by seriously injuring or destroying another man.

As noted elsewhere, neutralization in aikido is centered upon the aggressive action, not against the personality of the aggressor. That neutralization can be achieved with tremendous efficiency and power to spare, against one aggressor or against many; it does not destroy the bridge which, linking man to man, permits you to approach the remote or ethical aims of aikido.

Finally, this intrinsic energy is permanent in the sense that, like the Centre, its extension is "turned on" at all times, not only during combat. This requisite implies that the energy developed progressively through the specialized exercises of abdominal breathing and mental concentration in the Centre, extended consciously at first, will become a part of your personality —a way of being—through regular and properly motivated practice of the art of aikido.

As is always the case, the most difficult stage for everyone studying and training in aikido will be that of attempting to achieve the proper balance and integration between substance and manifestation, spirit and action—*ki* and technique. Those seemingly separate divisions are actually only closely related segments of the whole (the human being striving to be an individual who, as Pericles claimed for the free citizens of Athens, will be "able to meet every variety of circumstance with the greatest versatility—and with grace").

The Principle of Leading Control

"Control the Attack By Leading it"

The first principle dealt with the basic centralization of your personality, with its unification; the second principle explained the extension of energy, of *ki,* flowing outward for the purpose of controlling an attack. The next two principles will specify more exactly, just how that control is to be achieved.

In Chart 20, page 59, we saw how all the factors of an attack were combined in the Unified Power of Attack, i.e., your opponent's force as a totality converging upon you. We also noted that this UPA was extremely powerful along its direct line or pattern of convergence, but comparatively weak at the outer edges of that direct pattern or line, as well as beyond its intended functional point of impact, as illustrated in Chart 32, page 88.

Therefore, from the very first moment that you perceive an attack, you must control it through an appropriate "lead" which will direct its potentially dangerous and concentrated force into harmless channels. This lead must be smooth and continuous and never in direct opposition to the force of the attack, since halting or interrupting it would destroy the very momentum your aikido defense strategy requires. This lead will have certain definite points of control and certain precise dimensions.

In the illustrations which follow, you will see that the points of control to be established over the UPA as it converges upon you will be directed toward the areas where it is weakest:

At its source, i.e., at the point of its uncoiling, or where it is in the process of developing—inner limit (enter when pulled);

At its outer limit, beyond the point of its maximum extension, where dissipation of its force begins (turn when pushed), or

In the middle between its inner and outer limits, during the process of convergence upon you (see Chart 33, page 88).

32. THE POWER OF UPA

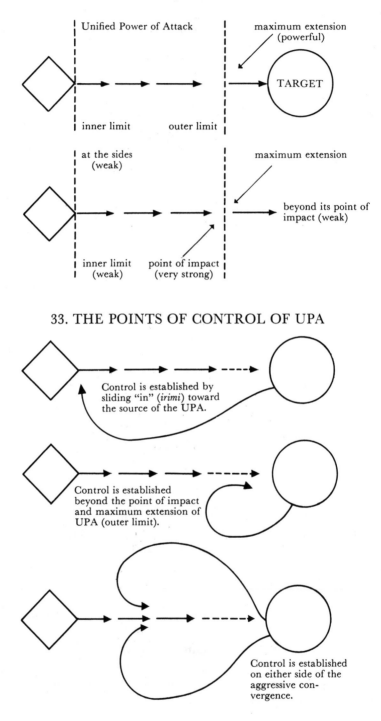

Unified Power of Attack

maximum extension (powerful)

TARGET

inner limit   outer limit

at the sides (weak)

maximum extension

beyond its point of impact (weak)

inner limit (weak)   point of impact (very strong)

33. THE POINTS OF CONTROL OF UPA

Control is established by sliding "in" (*irimi*) toward the source of the UPA.

Control is established beyond the point of impact and maximum extension of UPA (outer limit).

Control is established on either side of the aggressive convergence.

In all the cases indicated above, control through leading is assured by blending with and flowing within the aggressive convergence. Once you have established contact and control in this "non-abrasive" manner, you will then be able to direct that aggressive convergence, that attack, from within into an appropriate Circuit of Neutralization.

Readers familiar with the martial arts will recognize at this point the principle of nonresistance *(ju)* which figures so prominently in many of those arts. The principle of leading control is the specific form which the principle of nonresistance assumes in aikido practice.

If you do not establish control through this leading and blending motion and action as illustrated, you will be forced to clash directly with the concentrated force of that attack. It would mean strength directly opposed to strength, force meeting force head on, the exact opposite of an orthodox aikido strategy.

"Lead," in fact, does not mean "force" in the physical sense of pressure, a pull, or a push. If you push a man suddenly, he will instinctively push back. Grab his hand violently, and he will immediately try to shake you off. Any direct action taken against a man will almost inevitably result in an equally direct reaction.

This instinctive tendency to act and react directly will present you with your first stumbling block when you begin to practice the art. You will have to learn to spin when you are pushed and to enter when someone pulls you—in accordance with the principle of nonresistance, a principle which can prove much more effective in combat than that of strength or force directly opposed to an attacker's strength or force.

The dimensions of this lead will be simultaneously mental and functional (the latter being both dynamic and technical).

For example, you will move to evade your opponent's motion of attack, but evasion is only one of your dynamic purposes: centralization for the purpose of applying the appropriate technique of neutralization is the other. You will move, in other words, primarily because this is how you will begin to lead your opponent into the desired position. It is not simply to avoid his initial attack.

Against a direct thrust to your stomach or lower abdomen, for example (whether your opponent employs his fist or a knife), you will not pull back or pull in, mentally or physio-functionally. This would only draw him on. Instead you will move in tangentially toward the oncoming blow, spinning vertically at the same time. Following well-defined psychological and dynamic laws, such a spin will render the target (your mid-section) extremely elusive— as you lead the converging motion of attack around you.

Professor Tohei moves in and spins. Even if he does not touch your extended arm (which has already missed its target) you will feel drawn forward

and around him; his movement becomes a sort of suction you will find extremely difficult to resist.

This leading, which is a combination of intention (mental) and motion (physio-functional), will continue until your defensive strategy has been completed. You will keep your opponent's initial movement or attack going, leading him by a thin dynamic thread into whatever technique of neutralization is most appropriate to the circumstances.

This complex combination of psychological and functional factors (dynamic and technical) which work simultaneously to produce this principle of leading control, will reach its highest concentration in those techniques where you will seem to move hardly at all while under attack (usually in self-defense against a single attacker).

Several times the authors attempted to hit Mr. Tohei with full mental and physical concentration upon the part of his anatomy previously selected

as the target (his lower abdomen, his throat or chin, his head, etc.). Every time at the very moment when it seemed we would surely hit him, his hand would suddenly appear as if out of nowhere, and lead the oncoming blow or punch in such a way as to extend it out and away from its intended target, usually bringing it back to us. If a number of people attacked him he would lead the aggressive motion of one man around his own body, thus creating a vacuum into which he would draw the other attackers, only to send them spinning away from him across the mat.

Obviously this type of controlled, leading *ki* is not easy to develop. It requires a profound knowledge of the psychological and dynamic laws which govern human behavior: in general as well as in particular (combat).

To demonstrate even more clearly what is meant by leading, Mr. Tohei asked the strongest, most powerful members of our class to set themselves in the firmest position they could manage (standing). Then they were told

to concentrate totally upon remaining still, rooted to the spot upon which they stood. Even though their *ki* was thus flowing downward, a light movement of Mr. Tohei's hand traveling from the student's forehead to the back of his neck, or a rotating motion against his cheek, clockwise, brought each one in turn down to the mat flat on his or her back.

Mr. Tohei explained that he had led their *ki* upward from the front to the back where they had no support or balance, and then down.

This leading motion (defensive), if it is to be effective, must never be in direct opposition to the motion being led (aggressive). And once control has been assured by blending your lead with the line of attack, your leading motion will develop slightly ahead of the aggressive motion—not so close as to be easily captured, and yet not so far ahead that you will lose control over your attacker's dynamic momentum.

In the application of basic projection no. 1 *(kokyu nage)* from a static position, for example, you will allow your opponent to grasp your right wrist with his right hand. You will not try to pull away, but will allow your wrist to remain in his grasp as you move your body with a spinning motion, whirling to his side and slightly ahead of him. At the same time, you will extend your captured arm out, taking the lead as your hand projects slightly ahead of his grip and your pointing finger describes the dynamic pattern in the air which will lead to his fall.

The example given above is of the technique applied from a static position. It can also be applied dynamically: that is, before an opponent can secure his hold. But you must never pull or snap your hand away. Rather, you will move (arm in alignment with your body) at approximately the same speed and (initially) in the same direction as his original motion, keeping slightly ahead of his outstretched hand until full, centralized control has been established over his motion, body, etc.

A blow may be delivered to your head (attack no. 13, *shomen uchi*). You will pivot and kneel down, so that you are facing the same direction as your opponent. Your arm(s) will not "block" in the sense of stopping his motion, but will be extended so as to protect yourself. At the same time you will guide his motion (via his wrist or even sleeve) from the inside, lead him in full, circular extension forward and then down. This can be accomplished almost without touching him.

There is no pulling, no dragging; it is just a smooth, simple, circular lead, synchronized perfectly with your attacker's own movements. It is blended dynamically with them and, therefore, almost unnoticed until he is in flight. He falls, but yet does not know precisely how he came to fall.

The Principle of Sphericity

We have noted elsewhere that:

1. The mental attitude typical of aikido is strongly centralized.

2. The energy required in aikido is extended outward (either in a condensed or irradiating form) from the Centre.

Both of these principles—that of centralization and that of extension—imply the idea of sphericity or circularity in operation. And this circularity will characterize all aikido strategies of self-defense, regardless of how slight or barely noticeable that circularity may be when techniques are performed by advanced practitioners of the art at great speed. The authors refer to this general principle as the principle of sphericity.

In Asia, this principle is almost as ancient as the land itself. It is present in the doctrine of the Tao in China and in the *taiyoku.*

In India it appears again and again at the highest levels of that culture, i.e., in the Mandala, or the Wheel of Life, in Buddhism.

Sphericity was applied to the practice of many martial arts from the armed methods of fencing and spear fighting to the unarmed methods of boxing and wrestling. Moreover, it was usually a reflexively applied principle, i.e., a samurai would wait for another samurai to attack, using the attacker's dynamic momentum as part of his own strategy, leading and defeating it circularly.

According to many martial art chronicles, it was impossible to penetrate the guard of a skilled spear fighter—man or woman—who awaited an attack in the center of a sphere whose orbiting patterns could be traced with the razor-sharp blade.

It was also considered to be equally impossible (during the period when the sword was the most widely used weapon) to penetrate the defense of an Oriental swordsman skilled in the use of one, or, as in the case of the legendary Musashi, two swords.

The records of European martial arts, especially those of the Italian, Hungarian, and English fencing schools, also indicate that this principle was applied to strategies of combat devised for either sword or dagger. And this circular approach is still predominant in the use of the knife among the people of the Mediterranean from North Africa to Spain, and along the land arc which passes through the Middle East to the Balkans. It is also evident in the curved shape of many blades, including the Japanese *katana,* whose employment by the very logics of its design and structure, is based more upon the circular slash than upon the direct thrust.

The ancient principle of sphericity reached an exceptionally high level of functionality in the Chinese methods of Pa-kua boxing. It was neglected for a time in favor of the shattering power of the linear thrust so widely employed in the derivative schools of karate, in both the Chinese and Japanese versions. Many of the modern schools of karate seem to be returning to this ancient circular concept.

The principle of sphericity was also basic to the practice of judo at its highest levels as indicated by the records and films of early demonstrations. This principle was the nucleus of the teaching of the late judo Master, Kyuzo Mifune (black belt 10th degree), who in order to visualize it for his high-ranking pupils used an actual ball in his lessons. (Film Short, *Judo* with Master Mifune, Toho Cinema, 1964.)

It is in the practice of aikido especially that the principle of sphericity achieves a peak of functional excellence. In this art, in fact, the concept of sphericity almost becomes an absolute.

Circuits of Neutralization

In an aikido strategy, in fact, you may lead your opponent's aggressive motion/action into innumerable Circuits of Neutralization which flow around your Centre. These circuits are divided into three main groups, consisting of horizontal, vertical, and diagonal circuits.

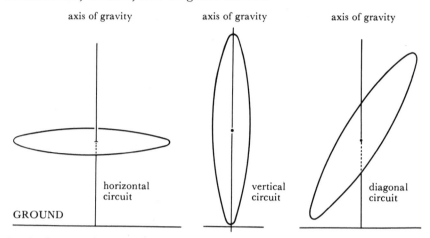

Basic Horizontal Circuits

The horizontal Circuits of Neutralization flow around your Centre in a circle parallel to the ground. They may flow from your right side to your left or vice versa.

These circuits are fundamental to aikido in both its dynamic and technical stages, and are known as *tenkan*, "turning or pivoting movements."

You will immediately recognize these circuits as the most commonly employed motions of evasion and centralization, and they will also figure prominently in many of the actual techniques of neutralization.

To give you a practical example of how these circuits will operate in combat, let us consider the case of defense against a direct thrust to your lower abdomen by an opponent who is employing either his fist or a knife.

As the blow is being delivered, you will move in toward it, even though slightly tangentially, spinning at the same time and hooking his extended arm as it passes by. Both the spinning motion of your body and the leading motion of your hand upon his arm will guide him into full circular extension around you in a circuit parallel to the ground (mat). When the dynamic momentum of his initial thrust, extended and expanded by your evading motion of centralization, has reached its point of maximum effectiveness, you will reverse your spin and the pressure upon his captured hand/arm, thus sending him whirling down onto the mat.

Basic Vertical Circuits

The vertical Circuits of Neutralization can flow around your Centre in a circle perpendicular to the ground. They may flow from front to rear, from rear to front, from the right side to the left side, and from the left side to the right side.

These circuits are found in many techniques of neutralization, some of which are illustrated at the moment of conclusion in the following examples.

Basic Diagonal Circuits

The diagonal Circuits of Neutralization flow around your Centre in a circle diagonal to the ground. They may flow on your right side (from front to rear or vice versa) and on your left side (from front to rear or vice versa).

These circuits are also embodied in many techniques of neutralization (see illustrations on page 99).

Spirals and Semi-Spirals of Neutralization

Your opponent's aggressive strategy, his motion and action of attack, may also be channeled into innumerable spirals and semi-spirals of neutralization flowing around your Centre. In fact, very seldom will a Circuit of Neutralization be as clear and determined as in projection no. 2 because very seldom will you remain on the same spot while your arms describe that clear, circular pattern around and above you.

As compared to the circuits examined above, the spirals and semi-spirals may be qualified as the ever-present and leading movement of your aikido strategy. (The "Dynamic Spiral" is actually the logical extension of the "Dynamic Sphere.") This is because your body, when executing a technique of neutralization, will move; you will turn or bend, thus enlarging upon or restricting the original circular movement.

The variety of possible operational spirals of neutralization can only be hinted at in the illustrations which follow.

These spirals may begin from a height and descend rapidly to the ground, or they may suddenly plunge down only to rise with increased momentum. They may be narrow or ample, simple or elaborate. But in every case, like the circuits, they will always enable you to "hook" an attack, drawing it into a vacuum of neutralization.

Examples of the semi-spirals are illustrated on page 99, drawn from the impressive immobilization no. 2 which is known as *nikyo*.

Circuits

Semi-Spirals

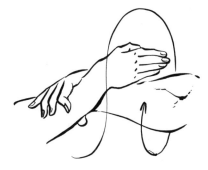

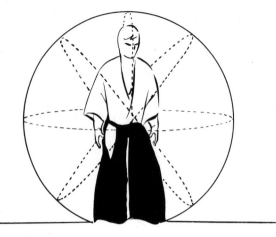

The Dynamic Sphere

If you combine all of those basic circuits and all the possible spirals and semi-spirals of neutralization around your Centre into a single image, the result is a sphere: a "Dynamic Sphere" of circuits enveloping you protectively as you channel any aggressive action into any one or combination of those circles according to the circumstances of each attack.

In the Dynamic Sphere, the concepts of the Centre (attitude) and the energy or extension *(ki)* as well as that of leading control are synthesized, providing a clear formula to which you can turn when seeking to resolve those functional problems which may arise during your practice of the art.

Any motion of attack (from in front of you, from behind you, or from either side), or any technique or method of attack (a blow, a hold, a combination) may be dynamically drawn into a circuit around your Centre and led away to its dispersion and/or neutralization.

Up to this point the Dynamic Sphere which we have examined, with all of its circuits, spirals, and semi-spirals of neutralization, has been linked to techniques of self-defense performed almost on the spot, usually against one attacker.

If you move along or across the surface of the mat, your functional command over an attack can be expanded to include the possibility of multiple attack, i.e., when two or more people attack you at the same time.

When you move your Centre, its protective sphere and its accompanying Circuits of Neutralization move with you, and spin around and about you in the direction of the attack, regardless of the side from which that attack may be launched.

Obviously it would be impossible to explore all the dynamic patterns which could be realized when linked to the Circuits of Neutralization discussed earlier.

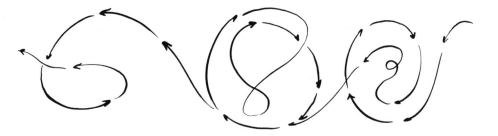

We can only attempt to clarify the basic idea of the Dynamic Sphere as it would be operational here, through a series of illustrations which indicate the main patterns of motion that sphere may follow in combat.

Accordingly, by pivoting within, and as the Centre of an extremely mobile sphere which rolls simultaneously along or across the surface of the mat and around your body, you will be able to face the simultaneous attack of several men—evading, spinning, always maintaining your centralized position in relation to your opponents, and using their aggressive *ki* (intention, dynamic momentum) to draw them into various Circuits of Neutralization, one or several, depending upon the number, tempo, or rhythm of the individual attacks which you must neutralize.

The typical circularity of an aikido defensive strategy, synthesized in the motion of the Dynamic Sphere, also characterizes the final stages of neutralization in which the aggression is either led circularly back to its source or deflected and sent spinning away.

First, "the closed circuit" is typical of those techniques of neutralization known as immobilizations. Through an appropriate extension of that aggression into a circuit around your Centre, you will channel that force back to its source. By leading that powerful motion/action originally aimed at you back toward your opponent, you will make him the target of his own attack.

Observe, for example, immobilizations nos. 2 and 3. In each, you will note this circular return of the opponent's attack to himself, usually through an immobilization which channels his power back to his own body. In fact, you will notice that in each of them, the opponent's captured hand is twisted back in the direction of his own body in a way that may be momentarily painful, but not permanently harmful.

Second, the centrifugal deflection is typical of those techniques of neutralization known as projections, in which, through an appropriate extension of your attacker's initial intention and dynamic momentum into a circuit flowing around your Centre, you will deflect his attack from its intended target and send him spinning harmlessly away.

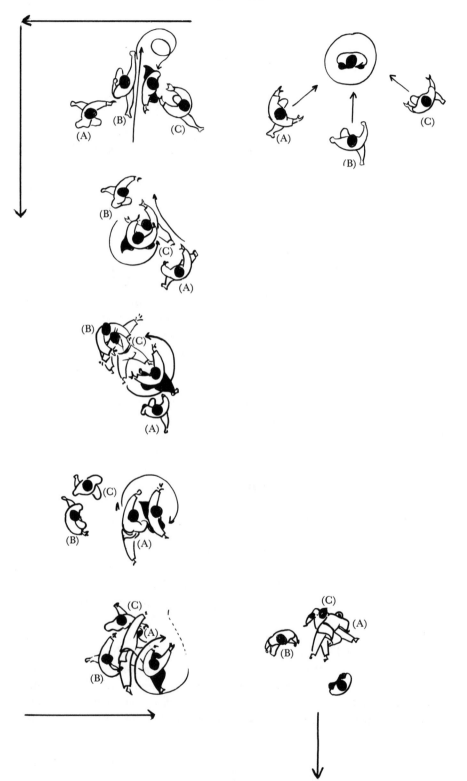

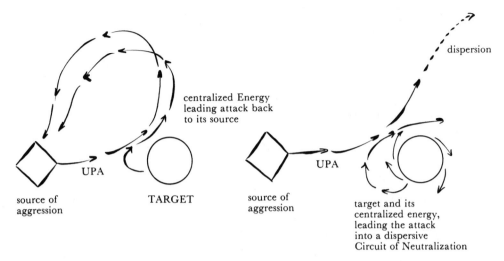

In synthesis, circularity of motion on the mat in preparation for the application of a technique, and circularity of action around your body (Centre), in concluding the process of defense with that particular technique, are the main characteristics of aikido in operation.

Once the principle of sphericity has been understood and recognized as being basic to every strategy of neutralization, then that strategy may be approached in relation to its two principal stages of practical application: the dynamic and the technical.

All the techniques and motions of aikido have been constructed around this idea of a circle, with you as the Centre and your opponents as whirling bodies flying along its periphery. Since this is such a fundamental principle, it is easy to understand why in aikido it is often said that you and your opponent form a whole, become a unit (controlled and directed by you), with an exact balance of the centripetal force flowing toward you and the centrifugal force flowing from you.

Fusion and Special Exercises

The first phase of centralization is concerned with coordinating the mental, physical, and functional powers of the student. The second phase involves the coordination of these powers with the action of combat, with the attack— in full fusion and control.

This centralization as used in aikido has two levels of development: the conscious or initial level of preparation, and the unconscious or advanced level of stabilization.

As has been noted repeatedly in ancient chronicles of the martial arts, concentrating all of one's attention upon the abdominal Centre, and therefore fixing the mind upon a single spot, does not differ substantially from fixing it upon an attacker, or concentrating upon his weapons, etc. In any one of these instances, mental independence would be lost and the entire process of defense necessarily impaired.

But a problem of possible confusion arises here concerning the initial stage in which centralization in the lower abdomen or Centre is developed through the special exercises which follow, and that stage in which centralization is or has become an accomplished fact (unconscious maintenance of balance— both mental and physical, extension of energy, circularity of motion and action, etc.). In the second stage, there is no longer any need for a conscious effort to stay centralized or to direct the attention to or upon the Centre, since at this advanced level of the practice a student will simply "be centralized," and his energy will always be "turned on." This condition thus becomes a continuous state which no longer demands conscious participation.

Centralization, extension, smoothness of control and circularity of performance are thus acquired through a disciplined concentration—at first, of your mental powers upon one spot, the Centre. When the feeling of centralization becomes "normal," i.e., familiar, it will then be tested in action through a conscious effort to maintain that feeling of centralization in the lower abdomen, even when walking or performing any of your normal daily activities. It is finally stabilized by maintaining it on the mat during aikido practice, during the performance of the basic exercises, and of all the techniques of neutralization of the repertoire.

If the conscious training has been thorough and well programmed, eventually the conscious part of the mind will not need to concentrate upon the Centre in order to maintain the necessary centralization and extension, since this will have become a continuing, unconscious state which will be maintained without conscious effort. The process of reaction at this point will become highly automatic and direct.

The Exercise of Posture

If one wishes to achieve a true centralization of the personality according to the natural law of gravity, posture in all of its possible forms and types is of paramount importance.

STANDING POSTURE

The distinctive characteristic of man's particular personality is represented by his upright posture straight between two spacial dimensions of his reality: the horizontal, the source of his life; and the vertical, the goal of his aspirations. It has been seen how this posture and its typical relaxed smoothness (or functional suppleness) determine the degree of centralization developed by man. But the simple standing posture can also be an exercise performed in order to achieve that centralization. In particular many schools of the martial arts never failed to devote a large portion of their training to this important initial attitude.

Judo, for example, has developed one of the richest systematic elaborations on standing postures, and so has karate. Very few disciplines, however, have emphasized the "normality" of a relaxed posture, even in relation to the dramatic circumstances of combat, as aikido and other related methods of self-defense have done.

This is the paradox of the theory on the *hara,* of the notion of a Centre, natural and already consistent with itself in the order of creation: a normal condition, pure and simple. What appears to be artificially contrived, i.e., a stiff posture indicating underlying menace or defiance, or the so-called solid postures of defense, are all abnormal because they are unnatural. An upright man learns to stay upright in a correct, balanced manner. His weight descends normally along the strong architectural patterns of muscle and bone without any tension manifesting itself anywhere or any stiffening of the muscles (in particular, those of the legs).

If he stands correctly, he will be centralized at the point of maximum balance between rest and motion (two opposites), and will be ready for either one.

The exercise of standing is performed by consciously relaxing and allowing the weight of the upper body to descend naturally according to the law of gravity. Still consciously, this centralization is felt at the Centre, kept in equilibrium there (not pushed or imprisoned), until the newly developed condition of natural centralization becomes instinctive.

SITTING POSTURE

Typical of the schools of thought (philosophy and religion) and those of representation (arts and crafts, calligraphy, painting, weaving) is the development of a theory of sitting and related exercises.

A panoramic survey of the most characteristic and representative sitting postures adopted in Asia from India to China and Japan, notwithstanding national differentiations of marginal relevance, will all reveal a typical closeness to and a peculiar identification with the horizontal plane of the ground. There is an unmistakable straightness, a verticality which becomes symbolic and universal in implication as represented in art, for example.

The exercise of sitting reaches its peak of perfection in Japan in the *zazen* posture which has come to be identified with the Buddhist sect of Zen. It shines in the plastic representations of Kabuki plays where the chorus, sitting in a characteristic manner, accompanies the action with comments sung in an abdominally deep, musical way.

The forms of sitting, as exercise, aim at the achievement of a condition of supple stillness conducive to the smooth centralization of the entire personality in the Centre. Its advantage is clearly due to the increased proximity of the ground, whose immobility is thus more easily shared. It is also invaluable for the contemplative purposes of men of thought who can transcend the physical barrier of reality, soar into the realms of the pure spirit, and be lost to the real world entirely. It is also of paramount importance for the artist, who, rooted to the "great mother," can nevertheless be free to move his brushes in a fluid manner. It is, however, less important in the schools of action where withdrawal from reality and static immobility are not primary objectives.

But in order to find and stay in the Centre, the sitting posture is definitely necessary to develop the feeling of centralization until it becomes continually present at all times, especially at times of stress, when in motion.

The Exercise of Stillness

One of the primary exercises for the locating and focusing of consciousness in the Centre is the exercise of stillness. It is aimed at dispersing the thick fog of sensorial solicitations which assail the student from every side, as well as activating his instinctive responses in the form of movement/action. It consists of assuming particular postures, sitting or standing (depending upon the school), and maintaining that posture for prolonged periods of time, holding physical responses in check until this stillness becomes a natural state.

Because of its strongly static outlines, this exercise is particularly suited to the metaphysical schools of religious or philosophical thought in which it is extensively practiced. But it has also been adopted by the more practical schools of action, which, like those related to the arts and crafts (painting, ceramics, theatrical presentations) and combat, use it as a preliminary discipline to establish self-control—"bridling the beast." Thus man learns to control his body and physical reactions so as to prepare it for the practice of other exercises and techniques typical of his school.

The Exercise of Concentration

This exercise, in many forms specific to each of the many schools of Asia, aims at directing the attention from the outside reality to the reality within man once his body has been stilled. This shift aims at illuminating those dark recesses of man's personality, at the roots of which the Centre is to be found.

Reacting against the dispersive solicitations of the outer reality, man withdraws within himself. He allows his body to relax completely, lets it fall under the natural sway of gravity, and concentrates his consciousness at the point of maximum intensity of that weight—the *hara,* or lower abdomen. Amidst a clamor of unaccustomed feelings—aroused and wildly fluttering about like bats in a cave which is suddenly filled with strange sounds—a man, if he perseveres, will emerge slowly and painfully from the confusion with a feeling of central balance, precarious at first, but increasingly stable as he repeats the exercise with disciplined application.

At that point, all of the anatomical elements of the body will appear to be magnetically unified; all the rambling thoughts will come to rest as a result of that implosive fusion. Thus one comes to perceive a new, central "self," a root so balanced that everything channeled there becomes still, in a state of rest.

The Exercise of Meditation

Finding the Centre, however, is only the beginning. Reality, both outer and inner, has innumerable ways of reasserting its autonomy, of recapturing the attention. It will continue to launch wave after wave of assault against that newly concentrated Centre, especially during the period immediately following its discovery. Meditation, therefore, is intended to make the discovery a stable, permanent condition as one attempts to stay centralized for increasingly prolonged periods of time.

Abdominal (Deep) Breathing

An exercise of particular importance for the development of that centralized energy which is the foundation of the principle of extension, is the practice of deep abdominal breathing which aikido (as well as many other martial arts) has adopted from other Asiatic disciplines such as Zen.

The characteristics of this exercise in the aikido dimension are of two orders: physio-functional, related to the way of controlling the two phases of inhalation and exhalation; and mental, related to the mental image you will use as a device for developing the proper rhythm and style of breathing.

One method commonly employed involves sitting Japanese style, *zazen* (Chapter III), while wearing loose clothing, in a well-ventilated room, and on a mat or some sort of cushioning material so that the pressure on your legs, ankles, and feet will not become too painful. Adaptation to this way of sitting should be built up gradually, increasing the time spent in this position by a few minutes every session. You should be careful when getting up at the end of this exercise because your feet and legs will most probably have "fallen asleep"—a common problem which many Japanese who practice *zazen* regularly have also mentioned. The Indian position for meditation (cross-legged) is also used, but if you prefer this position you should be sure to place a cushion underneath you in order to keep your spine straight.

When you are comfortably seated and relaxed, you may begin your breathing exercise. Inhalation should be prolonged, as a thin stream of air is drawn in through the nostrils at a regular, controlled rate. The sound of such a prolonged inhalation should be close to the letter "u." And this inhalation should be done relaxedly with no straining. Moreover, even though the air is drawn in through the nose, the glottis at the back of the throat should be used to control the stream. In other words, by drawing the air in through contraction of the glottis, instead of "sniffing" it you will be able to achieve the slow, steady stream of which we are speaking.

The air you inhale should fill the central part of your body, not only the chest cavity but also the lower abdomen which should thus expand normally, without undue strain or tensing of your stomach muscles. The idea is to breathe as fully and naturally as a child.

When you have inhaled all that you comfortably can, keeping your shoulders down during the inhalation, rest quietly for a moment or so before beginning to exhale. The exhalation should be through the mouth, again in a steady, concentrated, powerful but relaxed stream—the sound of the exhalation resembling an "aah." Again, there should be no straining or attempt to exhale suddenly with great force, since Mr. Tohei warns that this can cause stomach adhesions or other unfortunate side effects.

In order to coordinate the mental dimension of your personality with the physio-functional, thus working toward that essential fusion of mind and body which is the ultimate aim of any aikido exercise, many Zen masters advise their pupils to imagine that during inhalation a very thin silver thread is being drawn in uninterruptedly through the nostrils, flowing down the spinal column as illustrated, before being held for a few seconds in spherical suspension in the lower abdomen. The process is then reversed during exhalation.

Many martial arts practitioners declare that unless proper breath control is mastered, progress will always be limited in any of these arts. Since, as

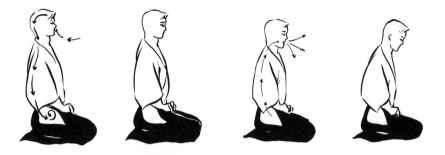

indicated earlier, this belief is also held by the best athletes, singers, and dancers, it does not seem an unreasonable one.

Breathing exercises should be practiced daily, and when combined with regular practice of the arts of aikido will result in surprising coordinated development.

Sitting Extension

As an examination of the various exercises for developing centralization and inner, coordinated power will reveal, aikido (like most martial arts) is heavily indebted to those doctrines of inner development such as Taoism and Zen Buddhism, which made ample use of, and actually are considered to have devised those exercises. But there are certain other aikido exercises which mark the translation of the Inner Factors of the art, into the outer, external dimension, thus transforming those factors into concrete and powerful actions.

Among these exercises, a position of particular eminence is accorded to an exercise of sitting extension known as *kokyu dosa,* which is usually practiced at the end of every aikido class—and sometimes even at the beginning of or during the class—any time you need to test the degree of your centralized extension, or relax into it again if you have lost it for any reason.

This exercise is performed in the sitting posture *(zazen)* described in Chapter III. Your partner, sitting in front of you, will grasp your wrists and hold them firmly. Moving from the hips with a powerful surge of energy from the Centre, you will extend your arms toward *uke* (the opponent), leading the power of his hold back to him, and circularly up to his rear. (This leading motion will often involve a slight initial "sliding below" or deflection of the line of his concentrated force.) You will follow him with samurai walk (Chapter IX) as he rolls sideways and down to the mat. Settling yourself at his side (one knee braced against his body), you will extend your arms and rest the knife-edges of your hands on the shoulder and arm of *uke*—firmly but without pressing down painfully. *Uke* will attempt to rise, trying to disturb

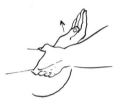

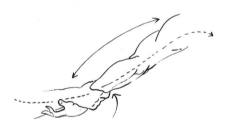

your downward extension. If you are properly centralized and your energy is flowing uninterruptedly downward "to the center of the earth," as some instructors say, you should be immovable, and *uke* should be unable to rise.

A variation of this exercise is also practiced as an introductory step to the practice of immobilization no. 4 *(yonkyo)*, illustrated in Chapter VIII. As *uke* grasps your wrists, you will turn your hands around his forearms, passing over them from the inside. You will then grip his forearm and exercise pressure on the nerve centers located above the wrist. His instinctive reaction to this pressure—trying to arch back and away from it—will allow you to extend his arms fully, setting them in direct alignment with the line of centralized energy that you will be channeling against his upper body through those paralyzed arms. You will project him sideways, since extending him straight back may cause severe pain and/or possible injury to his ankles or toes.

Tests

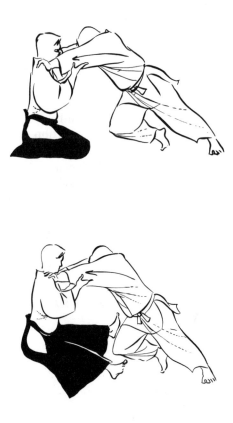

Aikido provides numerous ways of testing the quality and power of your centralized extension. The accompanying examples are only a sample of their range and type.

Sitting in *zazen,* you will relax and concentrate on your Centre, letting your *ki* flow outward from it. Remember to keep your back straight and do not be disturbed by your partner's efforts to topple you by pushing you backward (his hands on your shoulders) from above. Experienced aikido students can thus neutralize the power of two or three *uke,* even when sitting with legs apart as illustrated.

The same test may be performed in a standing position, with one of your arms extended in an "unbendable" arch, the edge of your hand resting against your partner's forearm. He will push and you will neutralize his power as if you were a rock against which his power was being discharged. In advanced stages of the art, you should be able to re-

channel the force he is trying to use against you, and even be able to push back several men as they strain against you to no avail.

Another test frequently employed consists of neutralizing the efforts of one or two partners as they endeavor to lift you from the mat. In this exercise you should be stably relaxed and centralized, your *ki* flowing downward and linking your whole body to the earth.

The test of the unbendable arm has already been described in Chapter I. When performed properly, the centralized energy flowing through your arm should be sufficient to neutralize any attempt to bend your arm if you do not wish it bent. This unbendable arm must be maintained continuously in every phase of your practice on the mat, and eventually become a constant state.

Other tests, whose number is limited only by the preparation and imagination of the individual instructor, may include the use of the stave *(jo),* or of the wooden sword *(bokken),* etc., but those which will introduce the aikido student to the use of centralized energy and extension in the performance of the aikido techniques of neutralization are briefly described under the heading, "Basic Exercises" *(taiso)*—Chapter VI.

The Physical Preparation

WE HAVE now reached the point in the aikido process of defense where you will move from the study of those "inner" dimensions characterized by the predominant role of your mind: perceiving an attack, evaluating its probable course, and deciding upon the appropriate measures for coping with it, to the "outer" dimensions characterized by the role of your body in carrying out those measures and neutralizing that attack.

We will now examine the physical and functional factors which will determine the correctness and efficiency of your strategy of defense in response to an aggressive solicitation which has been properly perceived and evaluated. These Outer Factors of your aikido defensive reaction will include first the physical condition of your body—the concrete instrument of defense (the authors prefer to avoid any reference to the body as a weapon of defense, for reasons explained in Chapter X).

These Outer Factors will also include the functional way in which you will position your body in the event of an attack; the way you will move, evade, extend, and control that attack dynamically; the way in which you will neutralize it with an appropriate technique of immobilization, projection, or a combination of both.

In this chapter we will examine how your body is to be prepared and conditioned physically through the practice of certain exercises for the specific purpose of keeping yourself fit and ready for the practice of the art, and, more generally, for the purpose of improving upon and maintaining a condition of stable health so that you may enjoy life—and living—more fully.

The exercises of physical conditioning and preparation adopted and practiced in aikido *dojo* are generally of two orders. The first group, qualified as preliminary, are all intended to develop and improve upon your body's

113

natural elasticity and suppleness which have always been associated with youthfulness and a natural feeling of well-being. The second or basic group of exercises includes a more specialized body of practices and movements intended to develop and improve upon your physical and functional co-ordination, in order to make your actions thoroughly coherent and smoothly effective, and thus the expression of an integrated personality responding appropriately to an attack.

Preliminary Exercises: Suppleness

The preliminary exercises performed at the beginning of most aikido sessions have the primary, overall purpose of loosening up your body, of stretching and relaxing your muscles, of limbering up your entire frame.

The development of suppleness and its correlative, speed, will be the natural result of regular performance of these exercises. Every muscle will be stretched and strengthened, every sinew freed from any "dust" which may have accumulated through inactivity or fatigue. Every part of your body will be flexed elastically in the pleasant manner of a natural extension similar to a morning stretch after a restful sleep.

When these preliminary exercises have been completed, you may then proceed to the more specialized or basic aikido exercises. They differ from the preliminary not so much in emphasis, but rather in their patterns of per-formance. The preliminary exercises, in fact, are intended to prepare your body in a general manner (to render it supple, flexible, and warm); the specialized or basic aikido exercises are intended to develop the particular aikido type of coordination and to register the basic patterns of the various strategies (extension of power, awareness, dynamic and technical reactivity).

The following sequences illustrate the preliminary exercises most com-monly employed in aikido *dojo* everywhere. They will be most helpful in impeding the creeping and relentless spread of muscular and skeletal rigidity affecting the spinal column and the joints which is usually associated with advancing age. The recommendation that you keep your body supple like that of an infant in order to counteract the rigidity and stiffness of the aging process is a very old one which ancient Japanese masters of martial arts often stressed to their disciples. This advice may be traced all the way back to ancient Chinese classics such as the Taoist texts, and having found its way into the manuals of martial strategy, soon became the foundation for that famous principle of nonresistance or fusion *(wa)* which according to a pre-dominant school of thought in this area underlies the principles of suppleness *(ju)* and harmony *(ai)*.

PRELIMINARY EXERCISE NO. 1

Sitting on the mat, your body erect, legs and arms outstretched, you will bend over to touch your toes (or the mat beyond your toes) with your fingertips, and your knees or thighs with your chest. This limbering motion may be repeated five or more times.

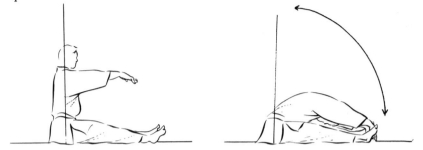

PRELIMINARY EXERCISE NO. 2

Sitting on the mat, arms in front of you, legs fully outstretched and spread diagonally, you will bend to the left, touching your toes with your fingertips and bringing your head down to touch your knee (or at least as close to your knee as possible). You may repeat this exercise five times on the left and then five times on the right.

Finally, grasping both ankles, or stretching your arms out in front of you, you will bend forward, bringing your head down as close to the mat in front of you as the elasticity of your spinal column will permit. This may also be repeated five times.

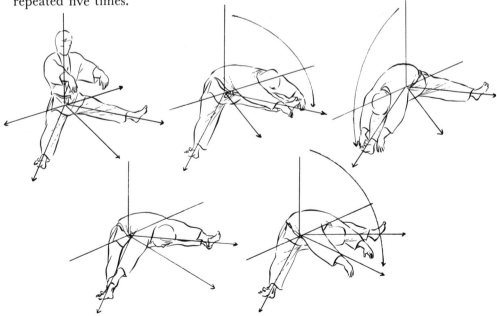

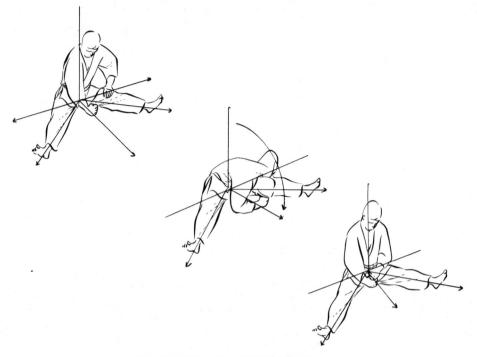

PRELIMINARY EXERCISE NO. 3

Sitting on the mat, legs outspread in diagonal, you will set one fist on the mat in front of you at arm's length and bend over to touch that fist with your forehead. If this is difficult at first, you may begin by putting one fist on top of the other to reduce the distance between them and your head. This exercise may be repeated five times.

PRELIMINARY EXERCISE NO. 4

Sit on the mat, Indian-style, with the soles of your feet touching and as close to your body as possible. This position will raise your knees from the mat. You will push down on both knees simultaneously (five times)and then bend over your feet five times, bringing your forehead down as close as possible to the mat in front of you.

PRELIMINARY EXERCISE NO. 5

Sitting on the mat, Japanese-style *(seiza)* with your feet tucked underneath you and your arms outstretched over your head, you will bend backward to touch the mat behind you with your hands. A partner will hold your knees so that you will be able to stretch up and back in full relaxed extension.

PRELIMINARY EXERCISE NO. 6

Standing with feet spread apart but on the same line, you will bend one knee and let your weight settle on that leg, stretching your other leg out fully. You will turn and twist your foot in order to stretch the ligaments. You may touch your outstretched ankle with one or both hands, thus bending your whole body at the waist. This exercise may be repeated five times on the left side and then five times on the right.

PRELIMINARY EXERCISE NO. 7

Standing, feet close together, you will bend your knees, keeping them close together and rotating them first in one direction and then in the other. After this, you will bend your knees deeply five times, sinking down as close to the mat as possible. (Do not move your feet or lift them from the mat while doing this exercise.)

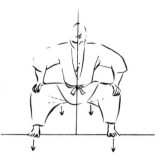

PRELIMINARY EXERCISE NO. 8

Standing with feet set apart but on the same line, toes pointing straight ahead, you will bend your knees deeply five times, spreading them apart.

PRELIMINARY EXERCISE NO. 9

Standing with your feet apart, you will swing both your arms from one side to the other, turning your whole body (including your head) as far around as possible without moving your feet. The difference between this circular motion exercise and basic exercise no. 15 *(ude furi undo*—spin) lies in the fact that this exercise is intended mainly to stretch and exercise your spinal column, while basic exercise no. 15 is directly related to the development of centralization, extension, and leading control via a swinging motion which will apply to your arms alone. There, your trunk and head remain facing forward as your arms swing from side to side.

PRELIMINARY EXERCISE NO. 10

Standing with feet apart but on the same line, you will swing your arms up and over, bending your body sideways as far as possible. Repeat this exercise five times on each side.

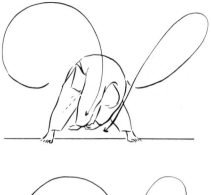

PRELIMINARY EXERCISE NO. 11

Standing with feet apart but on the same line, toes pointing outward and arms outstretched at your sides, you will swing your arms in an arc, bending as far back as possible and then as far forward as possible (five times).

Basic Exercises: Coordination *(aiki taiso)*

The specialized exercises, the *aiki taiso*—which you will practice either in class or by yourself whenever you can—are more precisely focused and at the same time more complex than the preliminary exercises.

Their primary aim, in fact, is to improve the coordination of all the various factors of the practice, as expressed through the disciplined blending of all your various powers and functional possibilities.

In the mental dimension, for example, the *aiki taiso* will help you to develop, exercise, and test practically your fundamental centralization (in the beginning, at least, at the *hara,* or Centre); the extension of *ki,* or Inner Energy, from and through this Centre (which will eventually expand to include your whole body); and the mental alertness and keenness of perception which should be the natural result of this extension of centralized energy.

In the physical dimension, the *aiki taiso* will also help to develop and stabilize that relaxed suppleness which is the main purpose of the preliminary exercises, as well as improve the rhythm of both your respiration and circulation. The weight of your whole upper anatomy will fall naturally into a central, supported position, vertically balanced upon your Centre without excessive muscular contraction or "hunching" of your shoulders, etc.

Your breathing will become calm and deep (abdominal breathing); your circulation will be enhanced as evidenced by a particular glowing feeling all over your body, and a tingling sensation will be felt at your fingertips upon the completion of these basic exercises.

In the functional dimension, the *aiki taiso* will operate as the basic formulas from which your defensive aikido strategies will be developed. They will represent the correct execution of the individual strategic movements and techniques in a formalized manner—much like the *kata* of other martial arts.

The disciplined repetition of these basic exercises is intended to register the basic strategic patterns or formulas of the art firmly in your mind, and to achieve through physical repetition their smooth, effective, and coordinated performance. At first these formulas will appear to be, and will feel very strange—often awkward and difficult. Through constant repetition and experimentation, however, your execution of these exercises will become a unified, coordinated, and strategically rewarding performance. Eventually their sequences of execution will be thoroughly programmed into your psyche, and registered in your subconscious where they will be transformed into automatic, conditioned reflexes.

As we have noted, these exercises are intended to develop total coordination of power (Inner Energy, or *ki*), of functionality (both dynamic and technical), of supple reactivity and awareness (centralization).

All the various factors of your defensive strategy of neutralization, however, must be brought into play simultaneously: mental exercises, physical exercises, functional exercises, must be fused together in a single formula of performance. Through the constant integrated repetition of the basic exercises, you will learn not only how to position and move your body, but how to be centralized in the lower abdomen or Centre, and how to extend your energy until this energy will flow outward automatically, enabling you to deal with any attack in a coordinated manner.

Aikido instructors may employ several methods to test the degree of your coordinated development in the execution of these basic exercises, ranging from the purely psychological: a sudden flick of the hand, to the physical: a strong pull or push. A few of these methods are indicated where they apply in the sequences which follow.

Some general recommendations for the correct execution of the basic exercises are:

1. Maintain correct posture throughout the practice of the basic exercises,

with your Centre properly positioned in a condition of balance aligned with the perpendicular force of gravity.

2. Begin and practice every exercise in a centralized position for static exercises such as nos. 1, 2, and 3 for example, moving from the Centre (from the hips) in all the others.

3. Extend *ki,* or Inner Energy, from the Centre in the specific direction of each exercise at all times.

4. When you turn your body or pivot (moving from the hips), remember to turn your feet (toes too) all the way around, so that your body will be in total alignment.

5. Start every exercise on the left, either with the left hand in exercises nos. 1, 2, and 3, or the left foot in all the others. After the required number of repetitions on the left side, change to the right and repeat the exercise.

BASIC EXERCISE NO. 1 (*nikyo, nikajo, kote mawashi-ho,* wrist turn-in)

Stand in a natural, relaxed, and well-centralized position *(shizentai,* left *kamae* or right *kamae)*. Grasp the back of your left hand with your right hand, your right thumb circling your left thumb. Now draw both hands up close to your upper chest (keeping your elbows down), flexing and stretching your left wrist inward until the fingers of your left hand touch your left forearm if possible. Some pain may be experienced at first, until your wrist ligaments develop the necessary strength and elasticity.

You should extend *ki* from your Centre at all times through that flexed wrist, thus considerably reducing the pain which you may feel initially, and increasing the index of curvature as well as that of rotation through the relaxed suppleness which centralization and extension will automatically produce.

This fundamental exercise will help you to develop a feeling for the correct hold upon the hand of *uke* (your opponent) in immobilizations nos. 2 and 3 through experimentation upon yourself. It will also teach you in a direct and personal manner how pain may be activated and where it will be centered in the wrist so that you will be able to locate and feel the right spot when necessary in combat.

You may perform this exercise— either at home or at the beginning of a class in the *dojo*—five times with the left hand, and five times with the right, then left and right hands alternated again.

BASIC EXERCISE NO. 2 (*kote gaeshi, kote gaeshi ho,* wrist turn-out)

Raise your left hand as high as your chest and rotate it outward at the wrist to your left with the knife-edge *(tegatana)* toward you, and your palm facing your left side. Place your right hand around your left hand with your right thumb between the ring and little finger knuckles of your left hand. The other four fingers of your right hand should circle your palm around the thumb mount near your wrist.

Now rotate your left hand outward, pressing down and around your fingers with your right thumb and using pressure on your ring and little fingers to increase the rotation. Your left elbow should be drawn gently in toward your body—your left hand thus bent toward the inside of your left forearm, and turned outward away from your body at the same time.

There may be some slight pain at the beginning. Extension of *ki* and correct centralization, however, will help to reduce this initial discomfort, as well as avoid excessive muscular tension in your arms and shoulders.

This exercise may be performed five times with each hand and then repeated at least five times more.

BASIC EXERCISE NO. 3 (*tekubi shindo,* wrist shaking)

FIRST VARIATION—Dropping your arms, let them hang relaxedly at your sides, no tension in your shoulders. Shake your wrists rapidly and limberly, extending *ki* from your Centre as if you were spraying the ground around you.

SECOND VARIATION—Hold your arms out in a horizontal position, hands relaxed. Shake them rapidly and intensely as noted above. When tired, drop your arms and rest before resuming the exercise.

THIRD VARIATION—Combine both the vertical and the horizontal variations of basic exercise no. 3.

This exercise, with its evident emphasis upon centralization and extension, is invaluable for stimulating your circulation and should result in that pleasant tingling sensation mentioned above.

This exercise is also used as an introduction to and preparation for the much sterner practice of aikido during the *kangeiko,* or winter months, when students in Japan often perform basic drills outdoors in the snow, or in the mountains. Its roots can be traced to Tibetan culture, through China and

India, and it is often referred to in the martial arts as a basic way of producing "inner" heat.

BASIC EXERCISE NO. 4 (rowing exercise)

One great dilemma in relation to the Centre and Inner Energy in the martial arts has always been how to render that centralized energy operative in real action in combat. The literature available on the subject amply documents the conflict between the static and the dynamic or operative schools of thought. The more contemplative discipline of Zen is typical of the former, while the latter has always been espoused by exponents of the martial arts.

In fact, as has been pointed out by many aikido instructors, it may be comparatively easy to be centralized in the lower abdomen and to keep extending *ki* while sitting in meditation *(zazen)* or standing still in a natural position. It is another thing entirely to maintain that condition of centralized extension while in motion, when there is real involvement with the highly distracting reality of everyday living—especially when you are dealing with a real attacker in the dramatic reality of combat.

In order to make that condition operative and constant, whether you are at rest or in motion/action, you will regularly practice an exercise which is known as the rowing exercise.

Assume a relaxed stance with your left foot ahead. When your instructor says "one," thrust your hips forward, shifting the weight of your body from your right leg onto your left—your right leg behind will straighten and your left leg ahead will bend at the knee.

Your arms will describe a small circle (as your shoulders are rotated) and then they will descend strongly, in full extension, following the forward motion of your hips, wrists bent inward so that your fingertips are pointed toward your body. Your trunk or upper body must be kept erect, i.e., you must not lean forward, since this exercise is primarily intended for the development of hip motion and at the same time the maintenance of balance.

When your instructor says "two," you will draw your hips back, straightening your left leg and bending your right one behind, as the weight of your body shifts back upon it. Your arms will again follow the motion of your hips, being drawn back easily to the sides of your body, fingers closing now to form a half-fist.

The accompanying motion of your arms will necessitate, as do all arm movements in aikido, the maintenance of an unbendable arm but there must be no sensation of pulling, since your arms will only be following the surging motion of your hips (forward and back again), playing their necessary but subsidiary role.

Your instructor may test your degree of coordination in several ways. He may stop you at the count of "one," and try to push your extended

arms up from underneath in the direction of your shoulders, or push you from behind at the hips. You should be immovable. Or your instructor may stop you at the count of "two," and push your shoulders back. He should not be able to upset your vertical stability.

BASIC EXERCISE NO. 5 (*shomen uchi ikkyo, ikkajo,* high parry, high extension)

Taking a half-step forward with your left foot, you will let your hips surge forward at the count of "one," bending your left leg and straightening your right leg behind as illustrated, trunk straight and in full balance. You will swing your arms forward and upward, fingers extended and *ki* flowing outward to the little finger edge of both hands and beyond. Your arms should stop naturally at about eye level. Your elbows should bend naturally according to the circular pattern of the centrifugal force flowing from your Centre, which should make your arm unbendable.

At the count of "two," you will shift your hips back, the weight of your body descending upon your right leg which will bend, while your left leg will straighten again. Your arms will swing back to your sides, following your hip motion, fingers closing into half-fists.

Your instructor may test the degree of your centralization and extension in several ways. In phase no. 1, in full extension, he may grasp your wrists and push against you, trying either to force your arms to bend or to move you backward. He may also step behind you and push your hips forward in an attempt to disturb your balance. In phase no. 2, he may place the knife-edges of his hands upon your chest near your shoulder joints and try to push you backward.

This exercise is intended to help you develop the centralization and extension necessary if you are to cope with blows coming from above toward your forehead or face.

In the *dojo* you may perform this exercise five times with your left foot forward and then five times with your right foot forward, repeating it five times more on each side.

BASIC EXERCISE NO. 6 (skip advance)

At the count of "one," you will take a half-step forward with your left foot, sliding your right foot up close behind it, while your arms swing upward as described in basic exercise no. 5.

At the count of "two," you will take a half-step backward with your right foot, your left foot sliding back to join your right. Your arms will swing down again to your sides.

The purpose of this exercise is to coordinate your centralized extension with your forward stepping (the straight motion in advance in *tsugi ashi;* see Chapter VII, "Follow-Up Step") and with your backward stepping.

You may perform this exercise five times with your left foot leading and then five times with your right foot ahead, repeating it five times more on each side.

Your instructor may test you by stepping in front of you and acting as either an obstacle which your extension will deflect, or as an attacker whose line of attack will be spun back to its source.

BASIC EXERCISE NO. 7 (*zengo undo,* static pivot)

This exercise is an amplification of basic exercise no. 5. You will perform phase one and phase two of basic exercise no. 5, and then, bringing your hips back and your arms down to your sides, you will wait for the count of "three" and "four."

At the count of "three," you will turn your hips 180 degrees to your right side (half-circle), pivoting on both feet but without taking a step. You will now be facing the wall, in the initial position of basic exercise no. 5, the only difference being that your right leg will be extended in front of you. From this position, you will let your hips surge forward, swinging your arms upward, as you did at the count of "one." At the count of "four," you will bring your hips back and your arms down again to your sides. At the count of "one," you will turn and repeat the entire series of phases and turns until full coordination is achieved.

The purpose of this exercise is to develop your application of centralization/extension against high attacks to your head, whether launched from in front of you or from behind you.

BASIC EXERCISE NO. 8 (dynamic pivot)

This exercise is another amplification of basic exercise no. 5 but this time combined with other types of motion—straight motion in alternation, and circular motion for the half-circle.

At the count of "one," you will slide your left foot a half-step forward, keeping your hips low (knees bent) and staying well centralized, while your arms swing in centrifugal extension up and out. At the count of "two," you will bring your arms down in an arc passing close to your sides, while your whole body turns 180 degrees (in a half-circle) to your right and you take

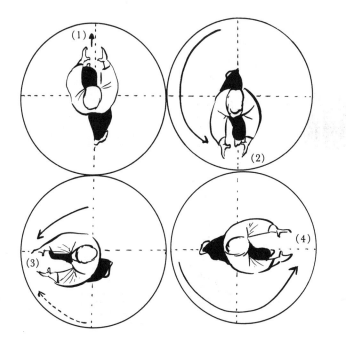

a step with your right foot, your left acting as the supporting and pivoting fulcrum for the circular motion. You will swing your arms up and then back down again as before. At the count of "three," you will pivot 90 degrees (a quarter-circle turn) to your left, taking a short, sliding step forward with your left foot, while you bring your arms up. At the count of "four," you will bring your hands down while you pivot on your right foot swinging your arms up and out once again. You will thus have covered four sides, pivoting on your left foot and then on your right, alternately.

This exercise may also be performed by stepping always with the same foot in the four directions indicated above, pivoting continually on the other foot.

BASIC EXERCISE NO. 9 (*happo undo,* eight-direction exercise)

The final amplification of basic exercise no. 5 is this exercise where straight motion (in *tsugi* and *ayumi ashi*) will blend with the circular motion of both the spin and pivot forms. The directions of your defensive extension will increase here from two (as in basic exercise no. 7) and four (as in basic exercise no. 8) to eight, as shown in the illustrations which follow.

At the count of "one," you will slide your left foot forward in direction one, drawing your right foot up behind in *tsugi ashi* as your hips surge forward and your arms swing upward in frontal extension. Then you will bring your hips back and let your arms fall naturally in an arc to your sides. At the count of "two," you will turn your hips 180 degrees to your right, pivoting in a half-circle on both feet. You will slide your right foot forward, bringing the left foot up behind in *tsugi ashi* and face direction two, as your hips surge forward and your arms swing upward. Then you will draw your hips back and bring your arms down again to your sides. At the count of "three," you will turn your hips 90 degrees to your left side, in direction three, stepping in that direction with your left foot *(ayumi ashi),* bringing your right foot up behind in *tsugi ashi.* Your hips will surge forward and your arms swing upward as indicated. Then you will withdraw your hips and allow your arms to fall back to your sides. At the count of "four," you will swing your hips in a 180-degree circle to your left, pivoting on both feet and facing direction four. Your hips will surge forward and arms swing upward. Then your hips will be drawn back and your arms will fall back to your sides.

At the count of "five," you will turn your hips in direction five—obliquely between directions four and two—taking a step in that direction with your left foot in *ayumi ashi,* your right foot being drawn up behind in *tsugi ashi.* As before, your hips will swing forward, your arms upward and outward. Then your hips will be drawn back, arms following, back and down to your sides. At the count of "six," you will pivot on both feet in a 180-degree circle, facing direction six, between directions one and three. Hips will surge forward and arms swing up in an arc. Then you will swing your hips back, and your arms

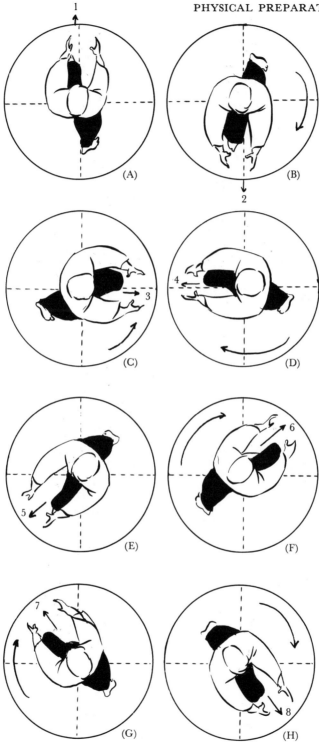

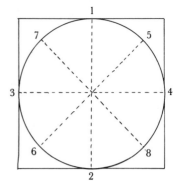

will fall naturally once again to your sides. At the count of "seven," you will turn your hips 90 degrees to your left side, stepping in direction seven—*ayumi ashi*—between directions one and four, your right foot following as it slides up from behind in *tsugi ashi*. Another surge forward with your hips, arms swinging up, and then you will swing your hips back, your arms curving down again to your sides.

BASIC EXERCISE NO. 10 (*kokyu ho undo,* wrist lead)

At the count of "one," from the left natural posture *(hidari gamae)*, you will extend your left arm in front of you, wrist bent inward and fingertips pointing toward you. You will slide your left foot a half-step forward, spin on it, and turn your body 180 degrees to your right (half-circle), withdrawing your right leg circularly behind you. Your hand will remain where it was at the

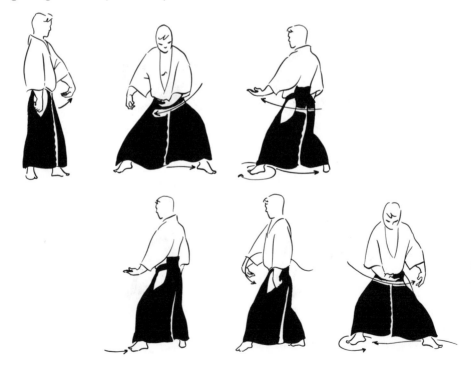

beginning of the extension; you will simply turn it so that your palm faces upward.

At the count of "two," you will bring that hand back to your side and extend your right hand forward, wrist bent and fingertips pointing toward you. Taking a long step forward with your right foot, you will pivot on that foot and withdraw your left foot circularly behind you. Your right hand will not move—you will simply turn it palm up.

Your instructor may test you in various ways. In phase one, he may push your bent wrist in the direction of your shoulder, which should not be raised. He may push your hips from behind, and you should not be moved. In phase two, he may try to pull your extended wrist from behind, but he should not be able to move or unbalance you.

The purpose of this exercise is to coordinate your defensive circular motion with an attacker's motion of convergence. When he grabs (or attempts to grab) your wrist, his movement will follow yours in the direction of your extended fingers while your Centre of power controls that movement. You will then be able to lead him into any one of a number of Circuits of Neutralization.

BASIC EXERCISE NO. 11 (*tekubi kosa undo,* double-wrist break)

You will stand, well centralized in the natural position *(shizentai),* feet apart and arms fully relaxed at your sides. At the count of "one," you will turn both wrists inward so that the fingers of both hands are pointing toward

one another, and swing your arms in front of your Centre, your hands crossing each other. You will return your hands to your sides and repeat five times with your left hand outside, and five times with it inside. *Ki* should be extended through your arms, down the back of your hands.

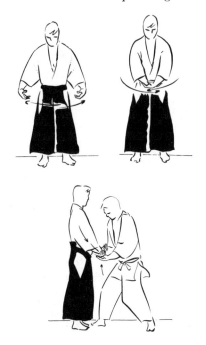

Your instructor may test you when your arms are at your sides or when they swing across. In the first case, to see if you are extending "down," he may push your arms up, trying to break your vertical balance. Or he may try to hold your wrists apart as you swing them back and forth. You must lead his own strength circularly underneath, following the turn of your wrists. Finally, he may stop you when your hands are crossed in front of you, and push them from underneath, toward your shoulders. You should remain immovable.

The purpose of this exercise is specifically that of training you to transform a hold on your wrists into a lead which will bring an attacker into position for the application of an immobilization or a projection.

BASIC EXERCISE NO. 12 (*tekubi joho kosa undo,* high wrist break)

This exercise is an amplification of basic exercise no. 11. You will turn your wrists with palms up, fingers pointing ahead. Then you will swing your arms upward to eye level, crossing your hands at that point, one cupping the other, palms facing you, fingers inclined ever so slightly inward.

Your instructor may try to stop the upward swing of your arms, or push directly against your wrists in the direction of your face. In either case, you should complete the swing and/or stand immovable, in full centralized extension.

BASIC EXERCISE NO. 13 (*sayu undo,* lateral swing)

Setting your feet comfortably wide apart, relaxing your whole upper frame, and centralizing yourself well, you will extend your arms in front of you palms upward. At the count of "one," you will swing your arms to your left side—your left arm projecting out (always unbendable)—your right arm extended across your chest, with the weight under. At the count of "two," you will bend your left leg and straighten your right. Your trunk must remain erect and in full balance (you must never lean to one side), and your head should continue to face forward. At the count of "three," you will straighten your legs and swing both arms from the left to the right—your right arm projecting out, unbendable, and your left arm extending across your chest also immovable. At the count of "four," you will bend your right leg and straighten your left; descending with your whole body, centralized and well balanced.

Your instructor may test both your centralization and your extension by pushing your hips from the side over the straightened leg toward the side of the bent leg; or by trying to bend the arm projecting out; or by trying to

lift the arm stretched across your chest. Mr. Tohei recommends that you "think heavy" under your arms, thus settling them so that a heavy concentration of descending power will develop which will later be unleashed in defensive action against an attack, when and if necessary.

BASIC EXERCISE NO. 14

This exercise is a dynamic variation of basic exercise no. 13. At the count of "one," you will step to your left with your right foot, sliding it behind your left foot. You will let your weight descend and then take an extended step with your left foot sideways, in the same direction, swinging your arms sideways as in basic exercise no. 13. At the count of "two," you will bend your left leg and straighten your right. At the count of "three," you will swing your arms sideways from your left side to your right, taking a step with your left foot which, this time, will pass behind your right foot. As your

weight descends, you will slide your right foot sideways, along the same general line. At the count of "four," you will bend your right leg, straightening your left leg.

This exercise may also be performed by stepping across in front instead of behind your central supporting foot. The coordination required will, however, be much greater because of the dynamic contrast with the movement of your arms, as illustrated.

BASIC EXERCISE NO. 15 *(ude furi undo,* spin)

At the count of "one," standing in the natural position *(shizentai),* you will extend your arms in an ample circle and swing them to your left side. At the count of "two," you will swing them to your right side, always maintaining your body (i.e., your trunk) in the correct vertical posture. At the count of "three," you will swing your arms back to your left side. Then, at the count of "four," as your arms swing back to your right side, you will take a short step with your right foot to your rear and prepare to spin forward.

At the count of "one," this time, you will take a long, sliding step ahead with your right foot, then pivot on it to your left, allowing your entire anatomy to spin, both arms whirling in the same circular direction and following the same circular pattern. Withdrawing your left foot circularly behind you, you will allow your weight to settle on that leg at the completion of the spin.

You should now be facing the direction from which you began the initial, whirling motion. At the count of "two," you will swing your arms to your right side, then take a long, sliding step with your left foot straight ahead, and pivot, turning your anatomy in a full circle. Your right foot will be withdrawn in orbital motion around you, your right leg settling down at the completion of the spin to receive the descending weight of your body.

In this movement (of fundamental importance to the practice of aikido), the following points must be observed:

Centralization must be maintained constantly throughout the dynamic phases of the exercise, in order to counteract the natural buoyancy of the spin which might result in a condition of unbalance or a sudden attack of dizziness.

The movement of your arms must be coordinated from the very beginning with the forward stepping or sliding of one foot and then with the retreating stepping or sliding of the other, thus making the entire exercise a single, unified, dynamic spin.

Your instructor may test the stability of your centralization at the very beginning—when you are simply swinging your arms—by pushing your hips in the same direction as your arms are swinging. Your body, regardless of the centrifugal effect imparted to it by that upper movement, should be firmly stabilized but at the same time relaxed. Your instructor may also attempt to stop your spin by moving directly across your path, or by gesturing in such a way as to break your concentration. You should continue to spin across the mat, back and forth, no matter what form his attempted interference takes. Finally, when you settle down momentarily at the completion of a spin, your instructor may push your advanced shoulder in the direction of the leg straightened behind, or push your hips from behind, in the direction from which you came. You should not "tense up," but you should not be thrown off balance either; instead you should remain in the correct position, secure and centralized.

The purpose of this exercise is to help you develop that subtle capacity to move circularly in any direction, which will allow you to deflect multiple attacks and to centralize yourself prior to their neutralization. As Mr. Tohei so aptly puts it, the principle involved is that of "a spinning globe."

BASIC EXERCISE NO. 16 (*ushiro tori undo,* forward extension)

At the count of "one," starting from the frontal posture *(shizentai)*, you will take a step forward with your left foot, letting your arms surge up, describing a half-circle in front of you. At the count of "two," you will bend your left knee, swing your left arm down close to your left toes and swing your right arm up behind you, turning your body slightly upon its own axis and straightening your right leg behind. Then you will resume your initial position, bringing your left foot back into *shizentai* and swinging your arms back to your sides. At the count of "three," you will begin the motion again, but this time with your right foot advanced; and at the count of "four" (as in "two" above), you will project your movement ahead but with your right side leading.

The points to be carefully observed are the following: Intrinsic or Inner Energy should be channeled from your Centre through both your extended arms; the inclination of your body over your bent leg should be as straight as possible, thus avoiding any exaggerated movement which would cause your hips to jut out directly across the path of an attacker's motion and thereby interfere with your techniques.

Your instructor may test your extension by trying to push your open arms back close to your body as you begin your motion or by pushing your hips from behind at the completion of the downward swing. Your arms should remain immovable and unbendable in the first instance, and your body should not be moved forward in the second.

The purpose of this exercise is to train you to capture an aggressive movement of encirclement from behind, and to lead it forward and then down through a dynamic "slide" or "chute," leading an attacker into open unbalance and down to the ground. (He should not be "loaded up," i.e., brought to lean heavily on your hips.) This movement will be especially effective against sudden attacks from behind consisting of a type of "bear

hug" or high encirclement around your biceps, as an attacker attempts to pin them to your body. In case of a low encirclement at the height of your elbows, which would make the necessary extension of the arms impossible, the general movement of your body will be the same—the forward surge of power from your Centre, and the stepping. However, your hands will clasp his hands and arms, securing a firm grip so that he will be paralyzed as you use your hip (i.e., total body) motion to throw him.

BASIC EXERCISE NO. 17 (*ushiro tekubi tori zenshin undo,* downward extension a)

At the count of "one," you will take a step forward from the *shizentai* posture with your left foot, turning your wrists inward so that your fingertips are pointing forward, palms up in a sort of cup. Sweeping your arms up to your forehead (fingertips pointing toward your face), you will then reverse your wrist position so that your fingers will be pointing toward the ground, palms down. At the count of "two," with a single motion, you will bend your body forward, describing a large circle with your hands as they descend toward the ground over your bent left knee. You will return to your initial position with your left foot drawn back into *shizentai* and your arms at your sides, wrists bent as illustrated. At the count of "three" and then "four," you will repeat the above, but taking a step forward with your right foot this time.

Your instructor may test your centralized extension at the beginning, by

pushing your wrists up, to see if your extension is flowing, if you are "projecting" or not. If you are not, your shoulders can be raised and your balance broken. When your hands are up, he may attempt to push them down. When you are bending forward, he may push your hips from behind to see if you will be thrown off balance.

In all these instances, your arms should not fold or bend, and your body should remain firmly in the chosen position.

The purpose of this exercise is to help you develop proper control over a motion of attack from behind—consisting of a wrist seizure. Your attacker's action will be captured and led first in extension upward, and then down to the ground, in a circular pattern which will neutralize his attack.

BASIC EXERCISE NO. 18 (basic exercise no. 17, downward extension b)

This exercise is similar to the preceding exercise, the only difference being that you will move backward this time, instead of forward. The extension will, however, still be channeled up, around, and down, as in basic exercise no. 17.

At the count of "one," you will take a step with your left foot, either directly to the side or slightly in diagonal behind you, and bring your right foot back, sweeping it behind your left and kneeling down on your right knee. The related movements of your hands, arms, and body will be the same as in basic exercise no. 17.

The functional differences between these two variations of the same basic movement will be represented by your centralization which in the first variation, basic exercise no. 17., will be positioned below your attacker's Centre of gravity in front of him, while in the second variation, basic exercise no. 18, the positioning will still be below his center of gravity, but to his side or slightly behind him.

Rolls and Somersaults *(ukemi waza)*

In aikido, your freedom of action and movement will not be restricted to the vertical dimension of defense, but will be extended to include (often primarily) the horizontal one, wherein you must learn to move and operate with equal ease and efficiency. The following exercises are intended to develop and stabilize this skill and control. They consist of rolls and somersaults in which the fundamental principles of centralization, extension, suppleness, and, above all, sphericity will be particularly evident and operative. The Dynamic Sphere will be functionally applicable here, because that freedom of action and movement insured in the vertical dimension by the unobstructed sphericity of your performance will be insured in the horizontal dimension, to perhaps an even greater extent by the sphericity of your body when contacting the surface of the mat, whether you are rolling backward or forward.

The sphere has always been considered by the ancient masters of martial arts to be the perfect figure. It has no protruding edges or angles which can clash against other surfaces, and it is intrinsically dynamic because its curved surface can meet all other surfaces tangentially and roll naturally along and/or around them. Your body must, when the occasion demands, become such a sphere, thus making your rolls and somersaults mechanisms of motion which you choose to perform for strategic reasons and for your own convenience.

Consequently, it is important to remember that these rolls and somersaults will not be "falls" in the strict sense of that word, i.e., mere methods for landing safely on the mat or the ground, and nothing more. In aikido, they will be forms of motion which will enable you to regain your vertical position by passing through the horizontal dimension.

BASIC EXERCISE NO. 19 *(koho tento undo, koho ukemi undo,* backward roll)

SITTING. You will sit on the mat as illustrated, with your left leg folded under your right leg (bent in front of you). At the count of "one," without changing this initial position, you will roll or rock backward, keeping your body "round." At the count of "two," you will return to your original position.

STANDING. From a left natural position (your feet in the triangular position of defense) you will descend to the mat at the count of "one," folding your back leg underneath you, so that you will not fall directly on your spine with possible jarring consequences, but will rather roll down and over that back leg. Once down on the mat, you will roll backward as in the sitting variation above. At the count of "two," you will roll forward again and in a single motion roll up and over your bent leg, stepping up onto the foot ahead and rising to your original position. This entire sequence should be repeated many times.

Your instructor may test your centralization and extension by trying to stop you either when you are "going down" or "coming up." Usually, he will pull your shoulders toward him from behind as you try to roll forward in the sitting variation, or as you try to get up in the second variation. In either case, you should complete the movement by extending your *ki* forward.

He may tell you to stop in the sitting position and then try to push you back or as you come up in the standing variation he may push strongly against your chest. In either case, as before, you should sit or stand immovable and relaxed, with your mind centered and extending ahead beyond any possible obstacles.

In both of these variations you may roll over your shoulders backward or forward as in basic exercise no. 20.

BASIC EXERCISE NO. 20 (*zempo kaiten undo, zempo ukemi undo,* forward somersault)

The forward somersault is performed in aikido in one of two basic ways: consecutively and/or rising up (the latter in short or long extension).

CONSECUTIVE (HORIZONTAL) SOMERSAULT. You will take a long step forward with your right foot, bend your trunk low with your right knee bent, while your left leg will be stretched out behind. Placing your left fist on the mat in front of your left foot, you will stretch your right arm in a curved extension alongside and over your head. With a single, circular motion you will insert your head and right arm between your left fist on the mat and your right foot. You will surge (don't throw yourself indiscriminately) forward, rolling along the arc formed by your unbendable arm, right shoulder, your back, and left thigh. Remember to keep your body round and your legs folded under you, in order to avoid hitting the mat heavily with your ankles (slapping the mat) at the completion of the circular movement along its surface. Using the same forward momentum generated by this roll, without getting up you will roll over again, and then again, following the same pattern. Alternate shoulders until this lower somersault becomes supple, relaxed, fluid, and natural.

It is important, in order to avoid soreness or injury to your shoulder, back, hip, or foot, that contact be maintained with the surface of the mat at all times. Pain is the result of a shock, of a direct frontal collision between two entities separated from each other. If there is no separation between them, there cannot be any shock, as boxers well know; i.e., when they "clinch," there is no room for maneuvering. Your body must *roll* along, not *fall* against the surface of the mat. And "roll" implies continuous contact with that supporting surface from the moment that your right hand touches the mat. Contact will be transmitted from your hand to your forearm curved below, then to your biceps, shoulder, back, and thigh, without any interruption. Usually the beginner sets his hand down, and then forgetting the rest of his arm, throws himself forward, landing heavily on his shoulder or back so that the entire weight of his body descends sharply upon those bones and muscles instead of rolling smoothly along an unbroken arc as indicated above.

At the beginning of this practice, some difficulty—both physical and psychological—may be experienced. The horizontal dimension is alien to man. It usually represents, in fact, some kind of inactivity: accepted in the case of sleep or rest, rejected in combat or in everyday living because of its possibly paralyzing qualities of inertia. But it is a dimension which, like any other, man must conquer and utilize for his own progress.

In aikido, therefore, you must overcome any physical block by concentrating upon your Centre, thus relaxing your entire anatomy and helping it to become, when required, a supple adaptable sphere. You must deal with the psychological problem by extending your Intrinsic or Inner Energy in the direction of the roll along the surface of the mat, thus using the somersault as another type of displacement (like walking), and not accepting it as an end in itself—as a fall, which would interrupt your movement and interfere with your motion. You must extend your mind in the direction of the somersault ("go beyond"), make yourself round and keep close to the surface of the mat at all times, rolling where and as you will.

VERTICAL SOMERSAULT. When you have become thoroughly familiar with the consecutive (horizontal) somersault, you may attempt the vertical, which will be technically identical with the former at the beginning (bending low) but will differ at the end, inasmuch as you will rise to your feet to face your *uke* once more. In other words, you will protect your central body by rolling down one unbendable arm onto the mat, across your back, and up again along the other arm; in effect, your roll will come "full circle" and you will spring up facing *uke* at the completion of this form of *ukemi*.

In this vertical form of the somersault you will notice the ample swing of your right arm over your head, circling toward the mat, contacting it with the outer edge of your right hand. Your arm and body will follow in continuous, tangential, circular contact, until your feet take charge once more as you roll back up again and into an upright position.

This somersault may be performed at a normal angle as described, always maintaining some physical contact with the surface of the mat (your feet first, and as they leave the ground, your arm). In the advanced stages of your aikido practice, however, the somersault may also be performed from an even greater height, your entire body flying through the air but even then extended in a semi-circle, unbendable arm ready for contact with the mat.

CHAPTER VII

The Posture and Motion of Defense

Stages and Unity of the Aikido Process of Defense

THE INNER Factors of your aikido practice—centralization, extension, leading control, and sphericity—which we have examined in Chapter V, and the physical preparation of your *soma* (see Chapter VI), will be finely and fully coordinated in and through the practical application of aikido techniques and strategies. In this chapter, we will discuss how and in what characteristic ways your body will function; how that physical instrument (not weapon) of defense will be employed in the process of neutralizing an aggression.

We will begin with a survey of those factors of your aikido practice which we call "functional" because they are directly related to the particular operations, the postures, the motions, and the actions. By them and through them, whether as regularly executed exercises or as a disciplined response to a specific and concrete problem, the goals of this art are to be attained.

Your strategy of defense in aikido will develop through three stages or strategic moments which, when performed properly, will become a unified, smooth and efficient process of defense. These stages will be: (A) the posture, (B) the motion, and (C) the techniques of neutralization.

the functional factors: the strategic activity of combat and its three stages.

the initial state: the posture

the dynamic stage: the motion

the technical stage: the techniques

The Posture

Your strategy of defense will begin with an initial posture typical of aikido, and with characteristic features of balance and verticality which, again, will be unmistakably *aiki*.

The Motion

The second stage of your strategy will be characterized by the predominant role of motion in space and along the surface of the mat. This motion is intended to simultaneously evade the direct line of convergence of *uke's* attack and to achieve a position of centralization (dynamic and technical) from which you will be able to successfully apply the technique most suitable for the neutralization of that particular kind of attack.

Taken together, evasion and centralization will become the foundation of, and establish the appropriate conditions for, the third and final stage of your defensive strategy.

The Technique

The third and final stage of your strategy of defense will be characterized by the predominant role of a particular technique of neutralization. Once having secured the necessary position of centralization which together with evasion was the purpose of your preliminary motion in the previous stage, your defensive strategy will flow from the dynamic stage (general) into the technical stage (particular). In this final stage you will:

Apply the technique of neutralization chosen from among those most appropriate to the type and circumstances of the attack launched against you (these techniques of neutralization are grouped under three main headings in Chapter VIII, immobilizations, projections, and combinations); develop that technique in the manner *(irimi* or *tenkan)* most suitable to the direction and speed of the attack launched against you, the number of assailants, the space available for maneuvering, etc.; and conclude that technique with either total immobilization of *uke* or his projection down onto the mat.

These three aspects of a singular, defensive process—posture, motion, and technique—must be first studied individually if they are to be understood ultimately as a whole.

Our analysis of these strategic moments of your defensive strategy, especially in its dynamic and technical stages of development must not, however, lead you to assume that any one of them can have a determinant relevance in either the theory or practice of aikido if taken out of context of the total action.

Motion, for example, with all of its dynamic characteristics, directional patterns, steps, etc., is only possible and characteristically smooth and rapid if your initial posture is correctly balanced between rest and motion, in full alignment with the perpendicular axis of gravity, coordinated and stabilized in the Centre. From this posture, motion can develop fully and characteristically, thus preparing the way through evasion and centralization for the particular technique of neutralization you wish to apply.

Conversely, this technique of neutralization, without the proper dynamic foundation, becomes meaningless in theory and very difficult to perform in actual practice.

We will study these areas separately here, with the understanding that it is only through the eventual synthesis and interrelation of the three stages that the process of defense in aikido will become relevant and effective.

The Posture

In the practice of aikido any study of the strategies of neutralization must begin with a consideration of the basic posture you should adopt when facing an attack, the basic distance which should be established and/or maintained between yourself and *uke,* and the basic positions or guard you should assume —all fundamental premises for an effective defensive response.

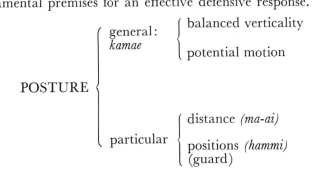

POSTURE
- general: *kamae*
  - balanced verticality
  - potential motion
- particular
  - distance *(ma-ai)*
  - positions *(hammi)* (guard)

The Basic Posture: Natural *(Kamae)*

In an aikido *dojo,* you will be taught to assume and to maintain a fundamental posture defined as "natural" *(shizentai gamae)* which has two variations, related to the positioning of your feet: right natural posture *(migi gamae)* and left natural posture *(hidari gamae).*

This natural posture will be characterized by the normal alignment of your body with the axis of gravity, thus achieving the first basic coordination of your physical self with the most important magnetic law of your environment. This identification of your anatomical centers (upper, central, and lower—each resting in full balance upon the one structurally below) with the axis of gravity begins with the positioning of your head. Hardly a single reputable martial art school has failed to point out—often in great detail— the importance of keeping the head in full vertical alignment with the spine. Many masters considered a correct positioning of the head the essential condition for maintaining the body's equilibrium, since even a slight deflection of the head from its vertical axis of balance will affect the muscles of the neck and shoulders, this tension being transmitted, in turn, to the central and lower parts of the body.

Head, spinal column, and lower abdomen, therefore, are the three anatomical centers which must always be kept in vertical alignment with each other and with the perpendicular force of gravity. This condition of natural balance should always be maintained regardless of the position of your feet, which may be side by side *(shizentai gamae)* or in combat stance, with your right foot leading *(migi gamae)* or with your left foot ahead *(hidari gamae)*. In any position, vertical alignment must always be maintained, without any self-conscious straining to keep your balance.

The adoption of the triangular position or stance *(sankakutai)* is typical of aikido, and introduces the potentiality of mobility into the natural posture.

This posture is a relaxed one, easily adaptable to normal daily life as well as to combat. But there is nothing static or intrinsically immobile about it. You will not be "firmly grounded" to the mat, nor anchored to its surface, but rather relaxed and ready.

Actually, the so-called defensive postures so frequently employed in any combat arts (both feet firmly planted on the ground) are often strategically negative and passive in conception because of their intrinsic immobility and rigidity.

The coefficient of friction between both feet and the ground is exceedingly high in such a posture and the full concentration upon vertical support implicitly negates mobility.

Ancient martial art masters often used the now-famous expression "motion in rest" to describe the desired state of balance. This expression, a philosophical interpretation of the principle of ultimate unity embracing all opposites or alternates in harmonious balance, was interpreted more specifically in the martial arts as a functional and fluid balance between rest and the dynamic possibilities of motion (in a potential state), or between motion and

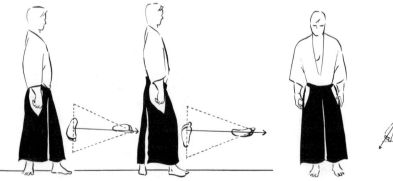

the vertical stability of rest (in a static position). From this centralized position in the lower abdomen—"floating" in a condition of dynamic rest—the weight of your body can be shifted at a moment's notice from one foot to the other, leaving the first foot free to glide swiftly in the desired direction, and to provide a new platform of balanced support for that weight (see "The Motion"). The choice of directions provided by this position is almost unlimited.

In conclusion, in the event of real combat, a sudden aggression may be launched against you at any time, from any direction, and from any distance. Therefore, it might appear superfluous to discuss a formal posture in the face of such a volatile and unpredictable event. But the problem of posture is not specific to combat alone, i.e., it is not related to the posture you must assume in the event of an attack and thus confined to this dimension alone. It is, rather, a general problem of the balanced, relaxed, and yet potentially dynamic posture which an aikido student should maintain under all circumstances. Thus, whether you know you are about to be attacked or not, whether you are walking or standing still, the balanced verticality of your posture and of your body should always be the same—centralized and ready to spin or to shift smoothly from one leg to the other in the desired direction, hands low or high as circumstances and/or events require.

Basic Distance *(ma-ai)*

This idea of distance is related to the natural measure of space maintained between men anytime they meet, for any purpose including that of combat. Disciplined aikido practice will help you to develop this sense of distance which should be maintained between yourself and other men, consciously at first, until finally it will become automatic. This natural distance will be exactly proportionate to your possibilities and capacities for reacting defensively to a sudden attack.

For training purposes, a particular method for developing this sense of distance has been devised and adopted. According to this method, the cor-

rect distance between you and your partner *(uke)* will be established by stretching your arm out so that you can touch his outstretched fingertips with yours. Given time and practice, maintaining this distance will become automatic and completely natural.

The Basic Stance *(hammi* or *hanmi)*

The natural posture *(shizentai gamae),* with its two basic forms—the right and the left stance—will finally be related to the positions of attack which may be assumed by an assailant. In this context, it will be identified as *hammi* or *hanmi* which the authors translate as "guard" or "stance" (initial position of defense), in order to distinguish its strategic application from the more generalized dimensions of posture examined previously.

Your initial defensive position in aikido will usually involve one of two basic stances with appropriate directional variations.

MUTUAL STANCE (*AI-HAMMI*)

When *uke* assumes a right posture, with his right foot forward, you may adapt your posture accordingly *(migi gamae)* with your right foot leading. This position is referred to as "right *hammi.*"

Or, when *uke* assumes a left posture with his left foot forward, you may switch to a left posture *(hidari gamae),* your left foot leading. This position is called "left *hammi.*"

REVERSE STANCE (*GYAKU GAMAE*)

When *uke* assumes a right posture, you may also face him with a left posture *(hidari gamae),* and when he takes a right position, you may assume a right posture *(migi gamae).*

| low *(gedan)* | natural *(chudan)* | high *(jodan)* |

The position of your hands, depending upon the circumstances of combat, may be low *(gedan),* natural *(chudan),* and high *(jodan).*

The Motion

In aikido strategy "motion" identifies the total displacement of your own body in space and along the surface of the mat. This general motion represents the prerequisite for any technique of neutralization which, accordingly, cannot be performed properly without it.

This initial displacement of your body can be of two basic types, straight or circular (with a third resulting from their combination). Whichever type of motion is chosen, however, and whatever style of stepping is selected, the aikido step will be unusually light and fast, feet gliding, toes turned outward, moving lightly along the surface of the mat, never dragging or hesitant.

This style of stepping about with the soles of your feet gliding very close to the surface of the mat "skimming along it" is also mentioned frequently in ancient martial art texts. It was said that a "solid" step settling heavily on the mat increased the coefficient of friction between the sole of the foot and the surface of the mat, thus simultaneously decreasing the coefficient of motion, and speed. By the same token, a "high" or raised step, while increasing the coefficient of motion considerably, decreased the coefficient of vertical stability and made the body extremely vulnerable to any push or pull however slight.

In aikido, therefore, you will not "drag" your feet, you will "glide," and you will resort to a leap only in the event of an unusually fast or close attack.

Straight Motion *(shintai)*

This straight motion will develop along a single line without curvature or angularity. The directions of straight motion are many, but the doctrine of aikido has broken them down into eight fundamental patterns, as shown in basic exercise no. 9 (Chapter VI).

A straight displacement along the surface of the mat may be performed

BASIC DIRECTIONS OF MOTION

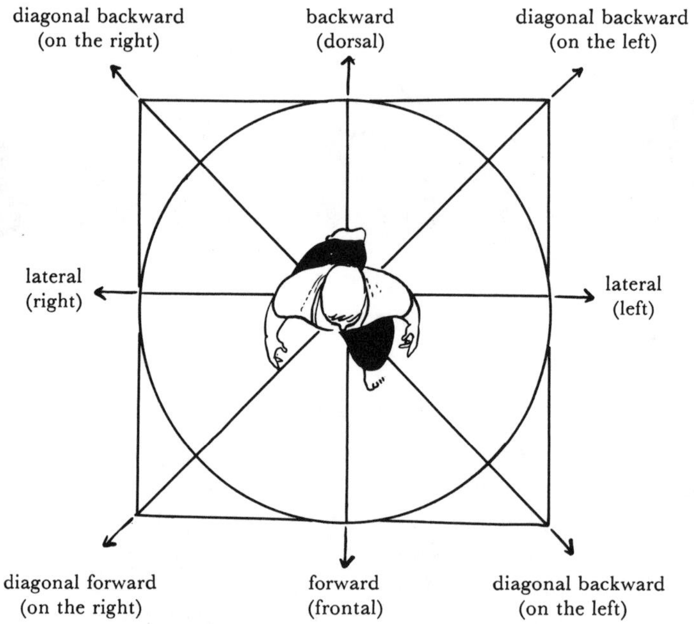

diagonal backward
(on the right)

backward
(dorsal)

diagonal backward
(on the left)

lateral
(right)

lateral
(left)

diagonal forward
(on the right)

forward
(frontal)

diagonal backward
(on the left)

from the natural aikido posture in three ways: the follow-up step *(tsugi ashi)*, the alternated step *(ayumi ashi)* and a combination of both.

The follow-up step *(tsugi ashi)* is fundamental in all the martial arts of Asia, and in the most popular martial arts of the West—boxing and fencing. It consists of stepping with one foot (the one leading) in the desired direction, toes pointing slightly outward, shifting the weight of your body onto that foot and then bringing the other foot (the one following) up close behind it.

The alternated step *(ayumi ashi)* is normal stepping: one foot glides freely in a given direction, settles down beneath the shifting weight of the body thus leaving the other foot free to glide over and beyond the former with a rhythmic alternation of function (support and motion) and operation (stepping).

The alternated step can be normal or crossed. It is normal when the whole body aligns itself with the leading foot, thus changing posture and stance at each step. It is crossed when the body does not shift but maintains the same side forward in the direction of the displacement.

As shown in the illustrated sequences, crossed alternated stepping may be performed with the leading foot crossing in front or behind the supporting foot.

Circular Motion *(tai sabaki)*

By far the most important type of motion in aikido is the circular displacement of your body when under attack. This displacement will develop along a single curved pattern, every point of which will be equally distant from the center of the pattern.

This type of motion has always been of fundamental importance to those martial arts applied in counterattack because it allows a man to evade the direct force of an attack, while strategically positioning himself for the launching of his response.

But it was in the arts of pure defense that circular motion became almost an absolute, and in aikido it assumed a distinctive form (see "The Principle of Sphericity," Chapter V).

The circular motion used in aikido may be performed in two basic ways: either by keeping both feet in light contact with the mat as you turn your hips (pivot), or by using one foot as the central fulcrum of a dynamic circle as the other foot glides smoothly around it, either forward or backward (spin).

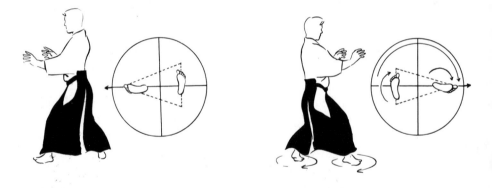

THE PIVOT

Turning on the spot to your right or left or to your rear may be accomplished, as explained in basic exercise no. 7, by pivoting on the balls of both feet, without lifting them from the mat. This pivot may be a quarter, or half-circle turn.

THE SPIN

The spin in aikido represents the ultimate in circular motion. It may be performed by leaving or setting one foot of the defensive triangle on the mat to act as the central element of support for your whole body and as the central axis of motion, while your other foot glides in orbital motion around that central support, either forward or backward.

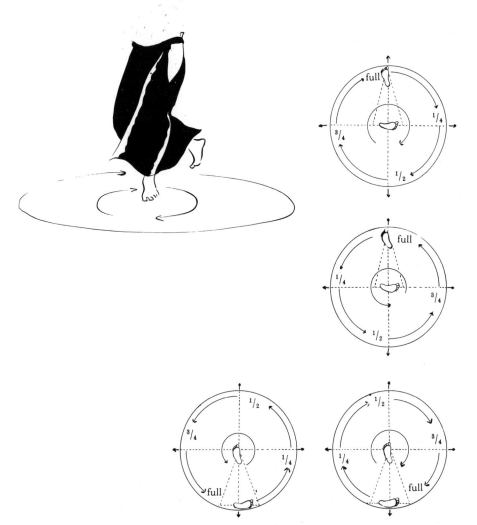

The range of circular displacements is immense, regardless of whether the foot at the apex of the defensive triangle or the one at its base acts as the pivoting fulcrum, and regardless of the direction in which the orbiting foot will move (forward in advance or backward in retreat).

Combination of Straight and Circular Motion

If you combine straight motion (the follow-up step, the alternated step, the combination of the two) with circular motion (the spin and the pivot) the choice of possible displacements in aikido becomes almost limitless.

It is important to practice each type of motion separately and with attention, before attempting to blend or combine them. However, it is this blending which will characterize the advanced practice of the art, as the various forms of motion are alternated and combined, fluidly, lightly, in full centralization, until finally they will become one—indivisible parts of a single, dynamic displacement.

Purposes of Motion

The purpose of your initial motion when faced with a real attack, will be: to avoid being overpowered by the direct, frontal stream of an attack by allowing its unified power (aggressive, negative *ki*) to flow past you, thus diminishing or dissipating itself in a vacuum of unbalance; and to slide simultaneously into a centralized position from which you will be able to operate (in full control) upon an attacker's weakened position, and lead him into the circular pattern of a technique of neutralization.

These purposes—both fundamental (evasion and centralization) and consequential or implicit (dissipation of aggressive *ki* and leading it into neutralization)—will constitute the dynamic premises for your conclusive defensive action or technique (see analysis in paragraphs which follow).

But again we must caution you to remember that the defensive motion of aikido is a singular phenomenon and that its various purposes are only individual aspects of a single unified goal, i.e., paving the way for the smooth application of an irresistible technique which will neutralize an unjustified and violent aggression.

EVASION

Evasion in aikido may be considered as an end in itself with the aggressive convergence of an attack being dissipated into nothingness; or the preliminary step to centralization for the purpose of neutralization. (In this second case, the aggressive convergence of the attack will actually be utilized to achieve the neutralization.)

In both cases, evasion does not mean trying to escape, in the sense of "running away" from that aggressive convergence of power, because if you retreat in this manner, you remain the "target," the passive, intended victim of an attack, which would continue to be pursued.

To evade in aikido means—and this is true of everything you attempt within the framework of the art—to "lead" in the sense that the unified power of an attack being discharged against you will actually be directed by you (through your own motion or action). You will lead it away from the intended target either into nothingness (pure evasion) or into a Circuit of Neutralization (evasion for the purpose of centralization preliminary to neutralization).

Simple evasion may be pivotal in aikido. Master Uyeshiba, whose smooth and fluid use of "pure" or pivotal evasion never fails to amaze and enthrall observers, has made an art of this form of displacement. It has even been said that if aikido were based entirely upon this initial motion it would still contain sufficient elements to cope with any attack, whatever its form, direction, or speed (see Chapter IX).

CENTRALIZATION: inside *(irimi)* or outside *(tenkan)*

Evasion as a preliminary step to centralization may be performed in aikido either by moving in toward the central source of aggressive power or by whirling away from that power, thus extending it beyond its natural limits. In both cases, this will be the point where that power will be weakest and where it may be controlled for the purpose of neutralization.

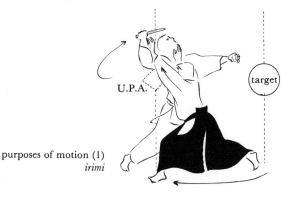

purposes of motion (1)
irimi

Examples of the first strategic dynamic possibility are offered by those displacements which bring your body very close to *uke* before he has been able to fully launch his attack. These displacements are called *irimi* or *omote* (entering motions).

Examples of the second dynamic possibility are those displacements which will shift your body circularly away from that attack, leading the aggressive convergence of *uke* out beyond the point of intended contact (either inside or outside his line of attack). These displacements are called *tenkan* or *ura* (turning motions).

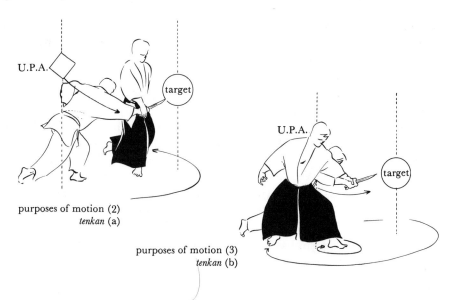

purposes of motion (2)
tenkan (a)

purposes of motion (3)
tenkan (b)

In both cases, whether moving toward the source of power or leading it beyond the outer limits of its effectiveness, the purpose of this motion will be to achieve a position of dynamic centralization from which you will be able to control *uke's* weakened attack and lead it toward its own neutralization.

As indicated in Chapter V "The Principle of Leading Control," it is a classic tenet of the most ancient schools of the martial arts that an attack should be deflected, i.e., not stopped directly through a frontal clash. Such a frontal, direct response to an attack would either be a strategic mistake, or, at best, a primitive, unsophisticated approach to the problem of self-defense.

There are certain *irimi* movements in aikido which to the untrained eye may appear to be direct frontal clashes. However, upon closer scrutiny it will become apparent that when performed properly these motions are always slightly lateral, either to the left or right of the direct, oncoming motion, or almost underneath it. An aikidoist's extension will then usually lead the attacking motion down or back to his attacker with a circular, defensive impulse imparted to the original motion of attack.

The lateral stepping may be almost imperceptible; the circularity of the leading motion also is barely noticeable, but anyone who tries to perform a technique without grasping the importance of this slightly lateral entering will find the technique exceedingly difficult to perform and—if his attacker should be stronger than he—perhaps even impossible.

But however complete or successful an evasion and the correlative dissipation of aggressive power, the primary aim is still that of positioning your body in the very center of the action, in a position from which you will be able to control, lead, and neutralize any attack. Whether you slide below the line of the motion/action of *uke* as, for example, when he attempts attack no. 13 *(shomen-uchi)* which you will counter with immobilization no. 1 *(ikkyo—irimi),* or whirl behind him in a *tenkan* variation of that technique, you will be establishing the same position of centralization and acting upon the necessarily extended and unbalanced body of *uke*. Whether he is preparing to attack or has been led past his intended target, his momentum is captured by your motion. It is from this point in space and place that you will launch your technique of neutralization.

A glance at the techniques of neutralization in Chapter VIII will be sufficient to indicate the functional relevance of this motion of centralization which will blend completely with the motion of evasion in every technique.

In using the word "centralization" one may think that it applies only to those techniques of neutralization which involve leading the aggressive power of an attack around your own body, in a circle parallel to the surface of the mat. But this term has an infinitely richer, more diversified dimension.

According to the operational principle of sphericity, that aggressive power (led beyond its intended target or cut off at its source) may be spun around you in a circle vertical to the ground, or in diagonal, etc., even in various combinations of complete circles, or in spirals developed in space in a series of infinite progressions. But in any and every case you will be the Centre while your attacker either floats in unbalance (static) if you have moved in toward him, or spins around in dynamic unbalance if you have moved away and led him out beyond his intended target.

In the case of pure evasion, the principle of centralization will be operative in the relationship established between the frame of *uke* converging upon you, and your own frame sliding inside his line of aggressive convergence, either laterally or underneath.

In the case of motion acting on the source of aggressive power, centralization will be acquired at the expense of the unbalance of *uke;* your body, well centered and in full balance, will be properly positioned for the extension and channeling of *ki* as you lead *uke* into a circular pattern of neutralization.

In the case of motion at the outer limits of aggressive power, centralization will be established more dynamically between your balanced and vertical spin and the dispersed motion of *uke* being led around in orbital motion.

The Basic Techniques of Neutralization

WITH YOUR motion of defense and the achievement of its main purposes—evasion and centralization—the process of defense in aikido enters its third and final stage, the stage in which an attack will be neutralized swiftly and efficiently. This neutralization may be achieved in one of three general ways: (1) through an immobilization which will make it impossible for *uke* to continue his original attack or initiate a new one unless you release him; (2) through a projection which will send him whirling away from you; or (3) through a combination of the first two categories. Each of the three general ways or methods has innumerable mechanisms for achieving the desired neutralization called "techniques." Each technique, in turn, contains a specific sequence of dynamic and technical actions that follows a pre-determined pattern or scheme of performance, so structured as to insure the effective neutralization of a specific attack.

According to some authorities, the possible number of these techniques of neutralization and of their combinations may well be in the thousands. In this vast arsenal of defensive mechanisms, however, there are certain techniques which recur frequently and which you will see practiced consistently in almost every aikido *dojo*.

159

Since the present book is only an introduction to the art, the number of basic techniques selected and illustrated here will necessarily be limited. They have been divided into three general categories: immobilizations, projections, and combinations, with numbers assigned to identify each technique individually.

Table 1 on page 161 offers a panoramic view of those basic techniques of immobilization and projection, identified by number and illustrated at the precise moment when they acquire their particular technical identity, the moment which differentiates each one from all the others.

Each technique is practiced in response to specific forms of attack. On page 162 Table 2 lists the techniques across the top, and the attacks down the left side; it indicates (with a check) the examples illustrated and explained in detail in the following sections. There are over one hundred such examples in this chapter.

General Recommendations

In the descriptions of techniques which follow, you will be referred to, according to the Japanese tradition in the martial arts, as *nage* (literally, the thrower, or he who applies the technique of defense to neutralize an attack). Your partner will be referred to as *uke* (the "receiver," or the aggressor whose attack will be neutralized by *nage*). Refer to the Glossary at the end of the book for a list of other words and abbreviations used.

For those readers who would like to use the descriptions which follow not only as a theoretical introduction to the art, but also as a practical guide, we strongly recommend that extreme caution be exercised when performing any techniques without the supervision of a qualified instructor. As even a cursory glance at the techniques in the following three sections will reveal, they can be dangerous both for you and—above all—for your partner. Aikido *dojo* have their share of accidents, the majority of which can be traced to uncontrolled applications of immobilizations and/or projections. Such accidents, which may discourage many students interested in the art, are absolutely unnecessary and almost always avoidable.

The student interested in the practice of aikido should proceed gradually by following a program of progressive development such as the one contained in this book. He should expand the range of his resistance, suppleness, and coordination through the practice of the preliminary exercises, the basic exercises and, of course, the special exercises intended to develop inner centralization, extension, leading control, and sphericity of performance before he attempts the techniques themselves. He should then try each technique with the cooperation of a prepared *uke,* at *kata* speed, i.e., slowly and carefully, with emphasis not so much upon practical efficiency at first, as upon correctness and precision of displacements, actions, holds, and leading control.

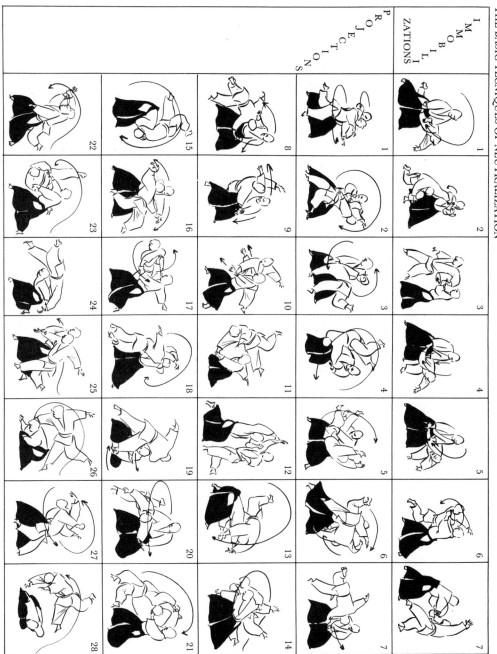

EXAMPLES OF BASIC TECHNIQUES OF NEUTRALIZATION ILLUSTRATED*

ATTACKS		IMMOBILIZATIONS							PROJECTIONS																										
		1	2	3	4	5	6	7	1	2	3	4	5	6	7	8	9	10	11	12	13	14	15	16	17	18	19	20	21	22	23	24	25	26	27	28
H	1	>>>	»	>>>					>								>	>	»											»	>						ANY
O	2	>		>			>		>	>							>	>	>		>																
L	3	>	>	>				>	>		>						>	>			>									»		>	>				
D	4			>	>		>		>			»															>										
S	5		>				>			>			>	>				>																			
	6				>		>		>				>	>									>														
	7							>							>							>														>	
	8								>																												
	9				>				>																		>	>									
	10		>													>																					
	11						>	>	>										»	>																	
	12								>																												
B	13		>	>	>		>		>		>	>							>			>					>										
L	14		>	>			>	»	>																>	>											
O	15	>			>			>			>	>													»									>			
W	16			>																						>			>						>			
S	17		>		>		>	>																													
C・O・M・B	18																																				

*Defensive Combinations Excluded

In aikido, efficiency should and will result from precision of operations; it will be a natural consequence of the correct performance of the various programmed motions which are the bare bones of each technique.

Particular care should also be exercised in the selection of a partner who, as *uke,* will be the receiver of your technique of neutralization. Ideally, he should have reached your own level of development since that would mean that both of you could practice at a compatible level of coordination.

But this ideal will seldom be possible. Your partner may be an advanced student of the art who will willingly and expertly provide you with the momentum of attack and the aggressive extension you will need to perform the techniques of neutralization successfully. You may then tend to become overconfident and careless about the control of your movements to the extent of actually hurting your partner. Experienced aikido players who really cooperate without "pulling back" are very often subjected to many such painful experiences due to lack of control and discretion on the part of inexperienced *nage.* Therefore, if an experienced student can get hurt, it is reasonable to assume that an inexperienced student will have still greater chances of being hurt if *nage* does not exercise caution and control over every stage, every motion, and every action of the strategy of defense.

In accordance with the fundamental principles of aikido practice in relation to combat, i.e., centralized extension of energy and spherical lead, when you secure a hold upon your partner (wrist, elbow, neck, etc.) you should not grip him too tightly, letting your fingers close around and press into his flesh like a vise. Not only is this a poor approach, but closing your fingers completely around any object will automatically close the circuit of your power and return it to you, thus weakening both you and your strategy. You should use your last three fingers (especially your little finger) and your thumb to hold, but your first finger should always be extended or pointing in order to maintain an open circuit of power so that your *ki* will be flowing outward all the time.

In relation to the techniques of immobilization that you will apply with the cooperation of *uke,* do not be misled by the feeling of power that may steal over you when you realize how painful they can be if improperly applied. As explained in Chapter IV, pain is only a transitional stage in any aikido technique (especially the immobilizations), not its primary purpose. Pain serves the limited purpose of dissipating the concentrated power of attack of *uke* by leading its force back to him for a brief moment, i.e., only long enough to lead him into the final immobilization or projection. Inflicting pain for its own sake has always been regarded in aikido (as is true of any superior discipline of development and coordination) as the surest sign of, at best, an immature, incomplete personality; at worst, a degenerate and absolutely negative personality.

In relation to the techniques of projection, do not hang on to *uke* when projecting him away from you or when bringing him down to the mat because the interruption of his dynamic displacement (which should flow smoothly into a roll or somersault) will inevitably cause him to fall heavily to the mat with the attendant possibility of serious injury.

Do not hurl him away from you either, since such a frantic disengagement (as is true of the tendency to "hang on" described above) will still be an indication of very poor control over yourself and accordingly over your actions. The negative effects of such lack of control will have to be absorbed by *uke,* and in some cases by you as well.

The idea to be kept in mind at all times is that of leading the attack of *uke,* not of interrupting it through a delayed hold or a premature "snapping" disengagement. If you lead his attack smoothly and circularly into the Circuit of Neutralization of a projection, you will be able to control him and his action from beginning to end. Eventually *uke* will come, almost automatically, to follow that lead and to cooperate more and more with you, thus giving you the full benefit of the unconditional coordination of his attack with your defensive strategy until they will become one; the practice itself will be harmoniously complete and beneficial for both.

You should also remember always to complete the technique with a follow-through motion. This will serve to complete the circle of the throw even after you have released *uke* and he is rolling away from you. This follow-through is very similar to the way a baseball batter completes his swing even after the ball has left his bat. If he should "check his swing," there would be a noticeable effect upon the ball and upon the direction of its flight.

This principle is particularly valid in aikido, where your follow-through motion will actually help *uke* to roll out of his fall and rise up safely, thanks to the impetus and guiding direction provided by your completion of each technique with an ample following gesture involving your hand, arm, and body.

As your experience in the art increases, your style will gradually become more and more coordinated so that it will become difficult to separate an attack from a defense and *nage* from *uke.* The two will move circularly together, without interrupting or sharply halting their motions and actions, but rather with a lively rhythm which will lend grace to the entire exercise. At this point your technique will finally become what it is intended to be— an exercise in total coordination.

Enjoy the practice of aikido and the application of its techniques of neutralization as exercises of coordination, exercises which must be perfected, polished, refined. If you are excessively concerned with the practical results of each neutralization (whether an immobilization or a projection), you will find that you have begun at the wrong end of the tunnel. The achievement of any purpose always presupposes a certain preparation leading to the achievement desired. The perfection of such a process has always made that ultimate achievement qualitatively superior and, eventually, natural.

Strive first to perfect the individual movements of the techniques, and the practical result—neutralization of an attack—will almost take care of itself. This is because, as noted earlier, it will be the result of the proper performance of the techniques themselves.

At all times "be centralized"; extend energy or *ki* from your Centre; lead the attack of *uke* and channel its force circularly into a circuit of dissipation and neutralization. Every technique, regardless of its particular operational complexity, is a concrete, specific application of those fundamental principles, which are their *raison d'être*. Without these underlying "energizers," the techniques will become simply "outer" exercises. Notwithstanding their undeniable value as calisthenics, they will lack that total fusion, the necessary coordination of Inner with Outer Factors. These factors represent the primary purpose of aikido and the preliminary step for your development on a superior spiritual level which will include ethics of conduct applicable beyond the limits of the mat and the *dojo*.

Immobilizations

The immobilizations of aikido are techniques of neutralization in which physical contact with your attacker will be maintained throughout, from your first defensive extension to the moment when he is effectively paralyzed in one of the five locks listed below.

There are many possible immobilizations which may be employed to neutralize an attack. Those which are considered basic in almost every aikido *dojo* include:

immobilization no. 1	*ikkyo*
immobilization no. 2	*nikyo*
immobilization no. 3	*sankyo*
immobilization no. 4	*yonkyo*
immobilization no. 5	*gokyo*

The following two techniques, which we include here with the five basic immobilizations listed above, mark the transition from techniques of immobilization to techniques of projection:

immobilization no. 6   *shiho nage*
immobilization no. 7   *kote gaeshi*

These last two techniques may be concluded with your attacker pinned to the ground or "immobilized"; or they may be turned into projections as you launch your attacker away from you across the mat (in the case of a multiple attack, against the other men converging upon you).

IMMOBILIZATION NO. 1
(IKKYO)

General Remarks

Immobilization no. 1, which is called *ikkyo* (form one) or *ude osae* (arm pin), is one of the most effective techniques of immobilization in the aikido repertoire.

You will recognize *ikkyo* by the position into which the arm of *uke* will be led (palm and elbow turned upward). His elbow may be almost fully bent or from half to fully extended; his arm may be turned at shoulder height or higher (in accordance with the attack being neutralized), but always in a smooth characteristic arch.

When you are bringing the arm of *uke* into any one of the above mentioned positions, you will usually be in front of him or slightly to his side. In the illustrations here, your original extension will sweep his arm back toward his face, your right hand guiding and/or grasping his right wrist while your left hand palms his elbow (i.e., his elbow will rest in your palm). The importance of not attempting to grab the initial blow can be easily understood here. And, of course, by sliding your initially extended hand (the left here) so that the elbow of *uke* rests in your palm, you will be able to rotate his arm easily without having to exercise undue pressure and without hurting him unnecessarily, since his arm naturally bends that way.

From this position, immobilization no. 1 can be concluded in either of the two basic ways: *irimi* or *tenkan*.

Irimi: In this variation, your extension and motion will flow in a large circle up and then down to the ground again, so that *uke* will be spun around or actually turned completely on the spot. The hand which is guiding his wrist will lead it downward in a large circle, while the hand cupping his elbow will rotate it smoothly, as illustrated. At the same time you will step forward (see illustrations), spinning *uke* around on the spot and bringing him down to the mat. Of course, both your arms should be extended (the unbendable arm) from the beginning of the technique to its conclusion.

You will descend in a single smooth sweep to the mat, sometimes with the aid of a slight, half-skipping step forward which is often used by those aikido practitioners who are not too tall.

When *uke* is flat on the mat you will be kneeling alongside him, pinning his outstretched arm to its surface as illustrated, palm facing upward, his

tenkan

irimi

wrist well secured, the knife-edges of both your hands controlling his wrist and elbow. One of your knees, the one closest to his body, will be firmly braced against his shoulder.

Tenkan: In this variation, you will step behind *uke,* pivoting on that foot and bringing your other foot around as illustrated. At the same time you are leading and guiding his extended arm around you in a descending spiral to the mat where you will secure his arm as in the *irimi* variation.

Let us now study a few examples of defensive reactions based on this technique of neutralization. They are used against various types of attack once the appropriate dynamic patterns of evasion, extension, and centralization have brought your *uke* into position for the smooth and effective application of immobilization no. 1.

irimi ←——— ↓ ———→ *tenkan*

IMMOBILIZATION NO. 1 AGAINST ATTACK NO. 3

Among the many ways of applying immobilization no. 1 against attack no. 3, we have selected the following: at the moment when both hands of *uke* contact your right wrist, you will take a step with your right foot to his left side, feigning a blow to his face in order to distract him. Then you will pivot on that advanced right foot and turn to your left while your right hand extends *uke* out, and you lead his unbalanced, moving frame in a circle to your left. You will then take a backward step with your right foot and bring your leading right hand downward, thus causing *uke* to bend forward, with his arms extended as he seeks to hold onto your wrist. In a single continuous movement, your left hand will grip his left wrist from the outside, while your right hand rises smoothly along his left side, turning his palm upward and detaching it from your own wrist with your left hand. At the point of its highest extension, the arm of *uke* should be in the position already encountered in the previous examples. From this point you will conclude the action with either the *irimi* or *tenkan* variation.

IMMOBILIZATION NO. 1 AGAINST ATTACK NO. 5

Uke moves to grab your shoulder or lapel—in the illustrated example, your left lapel—with his right hand. At the moment when he is dynamically committed and his hand establishes contact with your shoulder, you will retreat circularly on your left foot, using a smooth motion synchronized with the speed of his attack. You will then feign a blow to his head with your right hand which will move in an ample circle as it slides along his outstretched right arm and secures his right wrist on your shoulder or lapel. All of these synchronized actions and motions—his advance, your circular retreat—will have broken his balance for a brief moment during which he will literally "float" in the air. It will then be comparatively easy to turn your hips toward him (to your right side), thus putting all your power behind your left arm and causing the elbow of *uke* to rotate upward, while your right hand detaches his right hand from your shoulder or lapel. From this point, your may conclude immobilization no. 1 by using either variation— the *irimi* or the *tenkan*.

IMMOBILIZATION NO. 1 AGAINST ATTACK NO. 7

Uke tries to immobilize you by grabbing both your wrists from behind. At the moment when his hands begin to close around your wrists, while his dynamic commitment is still flowing downward toward and around them, you will turn your hands, palms upward (see basic exercise no. 8) and extend your arms initially in that same downward direction. Fingertips still pointing upward, you will then lead *uke* into a smooth extension which will soar up in front of you over your head where you will turn your wrists again, palms now facing the ground. Your hands will begin to lead downward again as you take a short step to your left side with your left foot, followed by a long sweep with your right leg deep to his left-rear side, dropping to the mat on your right knee. *Uke* will be led by the downward motion of your hands and body and his initially strong position will be considerably weakened by the sudden transposal of his target from in front of him to beside him, almost behind him. Your left hand will grip his left wrist from the outside, while your right hand slides along his forearm to his elbow. You establish the center of rotation which will be activated by the whole surging motion of your body rising up again from behind. You will bring him down in one of the basic variations of this immobilization—*irimi* or *tenkan*—simply by leading him down, either forward or if you choose to step further to his left-rear side, around your own body as you pivot in the center of the action.

IMMOBILIZATION NO. 1 AGAINST ATTACK NO. 13

A straight blow is being delivered to your head (nose, forehead, chin, etc.). As the blow is being launched your whole body will stretch fully toward it, both arms surging upward in front of you, as in basic exercise no. 5, the right leading and presenting an oblique surface to the blow itself. Thus, its force will be discharged not frontally as intended but obliquely and, therefore, ineffectually. That extended right arm, through which your *ki* should be flowing freely, represents the perfect set of "rails" along which the oncoming blow will slide, thus dissipating itself. Experienced aikido practitioners, as indicated earlier, continually practice this extension of their mental/physical powers in the direction of an oncoming attack, which—especially when a blow is involved—is thus psychologically deprived of its primary asset: the unilateral imposition of the attacker's will, and his initiative.

Upon contacting the forearm or wrist of *uke,* you should apply immobilization no. 1 in either of its two variations without the slightest hesitation or dynamic interruption. If you should choose the *irimi* variation, your right forearm will turn toward his attacking right wrist and you will grasp it, not at the moment when he actually hits or contacts you, but an instant later when the power of his blow has been dissipated along your obliquely extended right arm. Your left hand will contact his elbow and grip it as illustrated.

Care should be exercised at this point not to attempt to stop his blow with either or both hands as many beginners are inclined to do; i.e., trying to stop the blow with their outstretched hands, thumbs dangerously protruding across the path of the oncoming blow. Needless to say, a real chop or a straight right would crumple these flimsy barriers and the defender. The preliminary extension of your right arm and of your whole body surging upward toward the blow in a single powerful alignment will serve to "nip it in the bud" if it is still quite high, or parry, capture, and divert its force if it has already begun to descend. (Ideally, you should respond at the very moment when an attack is being launched: in this instance, when his arm is still raised high in the air.) In the *irimi* variation, you will parry first and then your hands will establish their respective holds on your attacker's wrist and elbow. From this point, as shown in the illustrations, you will step forward, bringing the arm of *uke* down firmly in front of you and leading him down to the mat. In the *tenkan* variation, the dynamic involvement of your body will be definitely greater because at the moment when the blow is being launched and/or begins to travel toward your head with blurring speed, you will extend

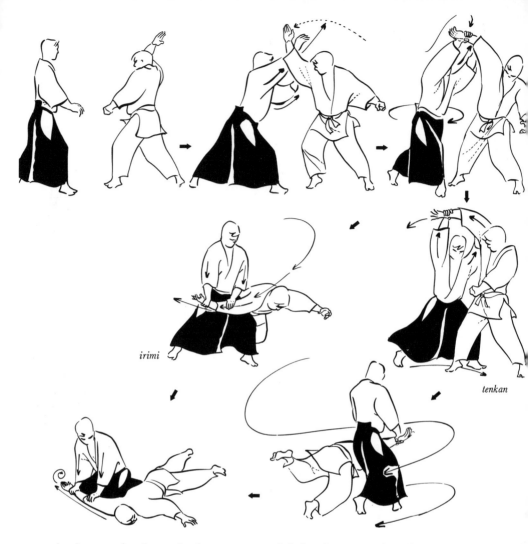

irimi

tenkan

both arms in the orthodox posture of deflection, stepping deep to his right-rear side with your left foot and then pivoting on that foot so that your body will whirl around, describing a large circle.

At the same time your hands will establish a firm hold on the arm of *uke* (his elbow and wrist) and lead the force of his blow centrifugally around you in an irresistible spin uniting both his motion and your own. Caution should be exercised during practice in order to avoid hurting a cooperating partner who really attacks you and does not pull back, because it is extremely easy to generate such momentum in the *tenkan* variation that your partner may be sent crashing to the mat. This variation should be practiced at moderate speed, paying close attention to details of extension, pivoting balance, and spiraling descent toward the surface of the mat. Do this in a smooth tangent and in a single sweep without pulling *uke,* but rather by employing the previously discussed "total body movement" *(kokyu).*

imi ←————↓————→ *tenkan*

IMMOBILIZATION NO. 1 AGAINST ATTACK NO. 15

Uke is about to deliver a blow to your lower abdomen or stomach with his right fist. As this blow travels toward its target, you will slide in toward his left side with your right foot, and then take a large, slightly circular step to your rear with your left foot. This will cause *uke* to be over-extended beyond the outer limits of his power. At the same time your right hand will swing over his outstretched arm, falling naturally upon his forearm and sliding along it until you secure a firm hold upon his wrist. Unbalanced and over-extended, *uke* will not be able to stop your motion as you swing his arm circularly up (see illustrations). By the time his arm reaches the apex of its extension, you will have secured your "cupping" hold beneath his elbow, thus locking him into immobilization no 1. You may now complete the technique with either the *irimi* or *tenkan* variation.

IMMOBILIZATION NO. 2
(NIKYO)

General Remarks

Immobilization no. 2 is referred to as *nikyo* (form two) or *kote mawashi* (wrist in-turn). It is one of the most powerful techniques in the aikido repertoire—one which, when correctly executed, can bring even the strongest man to his knees. Immobilization no. 2 (like immobilization no. 1) can be applied to neutralize almost any type of attack swiftly and efficiently, and can be developed from a variety of opening motions of evasion, extension, and centralization. Generally speaking, as shown in the illustrations, this immobilization is represented by his wrist being turned in one direction (toward his head), while a simultaneous pressure is brought to bear upon his forearm and elbow (bent at approximately 90 degrees), thus distorting and reversing the original force of his attack and the entire anatomical structure of his arm into a painfully closed circuit.

Such a positioning of the arm of *uke* can be accomplished by locking it in one of three basic ways: against your shoulder, with your hand alone, around your wrists. In all of these, as we shall see, the constant feature of immobilization no. 2 will be expressed by that characteristic form—resembling the letter "s"—which you will cause his arm to assume, and by the consequent reversal of its natural extension, both physical (structural) and functional.

	first lock: against your shoulder;		—the horizontal pin;
immobilization no. 2 *(nikyo)*	second lock: with your hands alone;	These three locks are applied in either the *irimi* or *tenkan* variation and concluded with:	
	third lock: around your wrists;		—or the vertical torsion

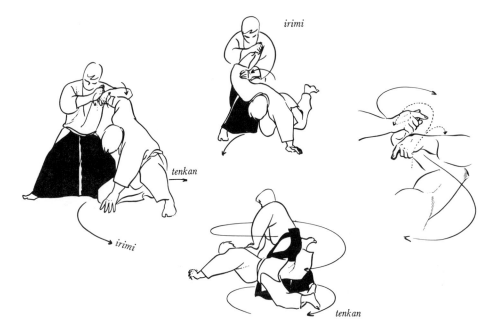

FIRST LOCK: AGAINST YOUR SHOULDER. The main point of reference in this first lock will be the position of the captured arm of *uke* against your shoulder, the position of your hands on his arm, and the position of your body in relation to his.

In the illustrated example, for instance, the right arm of *uke* is bent like an "s," with his hand firmly held by your left hand, his fingers kept close together within your grip (including his thumb) and pointing upward. Your left hand will grip his bent wrist; your forearm will rest on his. Your whole body then will be brought to bear behind the holding action of your arms which will not operate alone, as separate entities, but as natural extensions of your trunk. Notice, in fact, that your right elbow will be resting relaxedly against your right side, blending with your whole frame as you lean in, thus increasing the torsion.

The hand of *uke* will be held by your right hand, but the task of bringing pressure to bear upon his wrist will be carried out by your shoulder where his hand will be secured by your grip, his fingertips pointing upward. The pressure on that captured arm will be exercised in two directions: your right hand will turn his wrist circularly from your left to your right side, while your left hand turns in the opposite direction and your elbow sinks downward close to your body. The effect upon *uke* will be immediate and he will drop to his knees under the torsion. Your body will be positioned diagonally in relation to *uke,* with your left leg forward, offering a physical barrier and a protection against any possible attack he may attempt to launch (see illustrations).

SECOND LOCK: WITH YOUR HANDS ALONE. This second form of immobilization no. 2 differs from the first in that you will not bring the captured arm of
uke to your shoulder in order to bring him to his knees. You will operate
directly; both of your hands will work on his hand and wrist to obtain the
basic torsion without extending your own forearm along or upon his. This
is obviously a more difficult lock to apply and execute effectively since it
requires more than a passing familiarity with the intricate anatomical structure of a man's arm and the pattern of nervous centers imbedded there. Only
prolonged practice and experimentation with the first type of lock can ful-
fill those requirements. Once you have begun to feel at ease with it, however,
a tremendous range of possibilities will be opened in the area of defensive
strategies based on immobilization no. 2.

The central idea of this particular lock is closely related to that of immobilization no. 1, i.e., you will bring *uke* directly down to the mat without passing through the intermediate stage of bringing him to his knees. You could,
of course, bring him to his knees with this lock, but usually as soon as your
right hand locks his right hand in the inverted *nikyo* position, and your left
hand is free to operate either on his wrist or elbow, you will proceed to bring
him directly down to the mat in *irimi* or *tenkan* while keeping him extended
and maintaining the torsion upon his wrist. Once *uke* is stretched out flat on
the mat, you may complete the immobilization in either one of the two classic
ways: the horizontal pin or the vertical torsion against your chest.

THIRD LOCK: AROUND YOUR WRIST. A typical reaction against various aggressive holds is represented by immobilization no. 2 in this special lock which maintains the hand of *uke* in close contact with yours as you cut down across his wrist from above. In this example of a hold established upon your left wrist by his right hand, you will secure his hand against your own captured wrist with your free hand—the right one in the illustrations—and your left hand over his twisted right wrist from the outside, cutting down with the knife-edge of your hand across his forearm. The twisted position of his arm which will result is the classic one for the application of immobilization no. 2. Care should be taken to cut down as if you were "cutting your opponent in two with a sword, from top to bottom," a phrase used by many instructors. Needless to say, the motion and extension of your whole body will be behind that cut.

The same lock and consequent cut can be applied against his left hand holding your left. In this case you will secure his hand firmly with your free hand—the right one, as before—while you slide your left hand over his twisted forearm and wrist from the outside, cutting down as indicated above. In either case, such a cut will bring *uke* to his knees. From this point you may proceed to extend him out along the mat as explained previously, in either the *irimi* or *tenkan* variation, and complete the immobilization with either the vertical torsion against your chest or the horizontal pin.

Bringing *uke* to his knees with any one of these three locks, however, is not

an end in itself, but only a preliminary step in achieving his conclusive immobilization flat on the mat. Therefore, he must be brought down to the mat. This task may be accomplished in one of two ways—each with an *irimi* or *tenkan* variation.

SHOULDER PRESSURE

You will maintain the captured arm of *uke* in the *nikyo* position secured against your shoulder with one hand—the right one in this example—while you rotate his elbow around his shoulder and downward. Either you rotate by stepping across in front of him, typical of the *irimi* variation, or to his rear, spinning him around you in the descending spiral typical of the *tenkan* variation. In either case, *uke* will be brought down flat on the mat where you (kneeling at his side) will complete immobilization no. 2 in one of the two basic ways: horizontally along that surface, or vertically along the axis of your own body.

HORIZONTAL PIN. In the first case, you will remove the captured right hand of *uke* from your left shoulder, and maintaining the torsion on his right wrist, you will stretch his arm out along the surface of the mat as illustrated, in diagonal (where he has no support whatsoever). As usual, your left hand will operate on his elbow in order to keep his shoulder down. Once he is stretched out on the mat, your right hand will guide his right wrist back toward his head and away from you while your left hand pins his elbow, thus closing the circuit of his extension and increasing the pressure until the painful sensation at the joints causes him to surrender.

In this case too, as when applying immobilization no. 1, the angle of the arm pin in relation to his shoulder will be in diagonal forward.

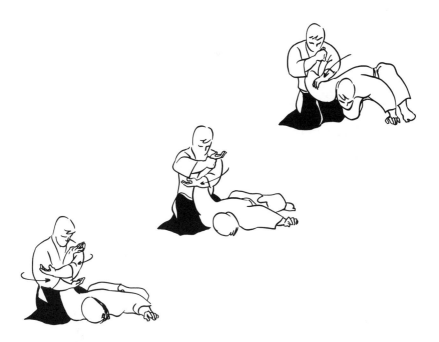

VERTICAL TORSION. In the second case, you will not remove his hand from your shoulder, but kneel at his side and secure that hand against your shoulder. This will be done by setting your left biceps across his wrist and forearm, thus locking them against your chest on the left side as illustrated. Your right arm will then "cut" into his imprisoned arm at the elbow. Thus secured, his arm will become almost part of your trunk as you pivot slightly at the hips and lean toward his head (keeping your back straight). You thus bring pressure and pain to bear upon that outstretched and locked shoulder joint.

WRIST PRESSURE

More simply, in order to bring *uke* down flat on the mat, you may remove his captured right hand from your shoulder while maintaining the torsion on his right wrist with your right hand. In order to control his possible reactions, rotate his elbow around the shoulder joint, thus bringing his face down either by stepping in front of him in the *irimi* variation, or pivot to his right-rear side in the *tenkan* variation. Once *uke* is flat on the mat you may complete immobilization no. 2 with either the horizontal pin or the vertical torsion described above.

Let us now examine a few practical examples of defensive reactions against various types of attack. These can be neutralized through the application of immobilization no. 2, after the appropriate dynamic patterns of evasion, extension, and centralization have established the premises for its success.

IMMOBILIZATION NO. 2 AGAINST ATTACK NO. 1

As *uke* grabs your right wrist with his left hand, you will take a circular step to your right-rear corner, leading him into a condition of extension and unbalance without pulling out of his hold. Rather, you will descend with him in the same direction as that of his original attack. Your left hand will feign a blow to his face, following an ample circle from your left side to the right and sliding along his outstretched left arm to establish a firm hold on his wrist from above (your thumb underneath).

Both of your arms will now continue to move along the same extended circular patterns which return upward toward his head. At its apex, when your hands are almost over your own head, you will disengage your right wrist and establish your hold upon the left wrist of *uke* with your right hand (now free). From that point you can slide into immobilization no. 2 by passing through either the first or second lock as shown in the illustrated sequences (in either the *irimi* or *tenkan* variation). Both will end with *uke* either pinned horizontally to the mat, or paralyzed completely and vertically against your own turning, leaning chest.

IMMOBILIZATION NO. 2 AGAINST ATTACK NO. 3

Uke moves to establish a hold on your right wrist, using both his hands. At the moment when his fingers close around your wrist, you will turn that wrist so that your fingers are pointing toward you and down, as in exercise no. 10, and step to the left side of *uke* with your right foot, thus allowing his line and force of attack to flow downward in front of you. Another retreating, circular step with your left leg to your rear will amplify the *tenkan* motion of evasion. It will lead *uke* out into a fuller extension through the action of your right hand which will describe a circle going up and then, in a smooth plunge, downward between the two of you. To make room for such a downward plunge of your arm, you will simultaneously take a long step with your right leg to your right-rear side.

At this point, *uke* is extended and unbalanced and with both hands still firmly attached to your wrist. Since you have not pulled out of his grip, you may easily apply the third lock of immobilization no. 2 on his right wrist by securing his hand firmly to your right wrist with your left hand, turning your right hand in a circle flowing from your left side to the right going over his bent arm, and cutting down across his wrist, as illustrated. You may also apply the third lock to his left wrist, of course. In this case, still securing his hand to your captured wrist, you will turn your right hand in a circle flowing from your right side to the left, going over from the outside of his left arm and cutting down across his left wrist. In both cases he will immediately drop to his knees.

If you wish, you may even apply immobilization no. 2 in the form of the first lock, by bringing his left hand to your shoulder after the downward plunge which follows your initial *tenkan* motion of evasion, extension, and centralization.

In any case, once *uke* is on his knees you may bring him down flat on the mat either through wrist pressure or shoulder pressure. The immobilization is then concluded with either the horizontal pin or the vertical torsion.

IMMOBILIZATION NO. 2 AGAINST ATTACK NO. 7

At the moment when the hands of *uke* establish contact with your wrists from behind, you will turn your hands—palms and fingertips facing up—and lead his line of attack down and then up again, after a smooth plunge below your Centre. Without interrupting the motion you will then lead his hands up over your head, where you will turn your hands so that your palms and fingertips now point downward. At the same time you will take a lateral step with your left foot to your left side, turning your hips to the right and taking another deep step with your right foot. You will thus slide under his left arm and, either kneeling on your right knee or with knees well bent, you will grip his left wrist with your right hand and surge up again while disengaging your left wrist, which will now secure a firm hold on his left wrist. From this position, you may bring *uke* to the mat via any one of the three locks explained previously. Once *uke* is flat on the mat you may conclude the immobilization with either of the two methods commonly employed —vertical torsion or horizontal pin.

IMMOBILIZATION NO. 2 AGAINST ATTACK NO. 13

Extend both your arms forward and take a step with your left foot to the right side of *uke* at the moment he delivers (or, ideally, is about to deliver) a straight blow to your head. Establish contact with his forearm from the outside with your right forearm and lead his blow downward, letting your left hand drop naturally onto his wrist. You will now be pivoting on your advanced left foot and stepping circularly to your rear with your right foot. Both of your hands will be on his right hand and wrist which you will extend downward in a large circle, then lead back upward toward you and into any one of the three locks explained above. You may then complete the immobilization with the vertical torsion or the horizontal pin.

IMMOBILIZATION NO. 2 AGAINST ATTACK NO. 17

With his left hand, grabbing your right lapel *uke* will attempt to deliver a circular blow to your head with his right hand. As the blow comes toward you, you will step circularly with your right foot to your right, pivot and sweep your left leg deep behind you, thus further increasing the centrifugal effect of such a pivot on the whole action. Your right arm feigning a blow to the head of *uke* will pass under his left arm and drop naturally onto his extended right arm, leading it downward, while your left hand will grasp his left hand, securing it to your lapel and turning it so that his palm and fingertips point upward. Continuing your original motion of deflection, your right hand will join the left on his wrist, your elbow will slide over his captured forearm. The first lock of immobilization no. 2 may be developed in either of its two variations—*irimi* or *tenkan* toward its conclusion in the form of the horizontal pin or the vertical torsion on the mat.

IMMOBILIZATION NO. 3
(SANKYO)

General Remarks

The main features of this immobilization are the position of the arm of *uke,* the position and functions of your hands on that arm, and the position of your body in relation to his.

His arm, as shown in the illustrations, is bent at the elbow, with his biceps almost parallel to the mat at shoulder height and his forearm perpendicular to the mat. His hand will be twisted in the direction of his head, palm obliquely downward. These indications are obviously relative in the sense that both the degree to which his elbow will bend, and the degree his wrist can be twisted inward will vary according to the different structure and size of each *uke's* arms—differences which will determine the degree of nervous response, and of the pain which those distorted and distended joints will be able to withstand.

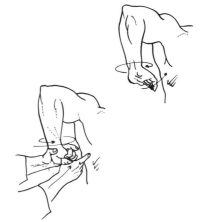

Your hands will usually be placed around his hand, your thumb and little finger performing the greater share of the gripping task, as illustrated. Your right hand will clasp his fingers, keeping them close together. Both of your arms will be extended so that *uke* will not be able to move in toward you. The action of your hands will be one of torsion on his wrist and arm, and one of extension of your entire body behind your arms in the direction of his head in an ascensional movement.

Your body will be positioned, at the moment when immobilization no. 3 is applied, either laterally to his side or diagonally, slightly to his rear corner.

The successful application of immobilization no. 3 will distract *uke* and divert his Unified Power of Attack, thus enabling you either to paralyze him completely on the mat, or project him away from you, possibly against other assailants (see Chapter IX). We will now illustrate these two possible variations.

IMMOBILIZATION. You may employ immobilization no. 3 as a preliminary step to the more complete and final subjugation of *uke,* bringing him down to the mat with either an *irimi* or *tenkan sankyo.* In the *irimi* variation as shown in the following sequences, you will twist his right wrist with your left hand up and toward his face and then down, in a circle. At the moment when the pain forces him up onto his toes, you will swing your right fist in a large circle, feigning a blow to his face and securing a hold from above on his elbow,

irimi

tenkan

which the twisting action of your left hand will expose for that very purpose. Simultaneously you will take a long, gliding step with your right leg (or a leap) in front of *uke*. That leg will now become the pivoting center for another circular step to your rear with your left foot. Your spinning motion, combined with the twisting action which you will be exercising upon his wrist, and the rotation of his elbow stretching his arm out in an extended line in front of him in diagonal will bring him down to the mat at your feet.

In the *tenkan* variation, you will step with your left foot to his right-rear side and pivot to your right, retreating circularly with your right foot. Simultaneously your left hand will twist his right wrist up and then downward behind him, while your right hand spins his whole body down in a circle around you. Upon the completion of the smooth, descending spiral of the *tenkan* movement, *uke* will land, as in the *irimi* variation above, at your feet.

In both of these variations, finally, *uke* will be pinned to the mat while you stand next to him or kneel at his side.

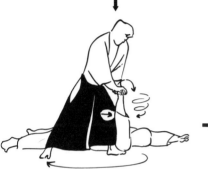

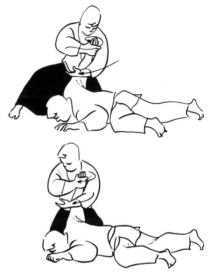

STANDING. Without releasing your left hand grip upon the wrist of *uke* you will step close to his right side with your left foot as illustrated, pivot on that foot and draw your right foot around circularly, close to his body. You will turn his right hand as shown, with his palm and fingertips twisted around in a continuation of the basic *sankyo* hold.

KNEELING. Transferring your hold on his right wrist from your left over to your right, which will grip his hand from the outside and hold it firmly against your left shoulder—you will kneel at his side as explained in immobilization no. 1 and "cut" with your left forearm across his extended arm. You will pivot on your hips to your right, leaning slightly in toward his head (but keeping your back straight) until he surrenders.

PROJECTION. Immobilization no. 3, finally, may be employed as the technical foundation for the projection of *uke* onto the mat, or you may use his body to protect yourself against other possible assailants. He may be projected down in one of two directions: backward or forward.

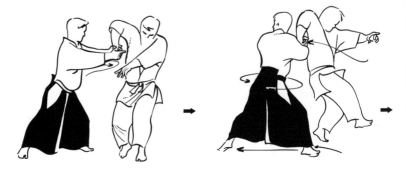

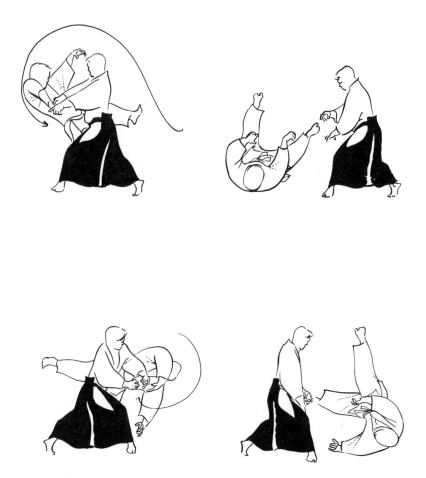

REAR PROJECTION. In the first case, you will bring the captured, twisted hand of *uke* back toward his face, taking a step with your left foot to your left-rear side, and leading his arm in a circle up over his head and then down.

FRONTAL PROJECTION. In the second case, taking the same step to your left-rear side, you will swing his hand back and up, causing him to bounce up onto his toes. Then, turning your hips to your right side again, you will swing his captured arm around you with a whipping motion closely resembling a baseball batter's swing. The pivoting turn of your hips will provide the power necessary to spin *uke* up and then circularly down.

Let us now examine a few practical examples of how immobilization no. 3 may be applied in response to a variety of basic attacks.

IMMOBILIZATION NO. 3 AGAINST ATTACK NO. 1

As *uke* grabs your right wrist with his left hand, you will turn your wrist so that your fingers are pointing toward you as in basic exercise no. 10, thus setting yourself physically and mentally in alignment with his line of attack. You will step to his left side with your right foot, pivoting on that foot and withdrawing your left foot circularly to your left side, while leading *uke* around your turning body. When he is in full flight, you will step with your right leg to your right-rear corner, as illustrated, leading his arm up and to your right. Another step with your left foot to his left side passing underneath his upraised extended arm, and a pivot to your right will bring you into the proper position for the application of immobilization no. 3. While sliding under his arm, your free left hand will clasp his left hand (which is holding your right wrist) as illustrated. You will then turn and bring both your arms in front of you, twisting the wrist of *uke* toward his head from underneath with your left hand and reinforcing this motion with your right hand which holds his fingers, keeping them close together. From this point you may bring *uke* down with either an *irimi* or *tenkan* motion, and immobilize him on the mat in either of the two ways illustrated (kneeling at his side or standing above him).

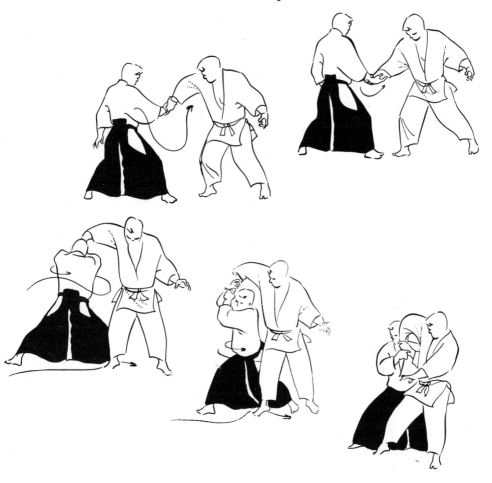

IMMOBILIZATION NO. 3 AGAINST ATTACK NO. 2

As the right hand of *uke* contacts your right wrist, you will lead him down and to your right in a circle which will extend him into a condition of unbalance—before rising up again on his right side, as illustrated. You will be simultaneously bending your knees and gripping his right wrist with your right hand. In a single motion, bring his right arm up, slide under that arm, step to his right side with your right foot, pivot on that foot and withdraw your left foot to your rear. Your left hand will assist your right in establishing the hold typical of immobilization no. 3, which will be applied when you swing your hips around to your left and bring both your arms up from underneath toward his face, twisting his wrist in the prescribed manner. Immobilization no. 3 may now be developed using either the *irimi* or *tenkan* variation, ending with *uke* flat on the mat while you paralyze him from either a standing or a kneeling position.

IMMOBILIZATION NO. 3 AGAINST ATTACK NO. 5

As his right hand grabs your shoulder or lapel, you will take a large, circular step to your left-rear side with your left foot, swinging your right hand circularly toward your left side, feigning a blow to the head of *uke* and sliding your hand along his arm to grasp his right wrist. You will turn your hips back toward your right side, putting your whole body movement behind your left shoulder against which his right hand will be pinned by your right hand. His right elbow will necessarily bend under this combined pressure. Your left hand will establish its center of rotation on his elbow and he will have to spin on the spot, while you lead his arm down in a circle in front of you. At the lowest point of this circle, your hands will change roles: your left hand will leave his elbow and slide down to grip his hand in the *sankyo* hold, while your right hand will grip his fingers as you drive his twisted hand up and back toward his face, as illustrated. Immobilization no. 3 may then be completed as indicated in the previous examples.

IMMOBILIZATION NO. 3 AGAINST ATTACK NO. 13

As a blow is about to be delivered to your head, you will extend both arms in front of your un-bendable arm—the right one leading—and let his right hand slide in tangent down your forearm which will turn on its own extended axis, thus allowing your hand to grasp his right wrist. Si-multaneously your left hand will contact his right elbow from underneath, turning his arm in a circle from your left to your right side and downward where your left hand, sliding along his forearm, will establish immobilization no. 3 on his right hand. Both hands will then lead his twisted hand back up toward his face. Immobilization no. 3 may now be completed as explained previously.

IMMOBILIZATION NO. 3 AGAINST ATTACK NO. 16

As the left hand of *uke* grasps your left wrist and his right forearm circles your throat from behind, you will drop your chin onto your chest to prevent the completion of the strangulation. There will then be two ways of applying immobilization no. 3: first, on the hand holding your wrist; and second, on the hand choking you.

ON THE GRIP. You will extend your captured left wrist down in front of you, where your right hand will be ready to grip his left wrist. You will then step sideways with your left foot and to the rear with your right foot, sliding under his left arm and leading his captured left wrist from underneath back toward his head. At the same time your left hand will grasp his fingers while you complete immobilization no. 3 in the manner described in the previous examples.

ON THE CHOKE. You will extend your left arm to distract the attention of *uke,* grip his right hand near your left shoulder with your right hand, and take a lateral step to your right side with your right foot, followed by another long step to your left-rear side with your left foot. You will either drop to your knee, or keep your knees well bent as you slide under his right arm. You will turn your body toward him, while your left hand joins your right on his right hand and now brings it back in front of you and toward his head. From this position you may complete immobilization no. 3 as previously described.

IMMOBILIZATION NO. 4
(YONKYO)

General Remarks

One of the most painful of all the basic techniques of neutralization (when properly applied) is immobilization no. 4, which is called *yonkyo* (form four) or *tekubi-osae* (wrist pin).

It involves essentially the application of sudden, sharp pressure upon the nerve centers of the forearm of *uke,* usually on the inside near the wrist (although *yonkyo* may also be applied on the outside of the arm). The initiation of this immobilization presupposes that you have already established a hold upon his forearm, after having successfully evaded his opening attack. The examples which follow include descriptions of how this technique may be applied upon the completion of your motion of evasion, extension, and centralization. In this section, however, we are primarily concerned with the application of the technique itself, with its development and completion, i.e., with *uke* pinned to the mat.

INSIDE PRESSURE. In most of the applications of this immobilization, you will extend you arm an instant after having established your hold upon his arm and cut down with the inner edge of your hand across the tendons, pressing deeply into the complex of nerves located two or three inches above the wrist.

Although this is an extremely effective immobilization, it is also one of the most difficult to perform correctly due to the fact that the exact location of the nerve centers mentioned above will vary according to the individual. Only continual practice will enable you to develop the necessary "feeling" or sensitivity which will tell you when you have contacted the proper spot, and where you should apply the required pressure on any individual's forearm.

Of significant importance in the application of this immobilization will be the part played by your little finger and the root of your forefinger when applying this pressure.

The impetus for this immobilization will come from the motion of your entire body, while your left hand, pressing upon his right wrist will bend his hand inward toward you. Both of your arms will describe a large circle in the air in front of you, leading *uke* up and then circularly down until he falls to the mat. While you are performing this circular motion with your arms you may either move ahead, cutting across his line of motion *(irimi),* or behind him, in which case you will spin him in a spiral that will end on the mat (the *tenkan* variation).

In either case the completion of this immobilization will find *uke* flat on his stomach. You meanwhile maintain the pressure upon his forearm, which your left hand keeps slightly diagonal in relation to the mat, thus permitting you to lock it in extension between the surface of the mat and your left hand,

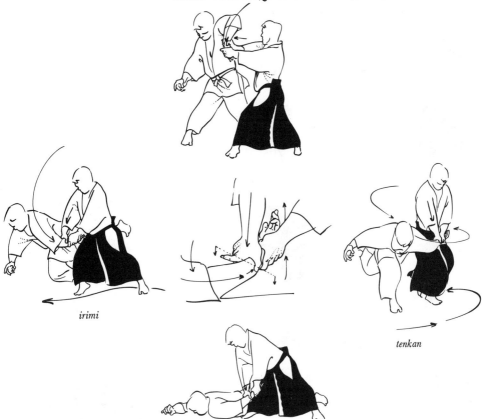

irimi

tenkan

and while the inside edge of your right hand continues to cut down, perpendicularly.

OUTSIDE PRESSURE. Immobilization no. 4 may also be applied on the outside of the forearm of *uke;* following the same general gripping procedure described for the inside of the arm, and applying pressure at almost the same height, some two or three inches above his wrist.

In the application of the inside pressure, *uke* will be led into a circle up, forward, and then down. In applying this outside pressure, exactly the reverse will occur: *uke* will be led up, backward, and then down, as he instinctively arches backward, away from the pain shooting up his arm (see *kokyu dosa,* Chapter VI). This variation of immobilization no. 4, therefore, is usually employed as a diversionary tactic to weaken the concentration of his Unified Power of Attack. Enlarging upon and developing the instinctive reaction of *uke* as he seeks to escape the sudden wave of pain, you may then apply the technique of neutralization most appropriate to the dynamic circumstances.

We will now illustrate some practical applications of immobilization no. 4 applied against various forms of attack.

IMMOBILIZATION NO. 4 AGAINST ATTACK NO. 5

As *uke* reaches out with his right hand to grab your left lapel or shoulder, you will withdraw you left foot, describing a large circle to your rear, and thus extending him out beyond the outer limits of his Unified Power of Attack. At the same time you will describe another large circle with your right hand, moving from your right side to your left, feigning a blow to his head or neck as you do so. Grasping his right wrist with your right hand from above (your thumb on the inside), you will surge upward from the hips and swing his arm in a large circle up and then down again, thereby causing his entire body to turn on the spot. Your left hand will slide into position for the application of immobilization no. 4, and you will conclude the technique as indicated in the general description, using either the *irimi* or *tenkan* variation according to the prevailing dynamic circumstances. The entire action should be fluidly synchronized with the speed and power of the motion of *uke*, so that both the attack and its neutralization seem to be part of a single movement.

IMMOBILIZATION NO. 4 AGAINST ATTACK NO. 9

As the hands of *uke* establish contact with your shoulders or neck from behind, you will take a step ahead with your right foot and then pivot on it, turning your whole body toward *uke*. Your right hand will grip his left hand as illustrated, and the twisting motion of your whole body will result in a partial form of immobilization no. 3. Grasping his left hand near his wrist with your left hand, you will then release your right-hand hold and slide this hand into position for the application of immobilization no. 4. You will then conclude the technique by employing either the *irimi* or *tenkan* variation, bringing *uke* to the ground with a single smooth, circular sweep.

IMMOBILIZATION NO. 4 AGAINST ATTACK NO. 13

As *uke* launches a straight blow, punch, etc., you will surge up toward it as in basic exercise no. 5, extending both your arms (the right one leading). Deflecting and leading the blow back toward his face with your right arm, you will establish immobilization no. 4 with your left hand and complete the neutralization in either the *irimi* or *tenkan* variation, as illustrated.

tenkan

irimi

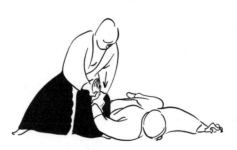

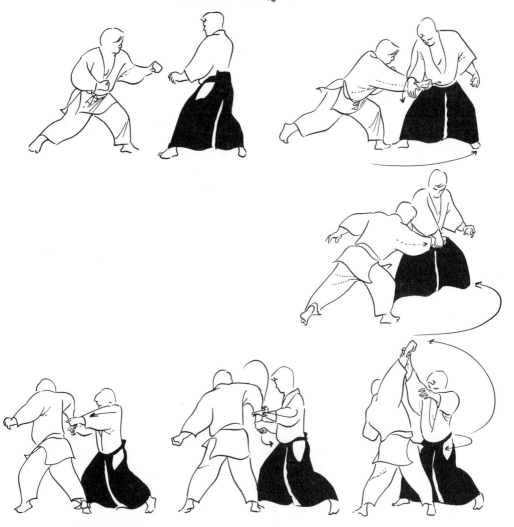

IMMOBILIZATION NO. 4 AGAINST ATTACK NO. 15

As *uke* is delivering a punch to your lower abdomen with his right fist, you will take a long circular step to your left-rear side with your left foot, thus extending him out beyond the limits of his Unified Power of Attack. Simultaneously you will describe a large circle with your right hand, feigning a blow to the left side of the head of *uke*. Let your hand drop naturally onto and along his extended right arm until your fingers close around his wrist. At this point, *uke* should be unbalanced forward, making it comparatively easy for you to swing his right arm up in an ample circle and apply immobilization no. 4 with your left hand. There should, of course, be no interruption in the unified flow of your motion/action. You may then complete the neutralization in either the *irimi* or *tenkan* variation.

IMMOBILIZATION NO. 5
(GOKYO)

General Remarks

Immobilization no. 5, called *gokyo* (form five), is usually taught in the advanced stages of aikido practice, although it is a basic immobilization. This technique is somewhat similar to immobilization no. 1 and is particularly applicable to the neutralization of an armed circular blow aimed at your head. *Gokyo* has been drawn from the ancient art of fencing in which lateral, slashing attacks with the *katana* were fundamental; in fact, the extension and leading motion of your arms in the initial phase of this technique provide a modern parallel to the samurai's extended, defending sword. This form is also illustrated in Chapter IX.

IMMOBILIZATION NO. 5 AGAINST ATTACK NO. 14

Uke attacks you with a circular blow aimed at your head, neck, or upper chest using his right hand. You will extend both of your arms in front of you as in basic exercise no. 5, thus parrying the blow from the inside with your left forearm contacting his right forearm as illustrated. Your right hand will feign a blow to his face or midriff, in order to disturb his aggressive concentration and, continuing that motion, will slide over your own left hand to grasp his right wrist. If he should be armed, this hold will effectively control the weapon and limit its maneuverability. From this point, you will lead *uke* out in the direction of his extended arm, turning your hips as you swing the captured arm with a circular motion back toward *uke* and over his head. Your left hand will exercise pressure upon the inside of his elbow as illustrated in order to bend his arm slightly. The same hand will then slide under his arm (not against it) as in immobilization no. 1 and lock it as illustrated. From this position you may bring *uke* down to the mat in either the *irimi* or *tenkan* variation, by stepping across with your left foot in front of him and leading his arm straight down; or by stepping behind him, pivoting on your left foot while drawing your right foot circularly around you as illustrated and leading his arm down, in a descending spiral.

irimi

tenkan

IMMOBILIZATION NO. 6
(SHIHO NAGE)

General Remarks

Immobilization no. 6, or *shiho nage,* which may be translated as the "four-corner throw," is a basic technique of immobilization also clearly derived from the fencing practices of Japan's legendary past. Moreover, it is a technique wherein two of the essential features of aikido (the characteristic turning of the hips and the dynamic reversal of the motion of *uke* back to its source) are so clear and practically demonstrated that this technique, together with projection no. 1 *(kokyu nage),* has assumed a position of primary importance in almost all aikido *dojo* where it is taught as the introductory technique or form to prepare the student for the series of immobilizations and projections which will subsequently be learned.

Immobilization no. 6 can be performed upon one or both of the wrists of *uke* but at first you will only grasp one of his wrists. You will extend that wrist (and arm) in one direction, then you will lead it circularly from above in the opposite direction and down. Regardless of the type of attack being launched against you, once you have succeeded in securing his wrist with both your hands as shown in the illustrations, you may apply immobilization no. 6, extending *uke* out and then—pivoting on your hips—reversing the motion and bringing his twisted wrist circled back to his shoulder.

His wrist should not be brought too far back and past his shoulder, or extended out too far to the side, since this could result in a break or dislocation. Admittedly, such a break or dislocation is the desired result in other methods

irimi

tenkan

of self-defense, but is considered crude, primitive, and unnecessary in aikido.

The entire body of *uke* at the apex of the hold will be brought into a characteristic condition of unbalance (tilted to his rear side, in diagonal) due to the twisting action you will be exercising upon his captured wrist.

Your own position on the other side must be observed in specific relation to your hands, arms, the angle of your body, as well as the location and functionality of your hips, legs, and feet.

After your initial motion of evasion, extension, and centralization, both your hands when you begin to apply immobilization no. 6 will be grasping his wrist (the right one in the illustrated example). Your right hand leads his extension to your right side, over your head and back to his shoulder as you turn with knees well bent. Your left hand follows through and closes over your right one on his wrist; it will reinforce the hold as illustrated, its role being subsidiary in an immobilization of this type applied against his right wrist.

Both your arms will be kept in front of you and well extended. They will move when the rest of your body moves, not before, and they will always be directed from the Centre. In immobilization no. 6 the functional relevance of your hips and your Centre cannot be overemphasized. This immobilization is actually motivated by the feeling of stabilized centralization which only a well-developed Centre can provide.

This technique is performed with a single smooth, circular motion in which no single element—technical or dynamic—will play the determinant role. Its efficiency depends entirely upon the "wholeness" of your motion (pivot/

spin-reversal) stabilized at your Centre. Your hips will pivot, your upper trunk will turn, your arms will be extended in front of you—but all moving as a unit.

At the completion of the pivot, when the arm of *uke* has been brought back to his shoulder and his extension reversed, your arms will be extended in front of you and your whole body will face his, in diagonal—arms, central body, legs, feet, even your toes—as illustrated. This cautionary note is particularly important in view of the fact that there is often an incorrect tendency to complete the pivot in a position too close to *uke* so that your arms will bend, or to be too far behind him so that your hands will be behind you.

Your hands and arms will have the important task of extending *uke* out, as you set your body in the correct position for the execution of this immobilization. In the illustrations we have included a dynamic series of displacements and actions cutting across the line of motion of *uke* in the *irimi* variation, as well as outside and around that line of motion in the *tenkan* variation.

Bringing *uke* down flat on his back is an operation which also requires a few words of caution. Normally such a task will be performed by bringing his hand over your head close to his shoulder, as you lead his body around and then down to your feet in a single smooth movement. It will be centered, as we have said, upon your pivoting hips. But there is room for a great variety of styles ranging from a very low immobilization no. 6 performed almost kneeling, to the circular fall of *uke* as he is brought around almost to your left side. Provided there is no danger of a break or dislocation and the whole movement is performed smoothly, they are all generally acceptable since they still fall within the limits of orthodoxy accepted by aikido.

The motion which will bring *uke* to the mat—as indicated above—can follow two basic patterns, one *irimi,* the other *tenkan.*

In the *irimi* variation, once you have established your hold upon the wrist of *uke,* as illustrated, you will step across in front of him with your left foot. As your weight settles on that foot, you will bend your knees and pivot on both feet, turning your hips completely to face *uke* again, as illustrated, his arm now locked into immobilization no. 6.

In the *tenkan* variation, you will not step across in front of *uke,* but instead will spin on the spot on your advanced left foot, bending your knees and withdrawing your right foot in a circle which will follow the turning motion of your hips. You will thus turn to face *uke* again and complete the immobilization.

Once he has been brought down to the mat, you will pin the wrist of *uke* as illustrated, and, if necessary, you may feign a blow with your left hand, kneeling at his side (or simply lean in), your whole body (left leg stretched out behind) supplying you with the power for the downward, pinning hold.

We will now examine a few practical cases of self-defense against certain basic types of attack which can be neutralized by immobilization no. 6.

IMMOBILIZATION NO. 6 AGAINST ATTACK NO. 4

As *uke* is reaching out to grab your wrists you will grasp his left wrist with your left hand and take a long step with your right foot across his line of motion, swinging his arm into a circular extension, out and over your turning shoulder. At the same time you will pivot and turn until you are facing him. Continuing your circular motion, you will bring him down to the mat. The illustrated example is based on the *irimi* variation. In the *tenkan* variation, you will spin on your right foot and lead *uke* out, turning to your left side.

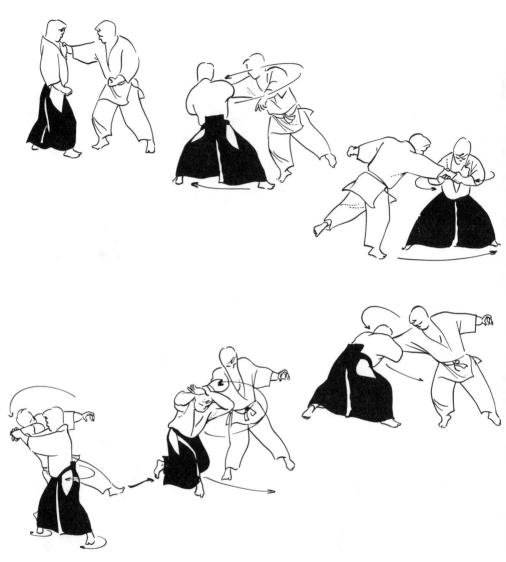

IMMOBILIZATION NO. 6 AGAINST ATTACK NO. 5

As *uke* is grasping your left shoulder or lapel with his right hand, you will take a step with your left foot to your rear, stretching him out and securing his right wrist with your right hand (if necessary, feigning a blow to his face). Then you will bend your knees, and taking a large step across his line of motion to your right side, you will lead the arm of *uke* down and then up again around and over your head. You will pivot on both feet until you are facing him, leading his twisted wrist back to his shoulder and bringing him down to the mat *(irimi)*.

IMMOBILIZATION NO. 6 AGAINST ATTACK NO. 7

As *uke* is grabbing your wrists from behind you will extend your arms either with your palms and fingertips facing up in the "s" extension, or with your arms opening diagonally in the diverging extension. Then you will slide out on your left side, take a step with your left foot, and lead his arm down in front of you, your right hand descending to establish the double hold of immobilization no. 6 on his arm. Then you will take another step with your right foot across his line of motion, extend his left arm out, up, and over your head, and pivot to your left side as you bring his wrist close to his shoulder and lead him down to the mat *(irimi)*.

IMMOBILIZATION NO. 6 AGAINST ATTACK NO. 13

As *uke* is delivering a straight blow to your head you will extend both
arms (the right one leading) toward the blow, and parry its momentum in
a tangent on the outside. You will then secure his right wrist with your right
hand and his right elbow with your left hand (your palm). Taking a step
with your left foot across his line of motion, you will pivot and face *uke*
again, bringing his right arm down between your body and his. You will
guide his motion down circularly to your right side, taking a step with your
right foot, followed by another across with your left, in front of him, while
simultaneously leading his arm up and over your head in the classic pivot
to your right side of this technique. At this point you will bring his wrist
back circled into his shoulder and then bring him down to the mat. You may
merely bend your knees deeply, or you may actually drop to one knee as
you follow his motion to the mat.

IMMOBILIZATION NO. 6 AGAINST ATTACK NO. 14

As a circular blow is being delivered to the left side of your head, you will step inside its line of motion with your right foot, extending your left arm from above and your right arm from below: the former will make contact with the arm of *uke* and guide it into the latter's grip. Now you will bring his extended arm down in front of you and apply immobilization no. 6 in either of its two variations. In the *irimi* form, following the same circular line of his attack you will step across his line of motion with your left foot leading his arm to your right side out, up, and over your turning shoulder. You will pivot outside and face him, bringing his arm down close to his shoulder as illustrated, and then bring him down to the mat. In the *tenkan* variation you will take a step on his left side with your left foot, spinning and bringing your right foot circularly around on the outside near his foot. You will lead his arm as specified above, and bring him down to the mat. Of these two variations, the former *(irimi)* is recommended because of its dynamic affinity to the directional pattern of the circular attack of *uke,* which will be led uninterruptedly around you as he flies along the perimeter of your dynamic circle in a descending spiral toward the mat.

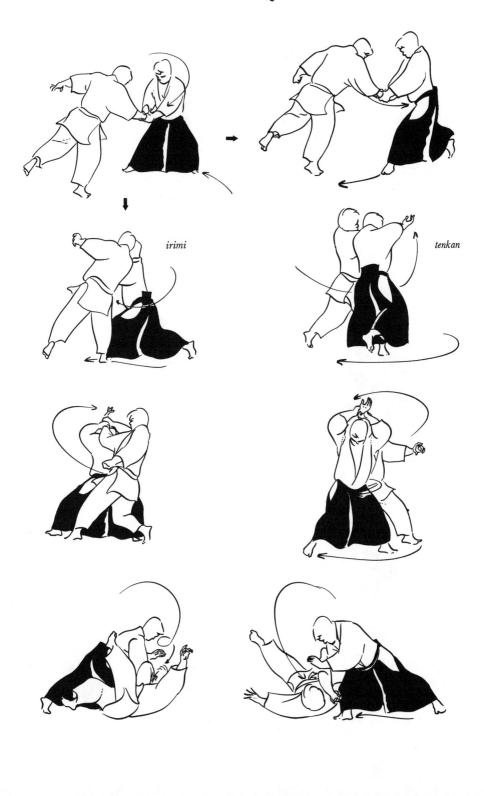

irimi

tenkan

IMMOBILIZATION NO. 7
(KOTE GAESHI)

General Remarks

As is true of immobilization no. 6, immobilization no. 7, or *kote gaeshi* (wrist turn-out), can end in either an immobilization or a projection. Its functional characteristics, however, as *uke* is being brought down to the mat, will be substantially the same. The illustrations show your basic position upon the completion of the preliminary motion of evasion, extension, and centralization. The hand of *uke* (the right one here) will be gripped as illustrated. Your left thumb will apply pressure upon his knuckles between the fourth or ring finger and the little finger. Your other fingers will close around his thumb and palm. From that position you will extend his hand back and over his forearm; this torsion upon his arm will unbalance his entire body and open the way for his fall. Particular attention should be paid to the angle of the wrist torsion. Since too wide an angle may cause dislocation of the wrist, the *aiki* method emphasizes that you should fold his fingers back toward his forearm rather than stretch his hand out and over in a *gyaku* position.

You should also try to keep his right hand low so that his fall will not be a heavy one and he will be able to slide down sideways onto the mat. Otherwise—and this is only safe for experienced performers—he may be forced to perform a high somersault over his own outstretched, turning arm. In either case, however, he will fall onto his back.

Immobilization no. 7, depending upon the circumstance of the attack of course, may sometimes end with the projection of *uke* onto the mat. This will usually be the case when you are engaged in a defensive action against more than one assailant.

You may, however, complete his projection onto the mat with a more involved form of subjugation which will prevent any resumption of the attack on his part. In this case, you must turn *uke* over so that he is face down on the mat. This may be accomplished in one of two ways—the first, or dynamic method, being preferable, since it is more in accordance with the smooth, largely painless, strategy of orthodox defense in aikido.

DYNAMIC. A human body falling to the ground, like any other physical body in motion, will be subject to the laws of dynamic inertia by which it can be

kept rolling with little effort if the motion and the dynamic momentum of that fall are not interrupted or distorted. Thus if you move rapidly, stepping with your left foot to the other side of his falling body at the very moment when he is actually hitting the mat or while he is still rolling on its surface, it will be comparatively easy to lead his arm over his extended body, thus causing him to roll over with a sort of "up and over" motion, as illustrated.

STATIC. The second method of turning *uke* so that he will be face down on the mat may be employed when his falling motion has ceased and he is lying comparatively still.

To attempt to roll *uke* over under these conditions is extremely difficult and unwise, since you will be fighting another type of inertia—static—which lends itself to his resistance (based on gravity and friction) as a body at rest. Accordingly, your left hand will bring his right hand down until his fingers almost brush his face, leading it in a circle over his head from his right side to his left, while your right hand rotates his bent elbow around the fulcrum provided by his right shoulder, very close to his head. Excruciating pain in his shoulder joint caused by the pressure upon and rotation of his elbow, and accentuated by the twisted position of his hand, will force him to turn over onto his stomach as quickly as he can. Due to the danger of shoulder dislocation which is intrinsic to this second method, and because this static form is reminiscent of other jujutsu methods, the first method is recommended as being the more orthodox, or *aiki* finish. Prospective aikido students are advised to concentrate upon the smooth speed of the action and the timing required to throw *uke* down, and—blending with and continuing the dynamic momentum of that fall—to spin to the opposite side, rolling *uke* over in a single, uninterrupted motion.

Once *uke* has been turned face down on the mat, he must be firmly pinned to its surface. This task may be accomplished in one of two ways, standing or kneeling.

STANDING. As *uke* hits the mat, you will step to the other side of his body, turn him over, and pivoting on your advanced left foot withdraw your right foot circularly, setting it near his fallen body. Without releasing his right hand throughout, you will turn his wrist toward his body and press down, arms extended, as illustrated. Your left knee will help to keep his elbow straight.

KNEELING. Once you have turned *uke* over, you will hold his right hand with your right; from the outside kneel down near his shoulder and cut across his elbow with your left forearm, as illustrated, securing it against your stomach. You will then pivot on your hips and lean slightly in toward his head (keeping your back straight), turning his arm vertically upon its axis at the shoulder joint.

Let us now proceed to examine a few practical applications of *kote gaeshi* against various types of attack, paying particular attention to your initial motion of evasion, extension, and centralization.

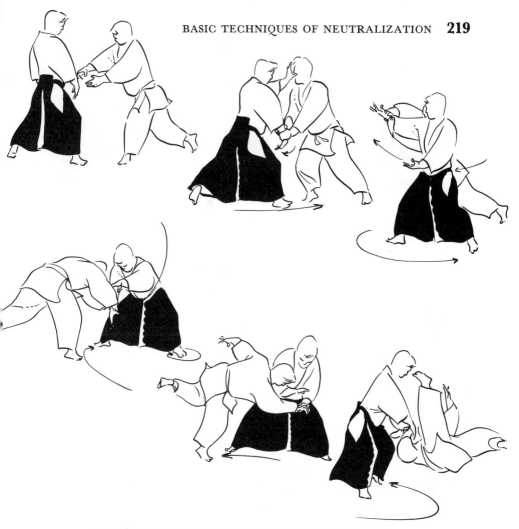

IMMOBILIZATION NO. 7 AGAINST ATTACK NO. 3

At the moment when the hands of *uke* are closing around your right wrist you will turn your fingertips in toward you and lead him downward in extension around you, as in basic exercise no. 10. Your right hand will lead him up. Using the dynamic momentum of his original line of attack plus that of his extended unbalance, you will describe a circle which will plunge rapidly downward between his body and yours as you take a long, deep step with your right foot to your right-rear side. At the lowest point of this descending circular pattern, you will grasp his right hand/wrist with your left hand and bring it up (reversed) to your right side, disengaging your right hand and using it to apply further pressure on his twisted wrist and fingers which you are pressing downward. To make way for his fall, you should take another deep step to your right-rear side as you bring him down. You may then complete the technique as indicated above.

IMMOBILIZATION NO. 7 AGAINST ATTACK NO. 8

As *uke* is establishing his hold upon your arms (above or at the elbows) from behind, you will extend your arms to the side and forward as if you were embracing a large sphere, extending fully forward in order to channel his two lines of attack into two new diverging (and dissipating) patterns. You will simultaneously take a step to your left side with your left foot, leaving room for the turning of your hips toward *uke* and for the long step which you will subsequently take to your right-rear side with your right foot.

Now you will bend over in his direction and grasp his right hand (still holding your right elbow) with your left hand in the manner prescribed for applying immobilization no. 7. You will continue to step around him to your right side, turning his right hand outward and taking a final, large step to your left-rear side as you throw him down over his locked right arm. You may complete immobilization no. 7 in any one of the various ways described above.

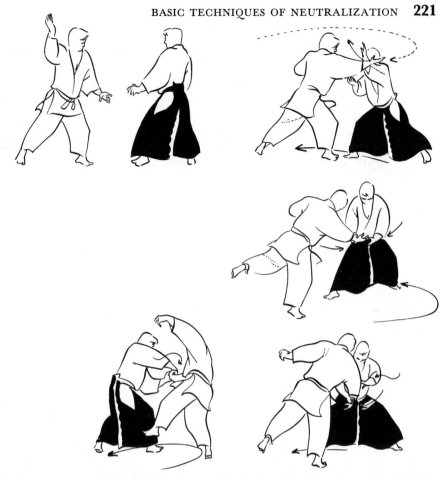

IMMOBILIZATION NO. 7 AGAINST ATTACK NO. 14

First Example (Under)

Uke is delivering a circular blow to the side of your head (ear, face, neck) with his right hand. As the blow comes in you will step inside his line of motion, sliding to your right side with your right foot and extending both arms to parry and guide his blow. Your left arm in extension from above will parry the blow circularly and indirectly, leading it into the hold prepared from below, by your right hand. Now you will take another step to your right-rear side with your left foot and bring his arm down in full extension in front of you as you hold his wrist with your right hand. Without interrupting the unified movement, you will continue to slide circularly to your right side around *uke,* who will have to spin on his advanced right leg. Your left hand will establish the prescribed hold for immobilization no. 7 on his right hand, and your right hand will assist in extending his fingers over and down. You may then project him down to the mat and complete this technique as indicated above.

over

Second Example (Over)

You will follow the same basic instructions as in the first example until the moment when your left forearm is leading the right hand of *uke* into the grasp of your right hand, which will this time be over his extended arm in front of you. Then, instead of continuing the circular motion to your right side with your right foot inside the line of attack of a *yokomen uchi,* you will step ahead with your left foot to his right side, swinging your left arm from above, pivoting on that foot and letting your left hand drop naturally onto his right wrist (kept extended by your right hand). You will withdraw your right leg circularly on your right side *(tenkan)* and when *uke* has been set in motion by this spinning, you will step with your left foot to your left-rear side, reverse your motion and project him down to the mat, completing the technique as explained above.

IMMOBILIZATION NO. 7 AGAINST ATTACK NO. 15

As *uke* is delivering a blow to your mid-section (or lower abdomen) with his right fist, you will slide forward with your left foot, turning your hips to your right side and evading the direct force of the punch. You will pivot on that advanced foot, withdrawing your right foot to your right-rear side and letting your left hand drop naturally onto his extended wrist in the prescribed hold for immobilization no. 7. Then you will lead *uke* in a circle around you before reversing your direction (if his initial momentum permits) or step directly to your left-rear side with your left foot. You will then project him down and complete the technique as indicated above.

Projections

The projections of aikido are techniques of neutralization in which physical contact between you and *uke* will cease (although your follow-through motion will continue) at the moment when he is thrown spinning down onto the mat or across its surface.

There are, as we have indicated, a vast number of these projections in the aikido repertoire. From those basic projections which are practiced in aikido *dojo* all over the world, we have selected 28.

PROJECTION NO. 1
(KOKYU NAGE)

General Remarks

The technique of neutralization which we list here as projection no. 1 is known as *kokyu nage* or the "20-year technique." This technique is usually the first throw taught to a beginner and is less specialized than many other projections you will meet later on. Projection no. 1 may be efficiently and smoothly applied to neutralize almost any type of basic attack, and can be developed from a great variety of introductory motions of evasion, extension, and centralization.

Projection no. 1, the series of immobilizations extending from no. 1 through no. 5, the two transitional techniques, and immobilizations nos. 6 and 7 comprise the central nucleus of the aikido technical repertoire and the basis for the development of numerous strategies of defense.

When you watch a high-ranking aikido practitioner (or *nage*) perform projection no. 1, it appears to consist of a blurring spin which—as *nage* suddenly reverses his original direction—will sweep the feet of *uke* from under him, bringing him down to the mat flat on his back almost before he realizes what has happened. Moreover, the entire performance at its best will be marked by the absence of any dynamic discordance, choking pain, or muscular spasms, etc., on the part of *uke*.

It may appear to be a very simple technique, its mechanism easy enough to operate when performed by a high-ranking practitioner of the art. When you begin to attempt it yourself, however, even with the best of partners you will soon realize why it has been nicknamed the "20-year technique"— in homage to Master Uyeshiba's painstaking efforts over a twenty-year period to perfect and polish the dynamic and technical complexity of this particular projection.

In its practical applications, as you will discover when studying the various examples of defense against a large variety of attacks, projection no. 1 presents certain characteristics, a number of specific features which are related technically to your hold on the body of *uke,* and to his position in relation to yours. Above all it is related dynamically to his motion around you, and to its pattern of extension which will eventually be reversed from above, flowing in an arc downward to his rear. In every example of a neutralization using projection no. 1, your initial motion of evasion will bring you into the position of centralization typical of this technique. Observe the details of this position closely. In the illustrated example, your right hand will be leading *uke* around your body as you spin in the center of the action. That hand, depending upon the type of attack being neutralized, may be grasping his extended right arm, simply guiding it from above, or possibly not touching it at all. But your left hand (never in a fist, but with fingers extended) will always be holding his head firmly against your shoulder (the right one here) —firmly, but not harshly or painfully.

Your palm may rest against his left temple (ideally), over his left ear, or along the left side of his neck; in any case this holding should be done in such a manner that your fingers will not gouge or inflict pain, since the intended target is not a particular area of his anatomy, but rather controlling the head to direct and then project the whole body.

Your body will spin upon its own vertical axis as you step behind *uke* with your left foot, withdrawing your right foot circularly to your right-rear side as illustrated. Your arms—in their respective leading and holding positions— will always be in front of you. Consequently, *uke* will have to spin orbitally around you, the axis of his upper body tilted in your direction. This will, of course, produce that condition of dynamic unbalance in his condition which is a prerequisite for the proper performance of this technique.

Uke will also be extended dynamically in the desired direction because your central spinning motion will be faster than his outer or peripheral motion as he whirls around you. His head, in direct contact with the spinning axis of the action (your body), will be extended ahead of the rest of his body following circularly behind; this, of course, is the reason for the characteristic forward lean of his body in motion.

The ultimate purpose of projection no. 1 consists in bringing *uke* down flat on his back on the mat. Starting from a motion that will lead him forward, it is clear that his orbital motion and frontal extension must ultimately be channeled back in the direction from which they originally came. And this dynamic reversal must be achieved smoothly, without the slightest dynamic interruption.

At the beginning, you may note a tendency to clash frontally against his line of motion, usually with some sort of choking thrust of your biceps across his windpipe. But this will result in a painful interruption of both your motion of reversal going from your right to your left side, and of his extended motion going from your left to your right side. The important point to keep in mind at this stage of projection no. 1 is that your dynamic reversal is and will remain throughout the technique a leading, guiding motion. It will channel his extension into the only circuit of reversal available: circularly upward, in a smooth arc stretching him further up and out, before returning downward from above behind his arched, extended body to the mat.

The action of your right shoulder (the fulcrum of rotation in this technique), of your elbow (describing the circle of extension and reversal), of your hand (leading and pointing in the desired direction)—all will be of determinant importance in insuring the success of this technique.

But they would all be ineffectual if they were not solidly based upon the continuous, spinning motion of your whole body as it pivots in a condition of dynamic balance stabilized at your center of gravity, or Centre. The dynamic motivation of the whole projection, its unity, is determined by this abdominal centralization or extension of centralized energy. It is an example of explosive stability which may appear to be a paradox in theory but remains an amazing, still relatively unexplored reality in combat.

Your motion of dynamic reversal from your right to your left side, and your spinning hip motion will usually be accompanied by a step in the same direction with your right foot. It will provide the following:

(1)   The platform of support for your whole frame as you sink down (bending your knees deeply) above *uke* as he falls to the mat in front of you or at your side.

(2)   A muscular barrier against any possible reaction (whether planned or instinctive) on the part of *uke*.

PROJECTION NO. 1 AGAINST ATTACK NO. 1

First Example

As *uke* reaches out to grab your left wrist with his right hand, you will evade his line of attack by extending your right hand between his right forearm and your left, stepping in to his right side with your left foot; you will then pivot on that foot while withdrawing your right leg circularly to your right-rear side, and lead his right arm around you (you may grasp his wrist after the initial extension, if necessary). Your left hand will secure his head against your right shoulder, passing from behind and over his left shoulder. You will continue to pivot around until his body is almost on your right side and in full motion. Then you will extend your right-side shoulder first ahead of him, leading him slightly down and out, then upward describing a circle with your elbow around your shoulder joint. At this point your hand, fingers extended, will lead him upward, and then circularly down. You will reverse your hip motion back to your left side, taking a step circularly with your right leg if necessary, and guiding him down to the mat.

Second Example

As *uke* grabs your right wrist with his left hand, you will take a long circular step to your right-rear side, leading him out in extension around you on your right side. Your right hand will describe a circle in front of him which will return from above, back toward his head. Your left hand will feign a blow to his face and slide under his extended left arm, helping to lead him up until the apex of this motion has been reached. At that point you will disengage your right hand in order to clasp his head on the right side, while you slide (or leap) behind him with your right foot. You will pivot on that foot to your left side, withdraw your left foot in the same direction, and let your left hand drop onto his left wrist, leading it in a single circular sweep downward. He will spin in dynamic unbalance around you, and when his body has almost reached your left side, you will channel his motion upward in an arc, thus reversing its pattern without interruption and leading it back to him. You will pivot to your right as illustrated; if necessary, take a long circular step with your left foot in the same direction.

Third Example

As the right hand of *uke* grabs your left wrist, you will turn your hand as in basic exercise no. 10 and lead him in extension forward. Then you will turn your hips to allow your captured wrist to pass freely, and step across with your right foot close to his right foot. Now you will lead him out to your right side in a circle returning behind him and passing over his right shoulder, while you take another long step with your left foot, further back on his right side. Unbalance him in that direction. Your right arm will slide around and over his left shoulder in a large circle and lead him downward, while you take another deep step with your right foot behind him, turning your hips as you do so. From here you will guide him down to the mat.

The element of apparent differentiation between this method and the other examples lies in the employment here of your captured left hand as the "leading" element of the projection, whereas in the more common form of projection no. 1 used to neutralize an attack on your left side, your right hand will perform that task. Your left hand will usually perform the task of holding his head against your right shoulder. However, if you wish, you may lead his right hand back to his right shoulder and grasp the collar of his jacket at the back of his neck as you spin him around, extending him up and back to his rear, directing his reversed motion circularly down to the mat.

PROJECTION NO. 1 AGAINST ATTACK NO. 2

First Example

This typical defense against attack no. 2 is featured in almost all aikido *dojo* as a standard introduction to the practice of projection no. 1.

As *uke* grabs your right wrist with his right hand, you will leave your hand there and concentrate on your hip motion, stepping with your left foot to his right side near or behind his advanced right foot. You will swing your left hand circularly and establish contact with the left side of his head which will thus be secured against your right shoulder. Spinning on your left foot, you will bring your right leg around circularly in a large sweep to your right-rear side. Your captured right hand, once you have moved to his right-rear side, will lead him out and around you. When he has reached your right side (his body still in full motion), you will rise up in a smooth circle and lead his extended upper body backward and circularly down to the mat. Your hips will turn back to your left side and, if necessary, you may take a step forward (to his rear) with your right foot.

Second Example

Another extremely dynamic way of applying projection no. 1 against attack no. 2 consists in turning your right wrist with the palm of your hand toward the extended right hand of *uke* and pivoting with your hips to the left side, while simultaneously withdrawing your left foot circularly to your left-rear side and extending your arm (and *uke*) toward his right-front corner. Your right hand will describe a large circle from below. You should bend your knees deeply to further emphasize the dynamic momentum of his unbalanced, circular extension. When the apex of this motion is reached, you will turn

irimi

tenkan

your hand (palm forward) on his extended and reversed right wrist, pivot back to your right side and step with your left foot to his right-rear side. Swinging your left hand around from behind *uke* (to contact his head), you will bring his right arm down with your right hand holding his wrist. Then you will pivot on your left foot, withdrawing your right foot circularly to your right-rear side and spinning *uke* around your whirling body by the combined action of both your arms—the right one leading his right arm down and around, the left one holding his head against your turning shoulder. At this point you will extend *uke* on your right side, leading him down and extending him out, then channeling his motion upward and reversing its dynamic pattern back and down, rotating horizontally at the waist, and vertically with your right arm. Finally, you may take an additional step with your right foot, if necessary, thus reinforcing his fall by the forward motion of your body.

PROJECTION NO. 1 AGAINST ATTACK NO. 3

First Example

As *uke* grabs your right forearm and wrist with both hands, you may apply projection no. 1 by evading his line of attack in either one of two basic, dynamic ways: with an *irimi* motion or a *tenkan* motion.

Irimi. You will lead both hands of *uke* downward in the direction in which he is moving, simultaneously stepping to his right side with your left foot, and swinging your left hand around and contacting the left side of his head. You will continue to pivot on your left foot, withdrawing your right leg to your right-rear side in a circle, and spinning *uke* around you, leading

his arms with your captured right hand. When his body is at your right side, you will extend him down, out, and then upward with your right hand, as your elbow rotates around your shoulder. At this point, you will turn your hips back toward the left, take a long step to his rear and guide his extended, reversed body downward until he falls to the mat.

Tenkan. As *uke* grasps your right forearm and wrist with both his hands, instead of moving in to his right side, you will move out to his left side with your right foot, pivoting on that foot and withdrawing your left leg to your left-rear side. Simultaneously your captured hand will lead his arms downward and out frontally, sliding them in a smooth circle around you.

Your hands must always be kept in front of you when you are turning in a *tenkan* movement. (When we say "your hands lead around," we do not mean that your hands will move while the rest of your body remains rooted to the same spot. "Leading around" means, more exactly, around your vertical axis; i.e., you will turn completely, hips first, with your trunk, arms and hands in proper alignment.) Now you will take a long diagonal step to your left side with your retreating left foot, and bring your captured right hand down in front of you between his body and yours. He will have to spin and expose his leaning, unbalanced right side to your defensive action. You will step in with your left foot to his right side, pivoting to your right-rear side and withdrawing your right leg behind in a circle. You will swing your left hand around his head from behind, leading him out and around with your captured right hand. Then you will spin, extend, reverse, and guide his motion downward.

Second Example

The action in this example will follow the same dynamic outlines as that of the *tenkan* motion explained in the preceding sequence, up to the point where you are leading *uke* out and around. Once he has been extended forward, you will spin him around without interrupting his motion by taking a long step with your right foot circularly to his left-rear side, thus practically moving around him. At the same time keeping your captured hand high you will describe a circle with it around his head in dynamic synchronization with your displacement around him. Your left hand will contact the left side of his head, your right hand will slide upward and then circularly down to his rear. Meanwhile, your body will be transforming your motion around him into a spin on your right foot, turning your hips to the left, and bringing your left leg back to your left-rear side. Now you will guide his reversed motion circularly down over his shoulders and to his rear. If you wish, you may achieve the same results by letting your captured hand drop down between your body and his once you have completed the initial opening motion in *tenkan* and he has been extended forward. This drop is highly dynamic in the sense that you will use the downward momentum of that hand to wrap your right arm around his head and at the same time spin him irresistibly on the spot. The position and motion of your feet will be the same as in the other relatively higher method, and so will the conclusive series of extending and reversing actions which you will perform to bring *uke* down to the mat.

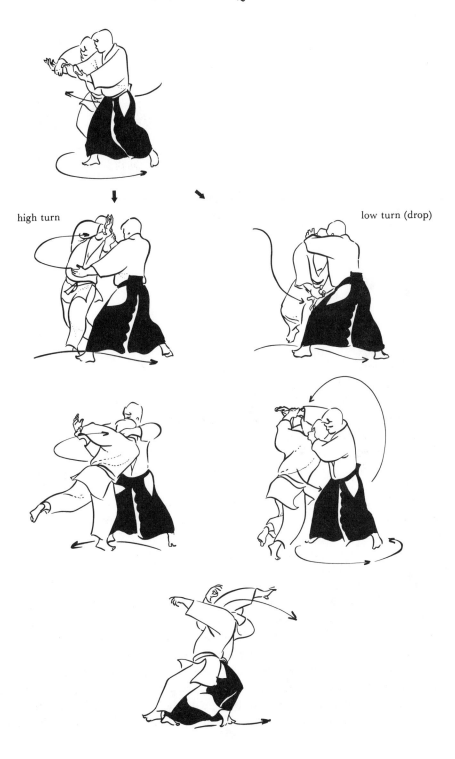

high turn

low turn (drop)

PROJECTION NO. 1 AGAINST ATTACK NO. 4

Among the many ways of neutralizing attack no. 4 with projection no. 1, we have selected the following example, a method frequently employed in aikido *dojo* all over the world. As *uke* grasps your wrists, you will lead and extend his left hand forward and his right hand down, taking a cross-step with your left foot at the same time. From this position you will take a second deep step with your right foot, as illustrated. You will be leading his left and right arms up and circularly back over his head, his left arm slightly ahead. Turning your hips and continuing this "windmill" motion of your arms, you will complete the technique as described previously.

PROJECTION NO. 1 AGAINST ATTACK NO. 6

As *uke* reaches out to grab your upper trunk with his hands (your throat, lapels, shoulders), you will take a large step with your right foot diagonally to your right-frontal corner, and thus inside the line of motion of his right arm. Then you will pivot on that foot, withdrawing your left foot circularly behind you to your left-rear corner. As you are taking the first step, your right arm will swing upward between his outstretched arms, feigning a blow to his face as a diversionary tactic, and then sliding down along his right arm, leading it down in front of you to your right side. Without any interruption of the movement, you will slide or leap to his right-rear side on your left foot, swing your left hand around to clasp his head against your right shoulder, pivot and step circularly to your right-rear side with your right foot. Then you will spin him around, and reverse his motion, leading him upward and then down to the mat. You may take a step with your right foot, if necessary, as you accompany him down to the mat.

PROJECTION NO. 1 AGAINST ATTACK NO. 7

As *uke* grabs your wrists from behind, you will bend them, palms and finger-tips upward, and lead his arms downward and forward as in basic exercise no. 17, then in a smooth circle flowing up and over your head and opening a path for your pivot of evasion. Or you may extend both your arms in front of you diagonally to the sides, rotating your wrists inward and bringing your elbows out, thus extending his arms over yours (this is the method illustrated here). In either case you will bend your knees deeply while turning your hips to the left. Once you have completed this pivot which brings you around to face *uke,* you will extend his left wrist (his left hand, remember, was former-ly holding your left wrist) to your left side, slide or leap to his left-rear side with your right foot, swinging your right arm to contact his head and bring it close to your left shoulder. Continuing your pivot, you will withdraw your left foot behind you, spin *uke* around, reverse his motion, leading him upward. Then, turning your hips as you step forward with your left foot, bring him down to the mat.

PROJECTION NO. 1 AGAINST ATTACK NO. 8

Held firmly from behind by *uke* who is clasping your arms at the elbows with both his arms, you will bow deeply as illustrated, almost touching your right knee with your forehead, and take a circular step to your left side with your right foot. Then you will bring your left foot outside and near his left foot, spinning on your left foot and sliding or leaping to his left-rear side (your right foot leading). The deep bow by its sheer weight, suddenness, and momentum, should have freed your right arm. You will now swing this arm around and secure his head, while your left leg is withdrawn circularly to your left-rear side. Spinning him around, you will extend his head circularly up; return in an arc down to his rear, turning your hips and taking a step with your right foot in the direction in which he is falling.

PROJECTION NO. 1 AGAINST ATTACK NO. 9

When you are grabbed from behind at the neck or shoulders by *uke* who uses both his hands, you will extend your arms out diagonally, rotating your wrists inward and your elbows out as illustrated. Then you will take a step forward with your left foot and slide your right foot to his left side behind you. Bending your knees, you will slide under—your right arm rising up again between his extended arms around his head on the left side (between his head and left shoulder). Your left hand will secure his head; your right foot will take another step inside and around on his left side. Then your left foot will follow with a circular stepping motion as you pivot to the left. Now you will spin *uke* around, extending his motion upward in a circle returning down behind him. Finally, you will turn your hips, taking a step with your right foot if necessary in the direction of his fall.

PROJECTION NO. 1 AGAINST ATTACK NO. 13

This typical defense has also been widely adopted as a standard introduction to the practice of this particular technique. As a blow is being delivered straight to your head, you will extend your arms—the right deflecting and capturing the dynamic momentum of the blow itself, as in basic exercise no. 5. You will step with your left foot to his right-rear side, spinning on that foot as you bring your right leg circularly around behind you. Your right hand will lead his right hand down and around, and your left hand will secure his head. Now you will spin him around and complete the throw by extending his head up and then backward, while you turn your hips, slide with your right foot, if necessary, in the direction of his fall.

PROJECTION NO. 1 AGAINST ATTACK NO. 14

As a circular blow is being delivered to your head on your left side, you will step diagonally with your right foot inside the line of the motion of *uke* extending both arms to parry the blow with your left arm and lead his right wrist smoothly into your right hand as illustrated. At the same time, you will step to his right-rear side with your left foot, securing his head with your left hand and extending him out and around with your right hand. You will withdraw your right foot and pivot on your left foot, describing a large circle behind you to your right side. Then you will spin *uke* around, extend his motion up, back and circularly down, turning your hips and stepping with your right foot, if necessary, in the direction of his fall.

PROJECTION NO. 2
(IRIMI NAGE)

General Remarks

Another basic technique of neutralization is projection no. 2, which like projection no. 1 is characterized by that dynamic reversal of the motion action of *uke* as you return it circularly back to him from above. This technique is referred to generally as *irimi nage,* or "entering throw."

Projection no. 2 can be applied to neutralize a variety of attacks; in each one, the main points to be observed (once you have completed your motion of evasion and centralization and are about to project *uke* down onto the mat) will be the following: *uke* must be spun around you in full dynamic extension; his body must be in full contact with yours; the total weight of your body will then shift around, slide down and rise up again in a powerful, wavelike motion, descending upon his unbalanced, upper frame; your balanced body, therefore, must be lowered for a moment (trunk erect, but knees well bent) and then uncoiled upward like a spring, following a spiraling pattern which will return down behind *uke;* at the moment when you reverse your motion leading *uke* around and down, his lower anatomy will still be in motion forward, while you are leading his upper trunk backward, where he has no support whatsoever.

These characteristic features of projection no. 2 are better visualized in the following examples of five ways to use this technique in response to a variety of basic types of attack.

PROJECTION NO. 2 AGAINST ATTACK NO. 1

As *uke* grabs your left wrist with his right hand, you will turn and extend your hand (fingertips pointing upward) in the same direction as his motion, taking a step to his right side with your left foot and removing your hips from the path of his now-controlled extension. You will pivot on your left foot and take a circular step to your right side with your retreating right foot, leading *uke* around you in the *tenkan* motion as you turn with him. He will whirl around you and you will bend your knees deeply, leading him down along a sloping pattern which will extend him forward and cause him to lean against you. At this point you will describe a large circle with your leading left hand, returning toward *uke* from above as your body rises and your weight shifts from your right leg to your left, as illustrated. The lower part of his body meanwhile will still be spinning around you, almost on your right side. Both your arms—the right one extended over his head or across his neck, the left one across his chest—will guide his motion down to the mat.

It is important that you maintain close contact with *uke* while his motion is being led up and back, because at that moment he will be extended into unbalance to his rear. In fact, it will be the dynamic use of your own body and its weight which will increase the momentum of his reversal.

Your arms will implement the spiraling rise of your body and its subsequent descent; they will not act alone. Your right hand may be used to feign a blow to the throat, chest, or stomach of the extended and therefore unprotected *uke*. If the motion of your body is really a total one, then its upward spiraling and powerful descent to his rear as well as the ample swing of both your arms should be more than sufficient to spin *uke* fully in the air and project him down to the mat. The function of your legs, therefore, will be extremely important in shifting your weight up and down in synchronization with his extension up and to his rear. The completion of the technique, however, will always find you in a condition of central balance.

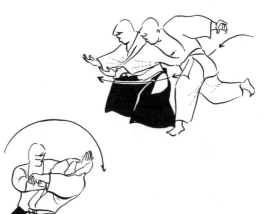

PROJECTION NO. 2 AGAINST ATTACK NO. 5

As *uke* grabs your right shoulder or lapel with his right hand, you will pivot on your left foot and withdraw your right leg circularly to your right-rear side. Now you will swing your left arm over his extended right arm and set it in frontal alignment with your right arm. You will keep turning and extending him around you circularly. When he is in full motion, you will swing both your arms in a wide circle in front of him and bring them back over his head to his rear. Your body will uncoil with a whipping hip motion, and your left leg will slide far back behind *uke*. At this point you will descend strongly on your bent legs, concentrating your leading motion upon his unbalanced upper trunk and causing him to fall to the mat. You will complete the technique by settling down centrally in full balance, feet spread apart, knees well bent.

PROJECTION NO. 2 AGAINST ATTACK NO. 6

As *uke* grabs both your shoulders or lapels, you will take a step to your left-rear side with your left foot, swinging your right arm between his two extended arms and disturbing his concentration by feigning a blow to his face. Now you will turn your hips to your right side and bring your left arm around down from above between his arms. Keeping both your arms in front of you in a diverging extension, you will describe a large circle to your right side as you spin and twist his body into a condition of spiraling unbalance. At the same time, you will bring your left arm up and then down to his rear while your right arm cuts across his chest. Your left foot will slide deep to his rear; your whole weight will rise up with that displacement and be brought to bear upon his unbalanced upper trunk. Then you will be settled centrally on both legs, knees well bent, feet spread apart, as illustrated.

PROJECTION NO. 2 AGAINST ATTACK NO. 7

At the moment when *uke* grabs your wrists from behind, you will lead his motion into the pattern of a diverging extension, thus draining his hold of most of its power. At the same time you will take a circular step to your left side with your right foot, setting *uke* in motion circularly around you. As he is stepping in front of you, you will sink down on bended knees and describe a circle on your left side, leading his movement back to his rear from above. You will shift the weight of your body up and then down to your right side, pressing on his unbalanced upper trunk and causing him to fall to the mat.

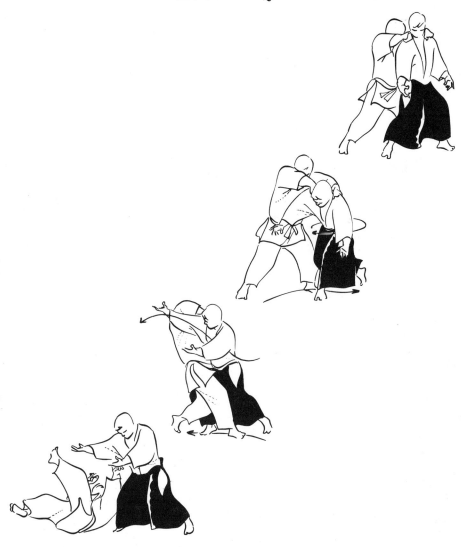

PROJECTION NO. 2 AGAINST ATTACK NO. 9

As you feel the hands of *uke* grasp your shoulders, neck, or biceps from behind, you will lead his motion forward into the pattern of a diverging extension. You will then take a step to his left side with your left foot, turning your whole body in that direction and swinging your arms as illustrated. At this point you will turn your hips back again to your left side, facing his left side and stepping far behind him with your right leg. You will swing your arms up and then down to his rear, extending his unbalanced upper trunk back and shifting your weight so that it will rest equally on your well-bent legs.

PROJECTION NO. 3
(KAITEN NAGE)

General Remarks

Another basic technique of neutralization is projection no. 3, known as *kaiten nage,* or "the rotary throw," and employed—like projections nos. 1 and 2—to neutralize a variety of basic attacks.

As you will note from the illustrations, the primary objective of this projection (as in projections nos. 1 and 2) consists in channeling the motion/action of attack of *uke* into a dynamic extension forward and then reversing its stream back to his rear in a large circle. The technical difference which imparts to this technique its unmistakable identity lies in the fact that in projections nos. 1 and 2, his dynamic extension is skillfully diverted and caused to flow from front to rear in a circular pattern passing over his unbalanced upper body. In projection no. 2 that same dynamic extension will be diverted and caused to flow to his rear in a pattern also circular, but running this time, beneath his unbalanced body, as illustrated.

We have included here three practical examples of neutralizations employing projection no. 3, chosen from the most representative methods taught in aikido *dojo* everywhere. In all of them, the following points will remain constant in the position of *uke* and in your own, at the moment when this technique is being concluded.

The body of *uke* usually will be bent forward and very low, in a condition of open unbalance: One of his arms (the one on the side where you will be centrally located) will be swung in a circle going first to his rear and up, then forward again from above and down in a full dynamic reversal launching him ahead while, at the same time, increasing his unbalance until it becomes dynamically irreversible and causes him to fall to the mat. The back of his head will be contacted lightly for a brief instant, causing him to bend down circularly.

Your own position of operational centralization will be a well-balanced one and you will shift your central weight fluidly from one leg to the other, without leaning too far past the vertical line of support of either leg: One of your hands will grasp the wrist which is closest to your body and swing his entire arm in a circle as illustrated, passing from the rear and ending in a frontal extension toward the ground. The other hand will brush his head down lightly and circularly in the opposite direction—to his rear; you will move out of his way, as you pivot in the center of the action and lead him down and around.

Psychologically, the intention of this technique is not to throw *uke* vertically down onto the ground, but to project him tangentially away from you, possibly toward other attackers as they converge upon you. Therefore, all of your motions and actions as you lead him into the throw must be geared accordingly and performed from a position very close to the ground. You will lower your body on legs spread apart and keep yourself well balanced, extending all of your powers in a direction flowing away from you toward the horizon. This is in order to avoid narrowing this otherwise open throw into the ungenerous mechanism of a tight and possibly ineffective reaction.

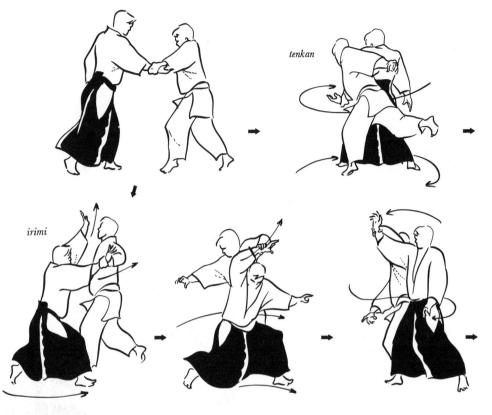

tenkan

irimi

PROJECTION NO. 3 AGAINST ATTACK NO. 1

As *uke* grabs your right wrist with his left hand, you may achieve the necessary position of operational centralization in one of two basic dynamic ways: *irimi* or *tenkan*.

Irimi. According to the dynamic laws of the *irimi* motion, as *uke* touches you, you will lead his motion down, and gaining control of his momentum, lead him out to his left side, sliding close to him on your right foot and feigning a blow to his face with your left hand. Then you will extend his left arm out and slide under it, stepping with your left foot to his rear. You will turn your hips until you face the same direction as *uke,* and lead his still extended left arm in a circle down between your body and his, withdrawing your right leg, as illustrated. As you reach the lowest point of this circle, you will withdraw your left foot to your left rear side, set your left hand on his neck or the back of his head, and swing his left arm to his rear, up and down again, frontally, and passing over his head as he leans forward. At this point you will spin him down in a frontal somersault, shifting your central weight behind the

action of both your arms. You should bring *uke* down very close to the mat so that he can roll safely away along the supporting arc provided by his right arm.

Tenkan. In this example as *uke* grabs your left wrist with his right hand, you will lead his arm in the same direction, stepping to his right side with your left foot, pivoting on it and withdrawing your right leg to your right-rear side, thus leading him out and around into the centrifugal pattern of the *tenkan* motion. As *uke* begins to gain momentum, you will lower your body into a strengthened position of balance on legs spread apart, leading his right arm down and causing him to bend forward. You will then set your right hand on his head, and pivoting to your right-rear side, increase the centrifugal momentum of his unbalance and make room for his fall as you whirl his right arm up, frontally from above, while your right hand leads his head down and rearward. In this *tenkan* variation, as you lead *uke* around you may also glide under his extended right arm as illustrated in the *irimi* variation.

PROJECTION NO. 3 AGAINST ATTACK NO. 13

As a straight blow is being delivered to the front of your head by the right hand or fist of *uke,* you will extend both your arms toward him—right arm leading—and contact his right forearm from the outside with your right, taking a step with your left foot at the same time to his right side. Then you will pivot on that foot, withdrawing your right leg behind you to your right side, letting both your extended arms drop naturally onto his right arm and lead it down to his side, thus causing him to bend forward in a state of unbalance. You will continue to pivot slightly to your right side while your left hand swings his right arm up, over frontally, and down toward the ground. Your right hand presses his head gently but firmly down and to his rear.

PROJECTION NO. 3 AGAINST ATTACK NO. 15

As *uke* is about to deliver a straight blow to your stomach or lower abdomen with his right fist, you will step forward to his right side with your left foot, thus removing yourself from the direct path of the blow. You will allow your left forearm to drop onto his extended right forearm and lead it downward until *uke* is unbalanced forward. Then you will pivot and withdraw your right leg to your right-rear side, spin him around you, lead his right arm up, over and down again in front of him—guiding his head down in a circle to his rear with a "windmill" motion of your arms.

PROJECTION NO. 4
(KOSHI NAGE)

General Remarks

Projection no. 4 focuses upon the movement of your waist and hips as *uke* is being lifted from the ground. Thus it is broadly defined as *koshi nage,* or hip throw. The use of a man's hips as the fulcrum of removal and rotation of another man's body in an effort to project him down onto the ground is almost as old as man himself. In aikido practice, we find many technical and dynamic applications of this type of technique in response to almost all of the basic types of attack.

The fundamental characteristics of this projection (in relation to the use of your hips at the moment when *uke* is about to be lifted from the ground) are generally related to the positioning of your hips against and across his lower abdomen as you establish an axis or fulcrum around which his body will have to rotate. In flight he will be turned upside down and will hit the mat reversed, on his back. This positioning is, first, markedly lateral in the sense that you will bring your side into contact with the frontal side of his lower abdomen, with the axis of your body cutting diagonally across the axis of his body. It is important that you do not cause his upper body to lean unbalanced over your upper trunk, because your main center of support will be much lower, i.e., the powerfully articulated structure of your hips and pelvic area.

Second, your lower abdomen must be lower than his because you will not be attempting to lift him muscularly, but rather causing his body to lean almost naturally and effortlessly upon your lowered hips. You will then be able to roll him easily around, over, and down to the mat. You must, therefore, sink low, bending your knees well to prepare for the rotation of *uke* over your lowered hips—this rotation, of course, being only preliminary to his fall onto the mat, flat on his back. However, due to your lowered position and to the comparatively short distance between the ground and his head as he falls toward the mat, there is a potentially dangerous moment in this technique. It is important, therefore, that you straighten your legs when his body has left the ground and is being turned upside down. At the same time you will lead his arms or body (depending upon the type of hold which his attack necessitates) upward in order to spin his head up and permit a horizontal fall. You should also release your hold upon him so that he may roll away, across the mat, assisted by the dynamic momentum of his own fall.

Now we will examine a few examples of basic attacks neutralized through the application of projection no. 4.

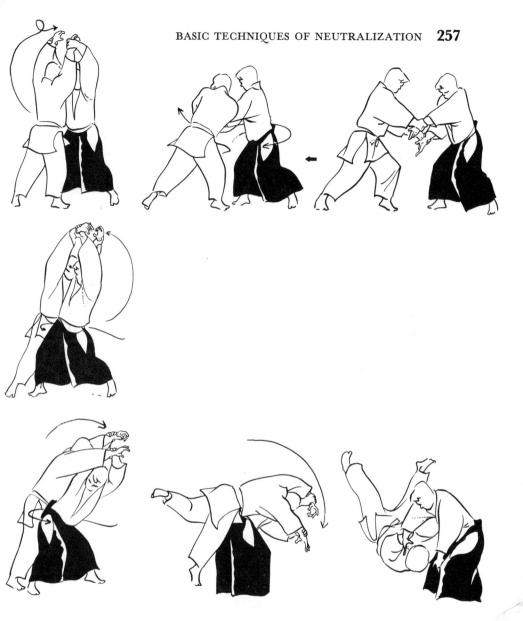

PROJECTION NO. 4 AGAINST ATTACK NO. 4

First Example

As *uke* grabs your wrists, you will swing your arms sideways in a large circle leading him out on your right side and returning over your head. Then you will step across in front of him with your right foot and slide your right hip diagonally under his center of gravity, leading his arms over your bent body and causing him to rotate over and around your right hip. At the same time you will lead his arms (or head) up and over, straightening your legs as he falls to the mat.

Second Example

As *uke* grabs your wrists, you will take a step to your right-rear side with your right foot and extend him in that direction. Without interrupting the motion, you will lead his left arm out and up circularly over his head, grasping his left wrist (reversed by your movement) with your right hand and stepping across in front of him with your right foot. Now you will slide your right hip diagonally under his lower abdomen and bring his left arm over his right arm (held by your left hand). As he slides up and over your lowered hip, you will straighten up and spin him in the air, releasing your hold upon his wrists an instant before he hits the mat.

PROJECTION NO. 4 AGAINST ATTACK NO. 7

As your wrists are grabbed from behind, you will lead his arms out and up as illustrated, and when his hands are over your head you will grasp his left wrist with your right hand. Now you will slide your right hip diagonally across and under his lower abdomen and lead his unbalanced body around and over your lowered hips, drawing a circle with your right hand. Finally, you will straighten up, letting go of his wrist an instant before he hits the mat.

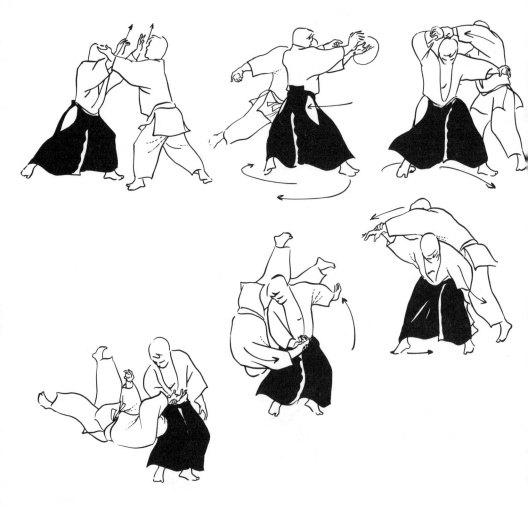

PROJECTION NO. 4 AGAINST ATTACK NO. 14

As *uke* delivers a circular blow to the right side of your head with his left hand, you will either extend your arms, the right arm leading (straight extension) as illustrated, or move inside his line of motion, stepping with your left foot and parrying the blow with that same right arm (circular extension). In either case your right hand will grasp his left wrist from above, your fingertips contacting his palm. After feigning a blow to his face, your left arm will slide along his left arm and lead his elbow from underneath. This is in order to extend him over your body which will pass across in front of him. You will step with your left foot, setting your hip diagonally across and underneath his lower abdomen. Finally, you will lead him over and around that fulcrum, guiding his left leg up with your left hand if necessary. You will straighten up and release his hand just as he is about to hit the mat.

PROJECTION NO. 5
(AIKI OTOSHI)

General Remarks

Projection no. 5—known as *aiki otoshi* or *aiki* drop—also depends upon the use of your hips in removing the feet of *uke* from the ground and projecting him back down onto the mat. This time, however, the positioning of your lower abdomen beneath his body will be different. Whereas in projection no. 4 it was your back which contacted the frontal section of his lower abdomen, in projection no. 5 it will be your frontal lower abdomen which will be brought into contact with his back. In both cases, however, the technical principle of your hips acting as the fulcrum of his removal, rotation, and projection will remain substantially the same.

This technique of neutralization can be applied against almost any of the basic types of attack. After your initial motion of evasion, extension, and centralization has been successfully completed, there will be a moment in which one of your legs will slide deeply behind *uke,* and the side of your body will come in diagonal contact with his body. Your upper trunk will be leaning forward, and your arms will encircle his legs. One arm will clasp the rear part of his thigh close to the knee, your other arm will go deep down behind his other knee.

You will sweep both legs of *uke* frontally, practically clasping them together; your lower abdomen at this point will become the operational center of the projection.

There are two possible directions in which you can throw *uke*. One is in front of you, a little to one side. Such a frontal projection may be accomplished by sweeping his legs up in front of him with a powerful turning motion of your hips. This kind of "whipping" motion, of course, must be performed in a condition of stable, centralized balance on legs well bent and apart. This motion will take the form of a small circle running up to one side and returning from above down to your other side. Such a dynamic circle will activate your whole body and lend power to your arms and trunk as they move together as a perfectly synchronized unit. You will release *uke* when his feet are high in the air and his trunk parallel to the mat.

The other direction in which this technique may be performed is over your hips to the rear, but the principles of execution will be essentially the same.

One important point: the central weight of *uke* must never fall on you. Your action in projection no. 5 will be channeled against the lower part of his body from his waist down to his feet. This part of his anatomy will be swept away rapidly, leaving his upper body no recourse except to lean, in full unbalance, in a vacuum for a brief moment—the moment needed to sweep his legs up in a circle.

Your total weight will always be in a condition of central balance, equally distributed on legs well bent and apart. His total weight, at the moment when his natural supports are being swept away, will be left floating in space (not resting on you). Therefore, the action will be swift and effortless, since you will not be "loading him up" onto your hips, which would be incorrect, but simply "cutting him down" from underneath. His legs, once his central weight is no longer pressing down on them, will become extremely light and easy to maneuver. Correct timing of his unbalance and your circular sweep, therefore, will determine the success of this projection.

Let us now examine two examples of the practical application of projection no. 5 in response to two basic types of attack.

PROJECTION NO. 5 AGAINST ATTACK NO. 5

As *uke* is reaching out with his right hand to grab your left shoulder or lapel, you will take a long step to your left-rear side with you left leg, feign a blow to his face with your right hand and slide that right hand and arm along his extended right arm from underneath to grasp his right wrist. Now you will extend him further into open unbalance until his grip on your shoulder loses its power. Then you will swing his right arm down to your right side, turning your hips and stepping with your left leg deeply behind him. At the same time your left arm will slide under his outstretched right arm and clasp his left thigh close to the knee. You will dislodge his right arm and grasp his other leg as well (the right one), keeping both legs close together. Now you will swing your hips in a small circle to your right side, up, and then down again while your body and arms sweep his legs away in front of his (up and then over to your left-rear side) as described earlier.

PROJECTION NO. 5 AGAINST ATTACK NO. 9

As the hands of *uke* fall upon your neck or shoulders from behind, you will extend your arms forward and out in the same direction as his hold, taking a circular step to his left side with your left foot as illustrated, and turning your hips. Then you will pivot on your left foot and slide your right leg deeply behind him. Both your arms will whirl into position and descend behind his legs. They will then be swept away in a frontal circle up and over your right hip.

PROJECTIONS NOS. 6, 7, AND 8

General Remarks

The projections which follow represent interesting and effective examples of the convergence of aggressive forces (originating from one side), which are extended beyond their intended target in the opposite direction, and thereby weakened to the extend of becoming easily maneuverable. In all of these projections, the force of *uke* regardless of the technique of attack (a hold, a blow, a combination), will be extended out in order to dissipate its original concentration of power and, consequently, lead it easily into the dynamic pattern of the projection. Among the forms this leading motion may take (each representing a technique), we have selected the following three projections which are widely practiced in various aikido centers of instruction.

PROJECTION NO. 6 AGAINST ATTACK NO. 4

Under-arm may be one of the following:

STANDING. As *uke* grabs your wrists you will step to his left side with your right foot very close to his body, pivot on that foot, and withdraw your left foot circularly to your left-rear side. At the same time you will be leading his right hand out, down, and around you while your right arm slides under his left arm, cutting over and down with the edge of your right hand as illustrated.

KNEELING. As *uke* grasps your wrists, you will withdraw your right leg circularly to your rear very close to him under his extended right side, and drop to your knees. Using his frontal momentum, you will lead his left hand down and around you while your left hand slides under his right arm as illustrated, and cuts down in an ample frontal circle. In case *uke* grabs your wrists and pulls up, you will follow him with a strong upward motion which will alarm him and result in an instinctive reaction (on his part) downward. You will then use that reaction, as indicated previously, to complete the technique.

PROJECTION NO. 6 AGAINST ATTACK NO. 7

As the hands of *uke* close around your wrists from behind, you will lead his movement forward with a scooping motion, as in basic exercise no. 17. You will then reverse that lead downward, taking a step to your left side with your left foot, pivoting on that foot and withdrawing your right foot to your right side, thus turning your body to face *uke*. You will lead both his arms down in front of you, but complete the circle with your right hand inside and under his left elbow. While your left hand describes a larger circle around you, you will spin *uke* down, as illustrated.

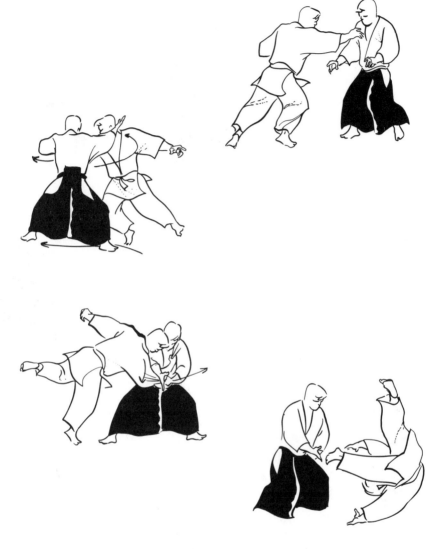

PROJECTION NO. 7 AGAINST ATTACK NO. 6

As *uke* reaches out to grab you with both arms extended, you will grasp his right wrist or sleeve with your left hand and insert your right arm over his left as illustrated, withdrawing your left foot circularly to your left-rear side. You will bend your knees deeply and spin *uke* over frontally making full use of his original momentum. Since this "cut" may result in a heavy fall for *uke,* you may drop to your left knee in order to guide his arm as close to the mat as possible.

PROJECTION NO. 8 AGAINST ATTACK NO. 14

As *uke* delivers a circular blow with his right hand, you will step inside his line of motion with your right foot, extend both arms diagonally in front of you, and pivot on that advanced right foot, withdrawing your left leg circularly behind on your left side. You will contact his right wrist with the edge of your left hand (or grasp his wrist from above if necessary) and lead it around you and down. Meanwhile your right hand, swinging circularly and high, will "hook" his left shoulder or neck and increase the centrifugal effect of your pivot. You will continue to whirl (arms always in front of you), describing a spiral which will end on the mat. This will send *uke* spinning around his own unbalanced axis before he rolls away from you along the mat.

PROJECTION NO. 9
(TENCHI NAGE)

General Remarks

The main features of projection no. 9 (known as *tenchi nage,* literally translated as the "Heaven-Earth throw") are that your circular motion will extend *uke* out on one side, and will be followed by that motion which you will use to cut him down on his rear diagonal side with a single flowing motion in space resembling a horizontal inverted "s." Your body, as usual, will lead the entire action, but your arms in diagonal extension forward will operate like the wings of a glider, describing a diagonal spiraling loop toward the ground.

This projection is particularly adaptable to the neutralization of almost any form of frontal attack, as you capture its extension and lead the Unified Power of Attack of *uke* into the pattern most suitable to your final aim—bringing him to the mat.

In this case the original force of his attack will be led out and back down to his rear diagonal side. The angle of his projection will be a narrow one; his fall, consequently, will be somewhat angular. If the technique is performed properly, however, he will be able to roll easily and safely across the mat.

Your own action will consist of a large, lateral step to his side for the purpose of extending him out in unbalance, followed by another large step, low and to his rear. Both your arms, openly extended, will perform the following functions: lead his captured arms out into unbalance, and cut the flight of his unbalanced body down, to his rear. The entire action must be performed smoothly and without any jarring motions.

Let us now examine the following practical applications of projection no. 9.

tenkan

irimi

PROJECTION NO. 9 AGAINST ATTACK NO. 1

As *uke* grabs your left wrist with his right hand, you will take a long step diagonally to your left side, leading his hand down and out in the same direction. (You may grasp his right wrist, if you wish, to insure his extension.) You will spread your arms, the left one leading *uke* out and down into a condition of unbalance on his right side, the right stretching across and over his left shoulder under his chin. His lateral extension will allow you to slide close to his unbalanced right side with a long step on your right leg to his right-rear side. You will swing both arms out and down, extending your well-balanced body behind them and propelling *uke* down to the mat. (This projection may also be applied in the *tenkan* variation illustrated here.)

Do not attempt to "load him up" onto your hips. His complete unbalance and the spin of his reversed motion should be more than sufficient to whirl him into the final *aiki* roll.

irimi

tenkan

PROJECTION NO. 9 AGAINST ATTACK NO. 4

You may neutralize this attack with projection no. 9 in two ways: an *irimi* or a *tenkan* variation. In the *irimi* variation you will take a long step with your left foot deep to the right side of *uke* with your left hand leading his right downward, and your right hand circling up in full extension. You will then take a second step with your right foot deep to the rear of *uke,* continuing the downward extension with your left hand and circling over and down with your right as illustrated, thus bringing *uke* down to the mat.

In the *tenkan* variation, while your left hand is extending downward and establishing the fulcrum for his centrifugal motion, your right hand will lead *uke* out and around you as you pivot on your left foot. His circular movement around you will permit you to step deep to his rear side with your right foot. As in the *irimi* variation, both your arms will extend *uke* and lead him down to the mat.

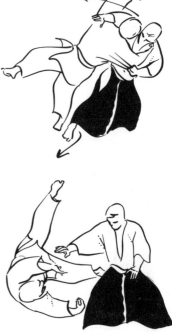

PROJECTION NO. 9 AGAINST ATTACK NO. 5

As *uke* reaches out to grab your left shoulder or lapel, you will grasp his right sleeve with your left hand and take a large, lateral step to his right side with your left leg, extending him out into a condition of unbalance on his right side. You will slide your right leg to his right-rear side, your right arm extending across his chest and over his left shoulder. Then you will lead his right elbow as illustrated, and spin him down to his right-rear side employing the whirling motion of your whole body to complete this technique.

PROJECTION NO. 10
(SUMI OTOSHI)

General Remarks

Projection no. 10 known as *sumi otoshi,* or "corner drop," is based on the semi-circular extension of your arms positioned beneath one or both of the arms of *uke* as you guide him up and then whip him down onto the mat.

In relation to the motion and eventual position of his body, you will channel the force of his attack on one side of his anatomy, that side becoming the axis around which he will rotate in unbalance until he falls to the mat. This motion involves a particularly delicate, spiraling pattern into which you must channel his original motion of attack. A well-developed sense of timing and dynamic synchronization will be necessary to blend his momentum with your own and spin him around your extended axis of projection (the arm closest to his body), which will be closely identified with the axis of his body. In fact, as you will notice in the examples which follow, the two will be almost one and the same—one is your arm, extended diagonally under the other, his leaning body.

There should be no anatomical pressure on his elbow joint in a misguided attempt to force him down. Instead, your entire action will be directed toward spinning his whole body down. Therefore, you will operate on and amplify his motion, rather than act upon any particular part of his body.

Your leading hand may grip his extended wrist in order to secure that lead. However, if your timing and coordinating are sufficiently developed this will not be necessary, since once his body has been spun into orbital motion the rest will be naturally consequential and he will almost seem to fall by himself.

This technique may be performed either frontally (inside) or beside *uke* (outside). Of the three practical examples illustrated, the first two deal with the former possibility, and the third with the latter. The functional or dynamic principle underlying both, however, will be the same: extension + centralization + spin = the projection of *uke.*

PROJECTION NO. 10 AGAINST ATTACK NO. 1

Irimi. As *uke* reaches out to grasp your left wrist with his right hand, you will take a diagonal step to your left side with your left foot and extend your left hand out on that side, in order to concentrate his central weight on his right leg. Then you will slide your right arm under his extended arm, as illustrated, and take a long step with your right foot to his right-rear side, turning your whole body in a circle to your left side—your left hand leading circularly down and the extension of your whole body animating your right arm. You will keep both arms in front of you and describe a circle with them which will descend toward the ground, turning your hips and bending your knees as indicated. If necessary you may grip his right wrist from the inside. From this point you will move circularly with your right side very close to and beneath his extended right side, thus contacting his anatomical axis as illustrated. You will then revolve his body smoothly and irresistibly in the air and bring him down to the mat.

Tenkan. The sequence of actions described in the preceding version of projection no. 10 will also apply here. The only difference will be in the opening motion.

As *uke* grabs your left wrist, you will step to his right side with your left foot, pivot on that foot, and draw your right leg circularly behind you on your right side. Your left hand will lead him out and around, as illustrated, into a condition of unbalance on his right side. You will guide his right arm down and then out to your left side by taking a step in that direction with your left foot. He will now be vulnerable to your defensive action—his right arm will be outstretched, his whole body will lean on the right side. At this point you will slide your right arm under his right arm as illustrated, take a long step with your right foot to his right-rear side, and spin him up, around, and down.

tenkan

irimi

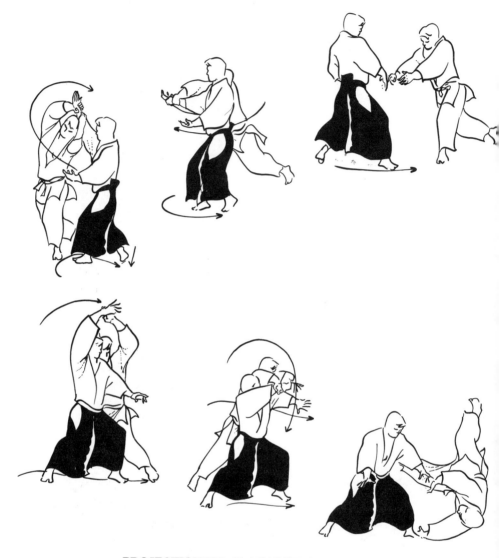

PROJECTION NO. 10 AGAINST ATTACK NO. 3

As *uke* grabs your right wrist with both hands, you will withdraw your left foot circularly to your left-rear side, pivoting on your right foot. You will then extend both his arms forward by leading him out and up to your left side in a circle passing over his head and returning down on your right side as illustrated. You will step across in front of *uke* with your left foot and extend your left arm under his left arm which is being led (together with his right arm) down. You will swing both your extended arms, turning your body against his unbalanced right side, then spin him up out, and down to the mat.

PROJECTION NO. 10 AGAINST ATTACK NO. 5

This is an example of projection no. 10 applied from the outside. As *uke* grabs your left shoulder or lapel with his right hand, you will withdraw your left foot to your left-rear side, swinging your right hand and grasping his extended right wrist with it (after feigning a blow to his head). Without stopping the motion, you will keep him extended on his right side and lead his right arm down diagonally in front of you, allowing your left arm to slide under his arm from the outside close to his body while you step in with your left foot. You will swing both your arms in a descending spiral using your whole body to spin *uke* up, out, and then down to the mat.

Never push against his elbow with your arm or side. Unnecessary pain or possible fracture are not the goals of this projection nor of any other technique in the aikido repertoire for that matter (including the famous immobilizations, where temporary pain is used only as a distracting device, preparing the way for the subsequent subjugation, and not as an end in itself). As has been stated before, any such pain should leave no permanent traces.

PROJECTION NO. 11

General Remarks

Projection no. 11 also belongs to the family of *sumi otoshi,* or corner drops. Its main feature will be represented by one of the arms of *uke* being led straight down while his body is spun around it. Naturally you will remain in the center of the action, with his captured arm locked temporarily to your anatomy.

This basic technique of projection may be applied to neutralize a great variety of attacks and its methods of application may be quite diversified, as the examples included here will demonstrate.

PROJECTION NO. 11 AGAINST ATTACK NO. 1

First Example

Sliding laterally to your diagonal front side with your left foot, you will lead *uke* with your captured left hand into extension and unbalance to his right-rear side, sinking down on your right leg close to *uke* and under his unbalanced frame with an *irimi* motion. You will cut behind his right heel with the edge of your right hand, sweeping his legs away from under him. The *irimi* motion, like the *tenkan* movement, is based on dynamic momentum. In the *irimi* variation, however, greater skill will be required and the initial momentum of *uke* will have to be sufficient in and of itself, while in the *tenkan* motion, the momentum of his attack will be amplified by your pivoting and extending action.

This example is characterized by the employment of your right hand to cut his legs away from under him and to block his retreat under a frame collapsing from above. However, skilled practitioners of the art can bring you to the mat with a single unified motion of the body (*kokyu*) and a leading extension of one hand/arm.

Second Example

As *uke* grabs your left wrist with his right hand, you will pivot on your left foot, withdrawing your right foot circularly to your right-rear side and leading him out into circular extension frontally and around you in a *tenkan* motion. As he gains momentum you will slide out and away from him with your left foot to your left side. This will bring you close to his right foot and almost perpendicularly under his unbalanced right side as you lead his right arm straight down along that side. Then you will kneel down, leading his arm downward. With the descending power of your whole body behind that lead, your body always being the operational center of the action. He will be spun almost on the spot as he falls to the mat.

tenkan

irimi

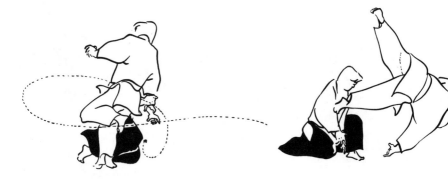

PROJECTION NO. 11 AGAINST ATTACK NO. 2

As *uke* grabs your right wrist with his right hand, you will take a first step to your right-rear side, grasping his now extended right wrist and taking another step to your left-rear side with your left foot, thus extending him out even further. Without stopping the flow of the motion you will bring his right arm into circular extension to your left side, sliding out with your left foot and kneeling down on your left knee close to him. You will spin *uke* over and then down, holding his wrist with both hands if necessary.

PROJECTION NO. 11 AGAINST ATTACK NO. 13

As *uke* delivers a straight blow to your head with his right hand or fist, you will extend both arms to parry the blow externally, your right arm leading while taking a step close to his right side with your left foot. You will pivot on the left foot to your right-rear side with a *tenkan* motion, withdrawing your right foot circularly to your right-rear side. Your right arm will guide his extended right arm down while your left hand will either grasp his sleeve at the elbow or encircle his wrist. You will lead that arm down in a pendular motion toward your left side. Then you will step out with your left foot and sink down on your right knee under his unbalanced right side. You will spin him over and then down to the mat. A final whiplike motion of your hands will further enhance the dynamic whirl of the projection. Do not attempt to hold onto *uke,* or his motion will be halted abruptly and he will fall heavily to the mat with the possibility of serious injury.

PROJECTION NO. 12

General Remarks

Particularly effective against blows to the head (and extremely dangerous when violently applied), projection no. 12 operates on an opponent's extended arm by using the centrifugal force of your spin to lead the force of his attack into a high circuit of projection. If this circuit is too tight and close to his body, his fall will necessarily be a sharp, almost vertical one. Accordingly, once the hold has been established and the spinning motion of centralization completed, you will extend his arm forward and lead his force of attack into an ample circuit of projection, which will bring his hand or fist close to the mat and thus allow him to safely somersault away from you.

PROJECTION NO. 12 AGAINST ATTACK NO. 13

As *uke* is delivering a straight blow to your head, you will extend your arms to meet it, parrying the blow and grasping his sleeve at the elbow while your right hand slides around to grasp his right wrist. You will pivot on your advanced right foot and slide underneath *uke* with your left leg close to his body as illustrated. You will then turn your hips to your right, withdrawing your right leg and kneeling down beneath his frame on that right knee. Your hands will maintain him extended in frontal unbalance as you whip him down to the mat in front of you.

Practice this technique correctly and slowly, step by step. When done quickly it can be dangerous for *uke,* since the fall, the unity of the motion, and the distance between his upper trunk and the ground, as well as the power of your descent beneath him may cause serious injury if not carefully controlled.

PROJECTION NO. 13

General Remarks

Projection no. 13 consists of a highly circular motion which will extend the original line of attack of *uke* into a pattern of unbalance and frontal projection over your body (usually lowered into a position of operational centralization beneath him).

Its essential characteristics are represented dynamically by your sliding motion in and under the line of his motion, while you simultaneously extend that motion into an arc curving downward to the mat. On the technical side, the "outer" characteristics are represented by your arms leading and guiding his arms into that descending pattern.

However functionally important they may appear to be in "hooking" *uke* and in leading his motion, your arms will not be the main instruments of projection no. 13. They will be—as always—physical extensions of the central body as you whirl in the center of the action and bend your knees in a condition of lowered, strengthened balance, spinning *uke* around in an orbit over, and finally down to the mat.

Let us examine three practical examples in which this principle of perpendicular centralization will be applied although the technical means of leading *uke*. The types of attack being neutralized may differ.

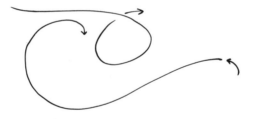

PROJECTION NO. 13 AGAINST ATTACK NO. 3

As *uke* grabs your right wrist with both hands, you will pivot on your right foot and withdraw your left foot circularly to your left-rear side, extending him out frontally. Utilizing the original momentum of his attack, you will continue to lead him upward as you turn toward him, making room between both your bodies for your next step which you will take across in front of him with your left foot. At the same time you will turn your hips to your right, and slide under his extended arms. Withdrawing your right leg, you will drop to the mat on your right knee facing in his direction. You will shift your body beneath him, parallel to his left side, leading his arms into a circular pattern which will descend smoothly in front of him. A slight "flipping" motion of your hand close to the ground will help *uke* to perform the somersault which will send him rolling away from you across the mat.

PROJECTION NO. 13 AGAINST ATTACK NO. 4

As *uke* grabs both your wrists, you will swing your arms to your right side and whirl them around and up in a circle flowing continuously over your head and then down to the mat in an uninterrupted flow of circular motion. At the moment when the circle has reached its apex over both your heads you will turn your hips to your left and step across in front of *uke* with your right foot, as illustrated. You will keep turning your hips to the left until the left side of your body faces his right side in diagonal forward. Then you will sink down with your whole body, withdraw your left leg, and sink to the mat on your left knee as you lead *uke* over and down, your hands having grasped his wrists at the moment when the circle passed over both your heads. The final movement will be the slight "flipping" motion which will help launch him into an *aiki* somersault.

PROJECTION NO. 13 AGAINST ATTACK NO. 7

As your wrists are grasped from behind, you will sink low, bringing your Centre close to the ground and leading the motion of *uke* out, frontally and up over your head with either a perpendicular or a diagonal leading extension. Withdrawing your right leg, you will drop to the mat, bringing your right knee close to his left foot a little to the outside. At the same time you will describe a large arc with your hands, arm and body, leading *uke* into a frontal somersault. (If necessary you may grasp his right wrist with your left hand and/or his left wrist with your right hand when your first extension brings them up over your head.)

PROJECTION NO. 14

General Remarks

Projection no. 14 was specifically devised to cope with an attack from behind which consists of a body-hold intended to pin your arms to your sides. The hold may be applied quite high—on your upper arm (attack no. 11), or lower down—at the elbows (attack no. 12).

The central idea of this projection is to use the original momentum of *uke* as he seeks to establish his hold. It is in order to extend him forward into unbalance before "flicking him off" with a powerful turning of your hips.

You will move forward, therefore, at the same speed at which he is moving —not faster, or you will lose him. You will slide one foot forward and extend your arms in response to attack no. 11, or your whole body in response to attack no. 12, ahead and down. Once your arms have been extended thusly, you will turn your hips sharply sideways and your whole upper body, almost with a recoil action, will fling *uke* off to your diagonal front corner or straight ahead if your extension is very low and his momentum considerable.

PROJECTION NO. 14 AGAINST ATTACK NO. 11

As the arms of *uke* are encircling your upper body over your arms and establishing their hold around you, you will extend both your arms diagonally forward and slide your right foot ahead, stretching your left leg out behind. Moving with you, *uke* will be brought into a condition of unbalance. At that moment you will turn your hips, swinging your arms out and bending your right knee as you lead his extended right arm under his left arm and against the left side of his body. Your right hand will plunge down toward the ground, and your left arm will rise up in a coordinated movement. The whole motion will have the effect of flicking *uke* over to your right diagonal side or straight in front of you. The synchronization of your motion with his attack is essential if this throw is to be successful.

PROJECTION NO. 14 AGAINST ATTACK NO. 12

As his arms are establishing their circular hold around your body, clamping your elbows against your sides, you will grasp his wrists or forearms in order to paralyze him completely and execute the movement explained in the previous example. You will slide your right foot forward, bending your knee and extending your whole body in the same direction before turning your hips sharply to your right side and flicking *uke* off over to your frontal corner. Be sure to release his arms at the moment when you turn your hip so that he will be able to roll safely away.

PROJECTION NO. 15

General Remarks

Projection no. 15 is also one which was specifically devised to neutralize a hold on your upper body and/or neck from behind. It consists of a simple deep bow forward, which, if perfectly coordinated with the forward motion of *uke,* will be more than sufficient to lead him over into the circular pattern of a frontal somersault.

Very often, however, your timing may be a bit off and *uke* may be able to complete his hold, thus settling himself in a condition of balance behind you. In that case it will be necessary for you to lower your Centre beneath *uke* by bending your knees. Thus you are re-establishing that condition of slight frontal unbalance over your lowered body which is necessary for the proper execution of this throw.

PROJECTION NO. 15 AGAINST ATTACK NO. 10

As the right arm of *uke* encircles your neck from behind—his forearm across your throat—you will lower your chin in order to prevent a full strangulation, and grasp his forearm with both your hands. Then you will perform a deep forward bow and allow *uke* to fly over you and down to the mat. In many cases, a few circular forward steps before the bow will increase the momentum of his attack, and greatly facilitate the execution of this projection.

PROJECTION NO. 16

General Remarks

Projection no. 16 consists of a vertical pivot performed on the spot, thus reversing the line of attack of *uke* so that it will flow circularly back to him. Included here are four practical applications of this projection.

PROJECTION NO. 16 AGAINST ATTACK NO. 7

As your wrists are grabbed from behind by *uke,* you will extend your left arm straight down in order to establish the center around which the entire action will rotate. You will pivot on your left foot to your left side, stepping circularly around to his left-rear side, while your right hand leads his right arm into a circular, frontal extension—up and then down to his rear, passing over his head. You will bring him down to the mat on his back, extending both your arms out and down as illustrated, and lowering your Centre on legs well bent and feet kept apart. At the moment when you are pivoting to his left-rear side, your right hand will be leading his right arm over his head and will cross his wrist which you may grasp if necessary.

PROJECTION NO. 16 AGAINST ATTACK NO. 16

As *uke* grabs your right wrist from behind with his right hand and slips his left arm around your neck, cutting across your throat with his left forearm, you will lower your chin, extend your right arm out diagonally, and grasp his left sleeve above the elbow with your left hand. Thus you establish the fulcrum of rotation for the whole action. You will pivot on your left foot to your left side, stepping circularly around with your right foot and setting it down on his left-rear side. You will lead his right arm in a circle which will return back to his rear, straight down passing over his head, while your left hand leads his left arm down—pinning his weight on his left leg. You will snap your arms open as if you were tying a large knot, and allow him to fall, unbalanced, to his rear. You may stay on his left side, or if the dynamics of the attack so warrant, you may whirl around him in a single displacement which will bring you to his right side.

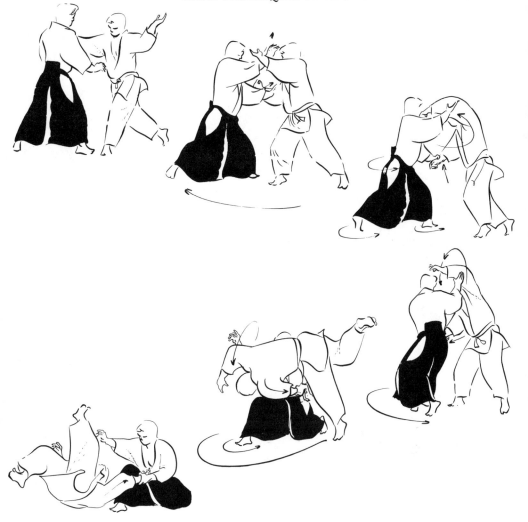

PROJECTION NO. 16 AGAINST ATTACK NO. 17

First Example

As *uke* is delivering a circular blow to your head with his left hand after having secured a hold upon your left lapel with his right hand, you will withdraw you right foot circularly to your rear while extending your right arm to parry the blow and dissipate its force around you. Your right hand will then slide under his left elbow and lead his arm in a circle upward, while your body spins on your right foot to your left side and your right leg slides as illustrated, almost to his right side, and you sink to your left knee. The "windmill" action of your arms will guide *uke* down to the mat. Remember to release his wrist a moment before he hits the mat so that he will be able to roll away safely.

Second Example

As *uke* grabs your right shoulder or lapel with his left hand and is about to deliver a circular blow to the left side of your head with his right hand, you will step circularly with your right foot in diagonal forward. You will pivot on that foot, swinging your left leg circularly to your left-rear side, and your right arm (which will feign a blow to his head) will swing along and then under his right arm as it is in flight toward its spinning target. You will extend him out to his right diagonal side, leading his arm up toward his head while your left arm encircles his left arm as illustrated. Both your arms will slide around his twisted arms and join hands on his biceps. You will continue pivoting to your left side, spinning *uke* around and up, reversing his motion as illustrated (whipping your hips to your right side and stepping to his rear with your right leg). Finally, you will steer his arms, spinning his unbalanced body down and away from you.

PROJECTION NO. 17

General Remarks

An interesting, more technically complex action of defense against a hold from behind, is represented by projection no. 17, which is described in relation to the aggressive combination it is usually called upon to neutralize.

PROJECTION NO. 17 AGAINST ATTACK NO. 16

Uke grabs your left wrist from behind, with his left hand and slides his right forearm across your throat in order to choke you. You will lower your chin, extend your left hand and lead his left arm out and up, contacting his right arm with your right hand, and taking a lateral step to your left-rear side. You will turn your hips toward him. Then, you grasp his right wrist with your right hand after sliding your head out of his hold. You will bring his left arm down and lock both his arms together at the elbows as illustrated. Then you will lead his left arm down and guide his right arm forward, taking a step forward with your right leg. This will bring him into a twisted condition of unbalance with his paralyzed arms functioning as the center of a wheel around which his body will spin in a somersault. You will release his wrists as he is about to whirl away from you across the mat. Caution should be exercised when locking his elbows together. They should be "wrapped" naturally one around the other, rather than set one against the other—*gyaku*.

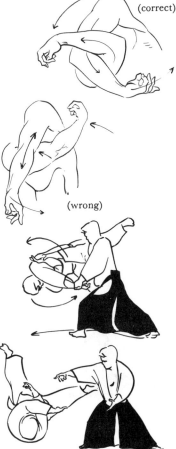

(correct)

(wrong)

PROJECTION NO. 18

General Remarks

This projection, throughout its various applications against a wide variety of attacks, demonstrates how it is possible to clearly lead an aggressor's force of attack converging upon you, back to him. It is often referred to as the "scarf," because its characteristic feature is that of wrapping one of your opponent's arms around his own neck, thus causing him to rotate vertically around his own spinal axis.

In the application of this technique, the principle of centralization is particularly evident, i.e., in the opponent's spin and in your own displacement which will begin around him (while his arm is being wrapped around his neck), resulting in his displacement and projection around you (when that encircling or "wrapping" motion has been completed and he is led downward in an ample arc toward the mat).

PROJECTION NO. 18 AGAINST ATTACK NO. 6

As *uke* is establishing his hold on your upper body, you will take a long step to your rear with your left foot, feigning a blow to his face in order to extend his arms out. Your right hand will then slide along his right arm to grasp his wrist, detaching its hold upon your shoulder with a single movement, and bending low as illustrated. Taking a large, circular step to his left side and bringing his head to rest against your shoulder, you will wrap his right arm around his neck and pivot on your right foot. You will then withdraw your left leg circularly behind, leading him down to the mat.

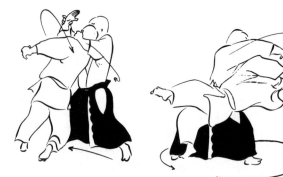

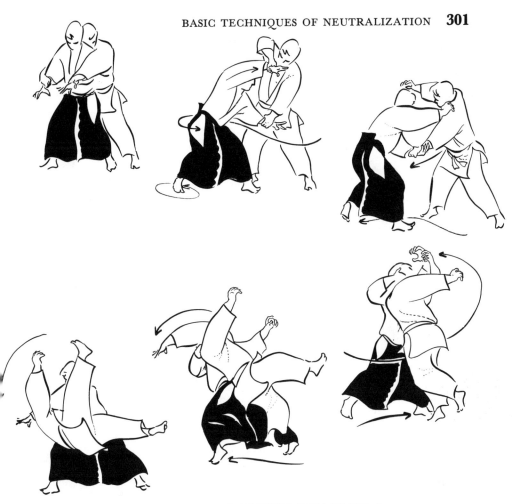

PROJECTION NO. 18 AGAINST ATTACK NO. 7

As *uke* grabs your wrists from behind, you will lead his motion forward as in basic exercise no. 17 and, spinning on your right foot, withdraw your left leg. This pivot will bring you around to face *uke*. You will grasp his left wrist with your left hand. Leading it circularly to your left side, across his body, and around his neck (as if it were a scarf) you will step with your left foot to your left side as your right hand swings around to clasp his head against your left shoulder. You will pivot on your left foot and sweep your right foot in a large circle to your right-rear side, spinning *uke* around you by the combined action of your right arm—holding his head against your spinning body, and your left arm—circling from high above to descend, rearward and down. The success of this projection will depend almost entirely upon the dynamic momentum created by: (1) your first step close to his body on his right side with your left foot; and (2) the powerful spin of your whole body, accentuated by the large sweep of your right leg whirling circularly behind you.

PROJECTION NO. 18 AGAINST ATTACK NO. 14

As *uke* delivers a circular blow to your head, you will take a long step with your right leg inside the line of his motion. Simultaneously parrying the blow from inside with your left arm, you will lead his arm down into your right hand which is waiting below. Grasping his right wrist, you will lead it in a circle downward and then up around his head. Taking a long step with your right foot frontally across to his left side and around him, you will secure his head against your right shoulder. Now you will withdraw your left foot circularly behind you (on your left side) and spin him in the air. Both your arms will extend him up and then down, while your hips turn to the left side. Your right foot may slide along in the direction of his fall if necessary.

PROJECTION NO. 19

General Remarks

Another method of neutralizing a large series of basic attacks is provided by projection no. 19, in which you will respond to an aggressive dimension above by establishing a contrary defensive dimension below. It is always in agreement, however, with the requirements of dynamic uniformity, centralization, and extension which are common to all the techniques of neutralization in the aikido repertoire.

Of the many attacks that may be neutralized by projection no. 19, we have chosen attack no. 6 since it is the one most commonly taught and practiced in aikido *dojo*.

PROJECTION NO. 19 AGAINST ATTACK NO. 6

As *uke* reaches out to grab your shoulders or lapels, you will take a step with your right foot, describing a large circle as you lead him out and around on his right side. Then you will withdraw your left leg circularly to your left-rear side and swing your right arm between his extended arms. You will feign a blow to his face, still maintaining your pivoting motion to your left side. Then you will sink down under his circular line of motion on your left knee. Hook his right ankle with your left hand as your right forearm cuts across his leg from the inside in the same direction as his original motion (which will also be the same direction in which his knee will bend, naturally). Finally, you will cut him down circularly to your left side, and as he falls to his right-rear side you will rise from your kneeling position.

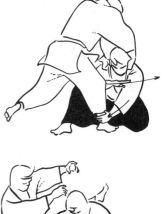

PROJECTION NO. 20

General Remarks

Another "spinning" technique typical of the aikido repertoire is projection no. 20 which is usually performed in defense against a low blow, but may be applied with appropriate dynamic adaptations of evasion, extension, and centralization to neutralize a variety of basic attacks.

PROJECTION NO. 20 AGAINST ATTACK NO. 17

Uke, having grabbed your left shoulder or lapel with his right hand, is delivering a straight or circular blow to your solar plexus or lower abdomen. You will turn your hips to the right, stepping in the same direction with your left foot. You will pivot on that foot, withdraw your right leg circularly to your right-rear side, and allowing your left arm to drop naturally onto his extended left arm, swing it down to your left side. As he is unbalanced and twisted to his right side, you will slide or leap in with your right foot to his left-rear side, and hook his head with your right hand as explained in projection no. 1 *(kokyu nage)*. You will then pivot on your right foot. Grasping his left wrist and holding his head down, you will spin him around you in an orbit, and fling him off in diagonal forward, guiding his left arm up in order to allow him to roll down and over onto the mat.

PROJECTION NO. 21

General Remarks

Projection no. 21, performed as a training exercise, is one of the best methods for developing your powers of perception, your sense of timing, and your coordination since its main characteristic will be your circular motion leading the force of an attack back to itself from above.

In order to achieve this reversal, you must rely almost entirely upon your past experience which will serve to alert you to the exact direction from which the attack is being launched, its speed, angle of inclination, etc. It has, however, as you will see in the examples which follow, a practical aspect which makes it one of the most powerful defensive actions in the aikido arsenal.

Projection no. 21 is usually practiced against a total attack such as no. 3, which has been chosen to illustrate how the neutralization may be achieved.

This projection may be practiced in one of two ways: leading only or leading and feigning a blow.

PROJECTION NO. 21 AGAINST ATTACK NO. 3

First Example (leading only)

STATIC. You will allow *uke* to establish a hold on your right wrist with both his hands. Then you will take a step to his right side with your left foot, and pivoting on that foot turn your hips to your right; facing his right side. You will extend your right arm down in front of him and lead his arms up again in a circle passing over his head and plunging down to the mat. You will continue to pivot behind him and complete the projection as illustrated, or pass to his left side with a single whirling motion. Your left hand will either grasp his collar in order to bring him down when he arches back, or lightly touch the back of his neck in order to channel his consciousness up. Thus you further increase his vertical extension and also his condition of dynamic unbalance to the rear.

DYNAMIC. As *uke* reaches out to grasp your right wrist or to hit you, you will guide his hands down in front of him and then up, stepping to his side and pivoting as explained in the previous description. At the same time you will bring your right hand straight down to his rear.

The difference between this dynamic form of the technique and the static performance previously described lies in the fact that in the former, *uke* will not have a chance to grab your wrist. Even if he has, he will not have time to grip that wrist tightly in full control. You will be moving your wrist, for example, in front of his hands and ahead of his motion, at approximately the same speed (not too fast or he will lose you and you will lose him; not too slow or he will be able to grasp your wrist firmly). This is a peculiar, tan-

talizing form of motion which makes a target appear to be so near and accessible at the very moment when that target is receding and drawing *uke* out into uncontrolled extension before he realizes what has happened.

In case he has already contacted your wrist, it will still be possible to lead him out into unbalanced extension, because "contact" does not mean "hold." A hold requires a few moments to become stabilized and thus transform a motion forward (reaching and contacting the target) into a punch (actually hitting that target), or a hold (tightening or securing control over the target). But a hold—if it is to be secure—requires some form of stability or balance. Providing you have moved in full coordination with the motion of his hands closing around your wrists, he will not have this balance because you will be fading away, and he will be stretching forward. His power will still be flowing out toward a target he cannot grasp and cannot stop.

Finally, when your right hand has completed the circular pattern of extension to his rear, you may then contact his forehead, bringing him down to the mat (your left hand on his neck as you do so).

Second Example (leading and feigning a blow)

Finally, a formidable and practical way of coping with a real aggression by applying the principle of dynamic extension and reversal typical of projection no. 21 is illustrated in this sequence. This method, however, is usually taught at a rather advanced stage of aikido practice, because the coordination required for its application and its intrinsic dangers are greater than in the method explained previously.

As *uke* rushes at you in any form of basic attack (provided he is totally committed to that attack) you will slide quickly to his right side and bring your right hand or fist up and sharply back, feigning a blow to his face. In the illustrated example, your right hand will lead *uke* forward, without touching him, and spread suddenly out from above before his eyes. If your coordination is correct he will arch back on the spot, landing on the mat at your feet. You will usually remain at his side in a condition of centralized balance.

PROJECTION NO. 22

General Remarks

Projection no. 22 in its two main variations—*irimi* and *tenkan*—is a leading technique particularly suitable to the neutralization of a series of holds, but also applicable to the neutralization of many blows once you have established your own leading hold on *uke*.

It is widely practiced in aikido *dojo* because the two main features of all techniques of neutralization—centralization and extension—are so clearly apparent in its execution as to make projection no. 22 one of the best exercises for acquiring a familiarity with the dynamics of those techniques, as well as with their inter-relationship.

PROJECTION NO. 22 AGAINST ATTACK NO. 1

Irimi. As *uke* grabs your right wrist with his left hand, you will extend your arm out to your right side as illustrated, feigning a blow to his face as you step in with your right foot. Then you will take another step with your left foot, and pivoting on both legs, turn your hips to your right, so that you are facing in the same direction as *uke*. You will lead his arm into a circular extension either frontally and down, or around you and down. In the first example, you will slide your right foot straight forward, sinking low and extending your whole body behind the forward motion. In the second, you will withdraw your left foot circularly on your left side. Do not pull your hand out of his grip. The idea is to accompany him into a forward extension, unbalance, and projection downward, with you leading the action to its completion.

Tenkan. As *uke* grabs your left wrist with his right hand, instead of stepping in and ahead under his arm, you will pivot directly on your left foot, turning your hips to your right side and withdrawing your right foot. Then you will lead his right arm up and by extending your whole body, project him down and away, or to your diagonal right side.

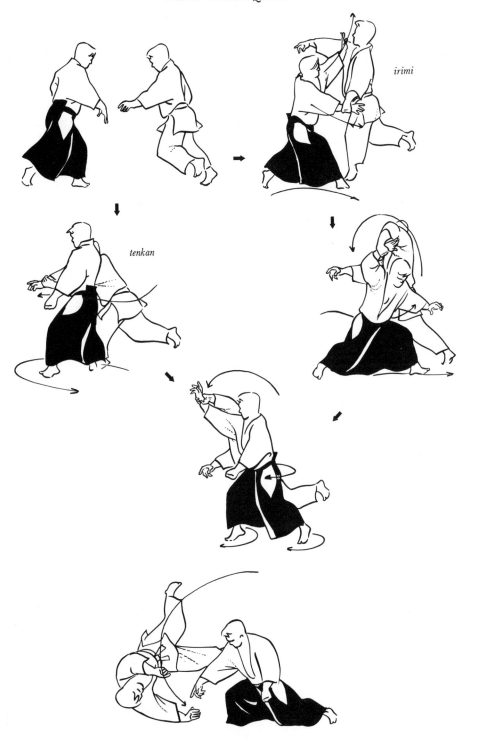

irimi

tenkan

PROJECTION NO. 23

General Remarks

A powerful projection devised to cope with an almost infinite variety of possible attacks is projection no. 23 (hip-pull). The central movement of your hips will generate a tremendous pull which will be remarkably effective, even when performed from a standstill. It is absolutely devastating in its effect upon *uke* or those he may hit, if the intense dynamic momentum of your pull is blended and coordinated with his motion of attack.

The movement of your hips followed by the snapping motion of your upper trunk and arms will resemble the recoiling of a whip—the lower abdomen acting as the handle. You will pull your hips back first to your rear, leaving your upper trunk and arms where they are for the moment and then taking a long step backward.

Finally, by either kneeling down or turning slightly, you will whip your upper trunk and arms in the same direction as your hips, the direction in which you will be throwing *uke*.

This projection may be performed efficiently against almost any type of attack—a hold or a blow from the front or from behind. It is, however, usually practiced in one of the two ways illustrated against attack no. 4: with your partner holding your wrists until the end of the technique, or with you grasping one of his hands or both at the moment you begin your hip-pull motion.

Naturally, against other types of attack—especially holds from behind—you will evade them first and then, grasping his wrists in the process, establish your own position of centralization for the effective displacement of your Centre and completion of projection no. 23.

PROJECTION NO. 23 AGAINST ATTACK NO. 4

STATIC. When performed as an exercise, *uke* will hold both your wrists and settle himself well, in order to offer some resistance to your action, and to test the muscular relaxation of your arms. You will forget about his hold and allow your arms to remain relaxed in his grip. You will concentrate on your Centre and swing your hips back, taking a step with your left foot in the same direction as illustrated. Then you will whip your body up and to your left side, snapping your arms up at the same time. Your right hand will grasp his extended right wrist. The pull will sweep your partner's feet from the mat and your circular lead on his right wrist, frontally and then down, will spin his body in the air, and land him flat on his back on the mat or send him rolling away along its surface. You will release his wrist as he sails through the air, thus allowing him to assume the correct, round posture for the aikido somersault or roll-out. The circular turning of your hips to your left side will have the effect of removing your body from the path of his spinning motion and of centralizing the entire action.

DYNAMIC. As *uke* reaches out to grab your arms or wrists, you will swing your hips back grasping his extended arms or wrists, and send him spinning through the air as explained in the previous example.

PROJECTIONS NOS. 24, 25, AND 26

General Remarks

Other examples of an aggressive convergence of forces which will be evaded and led into a dispersive circuit of projection around you, are offered by projections nos. 24, 25, and 26. In the first of these, the dispersion will pass centrifugally over you (from one side to the other). In the second technique, that force will be redirected in the original direction after a turn around you which hinges upon the opponent's outstretched arm. In the third example, the dispersion will again pass over you as in the first technique, but this time from behind.

PROJECTION NO. 24 AGAINST ATTACK NO. 4

As *uke* reaches forward to grab your wrists or arms, you will pull your hips back, taking a long step in the same direction with your left foot and lifting his arms up over your head. Taking another step to your right-rear side with your right foot, you will kneel down sliding under his body as it whirls by. Finally, you will swing your arms in an arc down to your rear, and then spin *uke* over frontally on his left diagonal side. (By kneeling down, you will remove your body from the path of his motion, i.e., you will slide under the orbital line of his displacement and—kneeling as illustrated—you will be slightly to the side, which is a necessary condition if you are to spin *uke* over in diagonal frontally from your position of operational centralization.)

PROJECTION NO. 25 AGAINST ATTACK NO. 15

As *uke* delivers a low blow to your abdomen, you will take a long step with your left foot to his right side, and spinning on that foot, you will withdraw your right leg behind you in a circle. Simultaneously your right hand will drop onto his extended right wrist and your left hand will grasp him as illustrated. Keeping his arm fully extended, you will lead him out and project him down onto the mat, continuing your follow-through motion as he rolls away from you. (The success of this projection will depend mainly upon the extension of his arm which will become the fulcrum of rotation of the whole action.)

PROJECTION NO. 26 AGAINST ATTACK NO. 9

Projection no. 26—known as a "body lead"—can be most dynamic and powerful if you increase the momentum of the motion of attack of *uke* by moving circularly ahead of him. As he touches your upper body, you will extend your arms diagonally out to your sides and move around in a large circle returning behind him. You will not "run away" or pull out of his grasp. As always, you will lead him into a circular pattern of extension and unbalance before sinking down so as to be able to lead that pattern to the mat and project *uke* over in a frontal somersault.

PROJECTION NO. 26 AGAINST ATTACK NO. 17

Uke, having grabbed your left lapel with his right hand, delivers a blow with his left hand to your face; you will spin on your left foot and withdraw your right leg circularly to your rear. As he spins in full extension around you, take another step with your left foot inside his line of motion, which you will then lead down onto the mat either by bowing deeply forward from a standing position, or by dropping to your knees as illustrated.

PROJECTION NO. 27

General Remarks

Sometimes referred to as the "double whirl," projection no. 27 consists of a spinning movement followed by a second spin. It can be particularly effective against holds from behind in confined quarters, or when surrounded by several opponents.

PROJECTION NO. 27 AGAINST ATTACK NO. 9

As *uke* grabs you from behind, you will extend your arms and slide your right foot out to your right, spinning on your left foot and bending low as you pass beneath his arms. Rising up on his right side, you will bend your knees and describe a second circle as illustrated. Rising up at the completion of this second circle, you will be close to his left side, your left hand extended up and over his head; your right hand is braced against his lower back, causing him to arch over and back toward the mat. Continuing your semi-circular sweep over and down, you will bring him to the mat.

PROJECTION NO. 28

General Remarks

Among the many techniques of aikido, projection no. 28 would seem to be one of the simplest and most effective ways of neutralizing almost any form of attack launched against you, whether by one or more opponents. Yet, it is one of the most sophisticated examples of that centralization coordinated with an opponent's movement of attack, which is the focal point of all the techniques. In projection no. 28, however, combat is shifted from the vertical dimension to the horizontal, suddenly and in full commitment, before the opponent realizes what is happening and can adapt his attack to the new combat circumstances. Projection no. 28, therefore, rests upon an accurate estimation of the opponent's commitment to a real attack—an essential factor in the successful employment of this technique.

PROJECTION NO. 28 AGAINST ANY ATTACK

As *uke* moves in from the front or from behind in order to either grasp or hit you in any form of basic attack, you will slide in under him or lead him out with a few circular steps in order to increase the momentum of his initial motion of attack. Then you will sink down deeply, under *uke* as if you were a huge stone suddenly thrown in his path. You rise up behind him, after he has soared up and over you in the somersault necessitated by the unexpectedness of your maneuver and by his own dynamic commitment to the attack.

Combinations

The various techniques examined up to this point are usually practiced with strong initial concentration upon their particular mechanisms or forms, i.e., the individual, pre-programmed movements which distinguish one technique from another.

As you become more familiar with many of the basic aikido techniques and your performance of them becomes ever more fluid and eventually instinctive, you may begin to practice the combination of these techniques—an intermediate step between the study of individual basic techniques and the advanced practice. Quite obviously, this method of combining various techniques will test and help to develop your coordination in a more comprehensive dimension as you begin—tentatively at first—to work toward going beyond technique. Flowing from one technique into another, your movements and actions should appear more and more to be natural responses to the particular form and dynamic outlines of any attack without any interruption in the continuity of your performance.

These combinations (used here to neutralize a single attack) will usually feature an immobilization followed smoothly by a second, different immobilization; or an immobilization closely followed by a projection; or a projection seconded by an immobilization. The number of possible combinations, even if limited to the basic techniques of neutralization examined up to this point, is staggering. It is sufficient to observe that immobilization no. 1, for example, can be transformed into or combined with almost any other technique (whether immobilization or projection) in the aikido repertoire. And this can be applied equally to almost all the others.

Illustrated below, however, are four examples of combinations typical of those practiced in many aikido *dojo*.

IMMOBILIZATION NO. 1 AND IMMOBILIZATION NO. 3
AGAINST ATTACK NO. 16

As *uke* blocks your right arm with his right arm from behind and encircles your throat with his left forearm, you will lower your chin to prevent completion of the strangulation, and grasping his left wrist with your free left hand, step to your left side with your left foot, turning your hips toward him. Withdrawing your right leg deep behind you to his left-rear corner, you will kneel down in order to weaken his balance and thus his power. You will withdraw your right arm from his now weakened hold and set your right hand inside and underneath his elbow, establishing the hold for basic immobilization no. 1. Rising up, you will step behind *uke* with your right foot and spin him around in the *tenkan* variation of that technique. You will release the leading hold of your right hand on his elbow as he completes a circle around you without releasing the hold of your left hand upon his

extended left wrist. As he spins around you, you will glide under his captured and extended left arm, your left foot leading. Meanwhile, your right hand joins your left on his left hand and establishes the hold for basic immobilization no. 3 which you will complete as illustrated, rising up at his side.

IMMOBILIZATION NO. 3 AND PROJECTION NO. 3 AGAINST ATTACK NO. 16

As *uke* grabs your left wrist with his left hand from behind while attempting to choke you with his right forearm, you will lower your chin to prevent completion of the strangulation. Extending your captured left arm, secure a hold with your free left hand upon his left hand. With both arms extended, you will lead his arm up in front of you while sliding your left foot laterally to make room for the withdrawal of your right leg. This second step will permit you to slide under his captured left arm and bring your body into the desired position of centralization—the left side of *uke* completely extended. You will bring his left hand down in front of you, controlled by immobilization no. 3 as illustrated. Without interrupting this downward motion, proceed to apply projection no. 3 setting your left hand upon his neck or head and bring his left arm up again from behind as you withdraw your left foot circularly and launch him away from you.

IMMOBILIZATION NO. 4 AND PROJECTION NO. 13
AGAINST ATTACK NO. 4

As *uke* grabs both your wrists, you will take a long circular step to your
right-rear side, pivoting on your left foot and withdrawing your right foot.
Leading his left arm up with your right arm, you will establish immobilization no. 4 on his left forearm as illustrated. Still leading him around you,
you will bring your right foot back to your left side and spin on it, withdrawing your left leg and kneeling down on your left knee. This will clear
the way for projection no. 13 and his frontal somersault.

PROJECTION NO. 26 AND IMMOBILIZATION NO. 3 AGAINST ATTACK NO. 5

As *uke* grabs your left lapel with his right hand, you will withdraw your left foot in an ample circle behind you, feigning a blow to his face with the right hand in order to extend him out and unbalance him. Spinning on your left foot, you will withdraw your right foot in a *tenkan* movement of leading control to your right-rear side, thus guiding him out and around you. A second *tenkan* movement to your left side this time (spinning on your right foot and withdrawing your left foot circularly behind you), will be followed by a deep bow toward the mat, bringing *uke* down. As he falls you will grasp his right hand (holding your lapel) with your left hand and proceed to apply immobilization no. 3 in any one of its possible variations.

CHAPTER IX

Advanced Practice

ONCE you have become familiar with the basic aikido techniques, your instructor will gradually begin to introduce you to what we call the "advanced practice" of the art. This will usually include: "mat" or kneeling aikido *(suwari waza);* the stave exercises *(jo* or *bo waza* and *jo kata);* the techniques of neutralization applied against a multiple attack; and free style *(randori).*

At this level of the art you will be able to test and develop your centralization and your extension of Inner Energy, since individual technical movements will not be as important in these forms as will be a total approach and response to any attack, i.e., the degree of unified and coordinated fusion of the powers of mind and body which you have achieved. It is at these higher levels of the art that aikido begins to emerge quite clearly as a discipline of coordination, with dominant emphasis upon a unified and harmonized personality. Knowing how to perform particular techniques will not be sufficient. You must move and respond in a smooth, flowing, characteristically aikido manner which will become more natural and constant as you continue your practice of the art.

323

"Mat" or Kneeling Aikido

Almost all aikido techniques can be, and often are, performed from or in a kneeling position. This form of practice is especially useful for developing your centralization and extension while testing your balance. At first you may find it extremely difficult even to move about on your knees, much less perform any particular techniques, but regular practice of what is often called "samurai walk" (see "Motion" section which follows) will help you to feel more comfortable in this kneeling position until you find that you can move about quite freely, and eventually perform various techniques in or from that position with a surging power that seems to come from the very earth itself.

This type of aikido has been derived from ancient samurai practices and much of the *suwari waza* performed in aikido *dojo* today is directly traceable to the Japanese feudal forms of fighting—whether with sword or dagger, or even unarmed—in a kneeling position.

The ancient Japanese reality was closely identified with the ground or the earth. Formal attendance upon the emperor at court or waiting upon a daimyo required a court attendant or samurai to remain for hours in an erect kneeling position, but always ready to move quickly and fluidly if and when necessary. Even meals and informal social occasions usually found them on their knees. From this heritage, the Japanese have derived an almost instinctive and continuing identification with the ground, which is reflected in their religions and preserved in most of their martial arts in certain formal exercises, or *kata*.

MOTION. The exercise popularly known as "samurai walk" begins from a left *hammi* position on your knees. You will step up on the ball of your left foot, keeping your trunk straight as you let your weight descend onto your left knee, pivoting on that knee and bringing your feet together as indicated. You will thus have described a half-circle as you moved along the mat. Your second step will be up on the ball of your right foot, right knee up. As your weight descends onto that knee you will pivot on it, swinging your feet together as indicated, and describing another semi-circle as you move ahead. It is imperative that you keep your shoulders down and concentrate upon being and remaining centralized.

In another extension of this type of practice, you will actually perform even the most difficult exercises—such as basic exercise no. 9 for example—on your knees, following the general outline provided in the section on the basic exercises, with the necessary adaptations to the kneeling position. Here, you will have to "move from the hips" if you are to move at all. And, of course, both your centralization and extension will be much improved by regular practice of the exercises from or in this position.

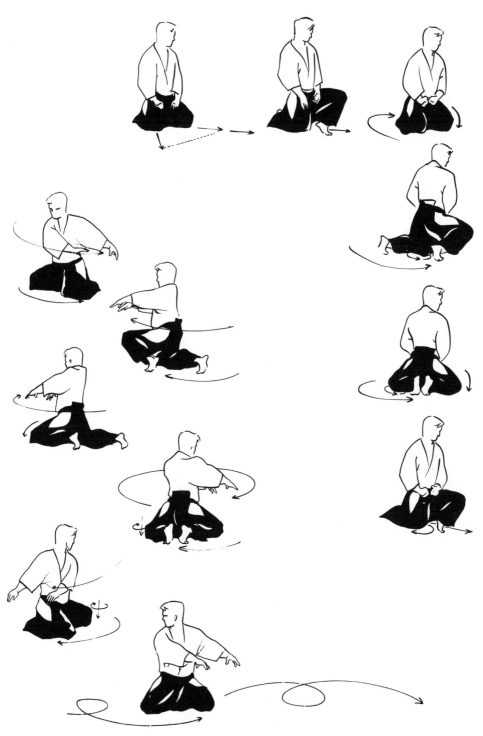

TECHNIQUES. By applying the basic principles of the samurai walk in combination with the various ways of applying the basic techniques or forms which have been outlined in Chapter VIII, almost all aikido techniques can be performed *suwari waza* style.

In the following sequences, we have endeavored to provide representative examples of this interesting form of aikido practice which you will observe advanced students of the art practicing in *dojo* all over the world.

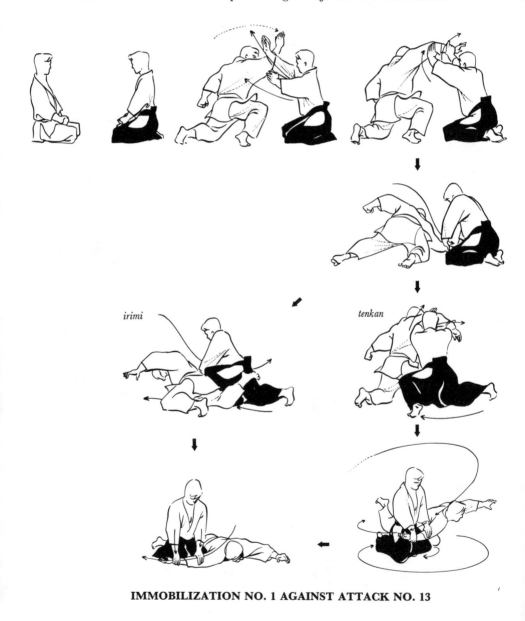

irimi

tenkan

IMMOBILIZATION NO. 1 AGAINST ATTACK NO. 13

IMMOBILIZATION NO. 2 AGAINST ATTACK NO. 13

irimi

tenkan

IMMOBILIZATION NO. 3 AGAINST ATTACK NO. 13

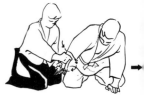

IMMOBILIZATION NO. 4 AGAINST ATTACK NO. 13

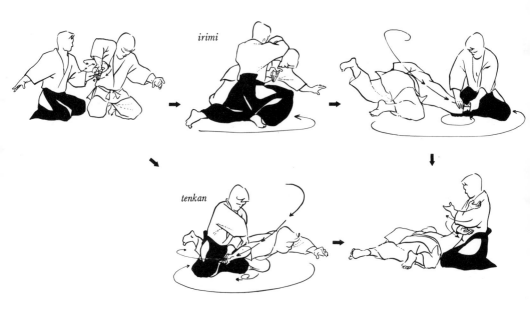

irimi

tenkan

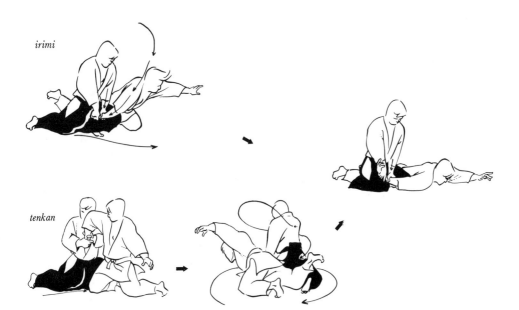

irimi

tenkan

IMMOBILIZATION NO. 5 AGAINST ATTACK NO. 14

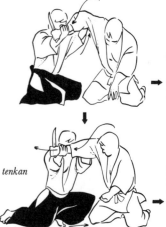

tenkan

IMMOBILIZATION NO. 6 AGAINST ATTACK NO. 1

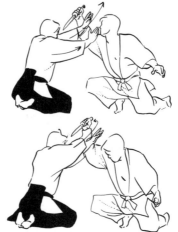
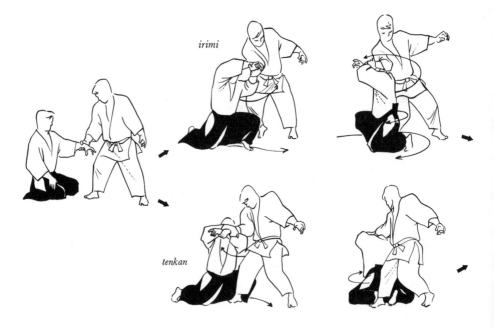

irimi

tenkan

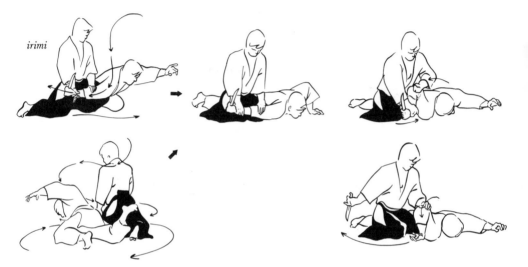

(This technique is performed from a position called *hammi hantachi*—with *uke* standing and *nage* kneeling.)

PROJECTION NO. 3 AGAINST ATTACK NO. 1

PROJECTION NO. 3 AGAINST ATTACK NO. 15

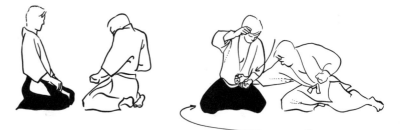

PROJECTION NO. 7 AGAINST ATTACK NO. 5

PROJECTION NO. 23 AGAINST ATTACK NO. 4

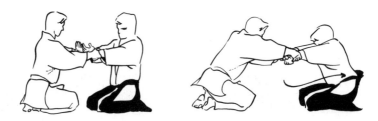

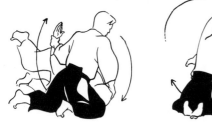

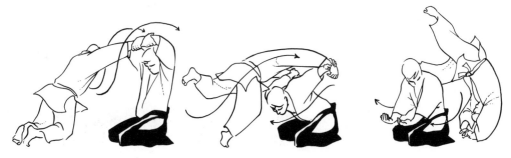

Various Opening Motions of Centralization

The first sequence which follows illustrates an opening motion of evasion, centralization, and extension against attack no. 1. The second sequence shows a motion of evasion, centralization, and extension against attack no. 5 which can then be concluded with basic techniques of immobilizations nos. 1, 2, and 3, as well as no. 4; or with a number of basic techniques of projection such as nos. 1, 2, 3, 6, 7, and so on.

The Stave Exercises

The derivation of aikido from the ancient arts of the spear and the sword is particularly evident in the practice of a complex set of exercises based on the *jo* (or *bo*)—the stave which was used in the ancient schools of martial arts as a substitute for the long sword and the short spear, together with the *hasshaku-bo* and the *rokushaku-bo* for the long spear and the halberd, and the *hambo* and *tambo* for the short sword and the dagger.

The *jo* is used in aikido in many ways: as a visible extension of your personality, as a weapon to be neutralized, or as an instrument of coordination.

Jo-waza for **Centralized Extension**

Using the *jo,* you may perform a number of basic aikido techniques by having *uke* grasp the other end of the stave and leading his motion/action just as you would if he had grasped your wrist(s).

This is a particularly useful way of testing your extension which must be projected all the way out to the very end of the *jo,* as well as developing the "total body movement" which will make the correct performance of the techniques possible.

The first sequence on page 336 shows immobilization no. 6 against attack no. 3, performed in the *irimi* variation, and the second sequence above shows projection no. 21 used to neutralize the same attack—both employing the *jo* as the physical instrument of leading control through which your centralized energy will flow outward and into the circular patterns of neutralization.

Jo-waza for Defense

The stave may be employed by *uke* as a weapon of attack which you will be required to neutralize with an appropriate basic technique. Such a neutralization of a direct, low thrust (attack no. 15) may be achieved in various ways.

Projection no. 22, illustrated in the first sequence, and immobilization no. 6 in the second, are two examples selected from the many techniques which you may employ to neutralize this type of attack.

Jo kata for Total Coordination

From the many sword and spear cuts and thrusts developed and perfected by the samurai during Japan's feudal period, certain movements were combined and practiced in the slow, stylistically controlled manner of the *kata,* or formal exercises, employing the stave. One such *kata*—regularly practiced in aikido *dojo* (either alone or with a partner)—consists of a series of 22 programmed movements which are illustrated here.

It is extremely difficult to portray these movements individually, since they flow into one another in actual practice. It is also almost impossible to indicate the stepping ahead, the pivoting, and the reverse stepping as they are performed on the mat. To do justice to this kind of exercise, you would have to see it performed "live" or else on film. We have, however, outlined these 22 movements here, because of their importance to the "advanced practice" with certain precautions:

First of all, the sliding, "entering" extension of the first movement (and all those which are repetitions of the first movement) does not involve a straight stepping in, but is, instead, an ever-so-slightly circular "entering" (in the illustrations it is being portrayed on the left side).

Your left foot will slide forward semi-circularly to the left side; your right foot swings behind it. You will return to your original position and perform the second movement which is a repetition of the first. When you perform the third and fourth movements (and the seventh and eighth, which are repetitions of the third and fourth), you must take a large sliding step to the side (first to the right in the third movement and then to the left in the fourth movement), describing an ample semi-circle and bringing your other foot around to join your stepping foot.

Each one of these stave forms will require you to move along the mat. You will never just stand in one spot and swing your *jo* around. You will be sliding forward, you will be pivoting, and you will be reversing or retracing your steps, but you will always be moving.

In the passage from one form to another, the stave will whirl upon a central axis provided by your hand/arm (which, of course, is an extension of your centralized body) tracing in the air—the circuits of that Dynamic Sphere which is at the very heart of the *kata* itself.

The Techniques of Neutralization Applied Against an Armed Attack

An especially demanding form of practice, one which will test the functional power of your centralization and relaxed extension in a particular way, is the application of the basic techniques of neutralization against armed attacks.

As was noted previously, the neutralization of this type of attack will not differ in a functionally substantial manner from the neutralization of a similar, unarmed one, i.e., the aikido technique employed in either case (armed or unarmed), will be basically the same.

AGAINST KNIFE

In the sequences above and on the opposite page you will see a knife attack from behind, a knife attack from the front at the throat, and a knife thrust at the stomach—all neutralized by immobilization no. 7.

In each and every one of these examples, the centralized spin which disperses the dangerous concentration of that attack tangentially, the extension of motion, and the centrifugal lead around you and then down, will be the most important functional characteristics of your defensive strategy (see Chapter V, the principles of centralization, extension, leading control, and sphericity). They will help to insure the necessary speed and efficiency of the immobilization applied.

Two other examples of armed attack using a knife—one neutralized through immobilization no. 3 and the other by an arm lock belonging to the advanced technical stages of aikido practice—are illustrated in the sequences which follow.

As we have observed in the general remarks to immobilization no. 5, this basic technique may also be employed to neutralize circular attacks with a knife or sword. In this example, the knife is taken away from *uke* once he has been brought down to the mat with the *irimi* or *tenkan* variation of immobilization no. 5.

tenkan

irimi

AGAINST SWORD

The sword is also used in an attack that must be neutralized *aiki* style. Almost every aikido *dojo* has at least one traditional *bokken* (the wooden sword used today for training purposes and once used by the samurai in relatively bloodless contests of fencing skills).

In the first sequence a straight cut to the head (attack no. 13) is neutralized by projection no. 1, completed through an arm lock; while in the second sequence, a circular cut to the upper part of the body (attack no. 14) is neutralized through immobilization no. 6.

AGAINST CLUB

Techniques of neutralization against attacks with a club are part of the training program in most aikido *dojo*. Two examples have been included (see "The Stave Exercises").

The Techniques of Neutralization Applied Against a Multiple Attack

The development of your inner centralization and outer extension will be tested in the performance of techniques of neutralization applied against a multiple attack, i.e., one involving two or more men. These techniques may be performed in two basic ways: either statically with your partners' holds already established, or dynamically, at the moment when they are about to converge upon you. A number of examples follow to describe the static method; the dynamic method will be shown through free style *(randori)*.

The static method of defense against a multiple attack is a means of familiarizing yourself with the inevitably greater number of impressions and increased range of resistance which will flow from the various aggressive personalities surrounding you. The constancy of your inner independence from the distractions of such a forbidding reality and the continuity of your extension of centralized energy must, consequently, be superior in quality, depth, and range.

A defense against multiple attack performed statically will usually involve one more of the basic techniques of neutralization examined in Chapter VIII. The same technique may be applied against two *uke,* or two basic techniques may be combined.

In the first example here, arms of both *uke* are brought into alignment through a powerful hip-pull (projection no. 23), and then immobilization no. 6 *(irimi* variation) is applied against both men at the same time, keeping their arms entwined.

In the second example, both *uke* will be dynamically displaced through a forward motion, followed by the deep plunge to the mat of projection no. 22.

In the third example, a powerful surge forward will set both *uke* in motion, followed by another deep plunge, ending in the double spiral of projection no. 18, which will spin both *uke* in opposite directions and bring them down to the mat at your feet.

In the fourth example, you will detect the initial leading plunge of immobilization no. 6 against the *uke* on your right side, followed by the hip-pull of projection no. 23 against the *uke* on your left side—bringing his outstretched arms under those of the first *uke*. From that position, without any interruption in the flow of the motion, you will lead the arms of one *uke* in a circle from underneath, against those of the other *uke* with a "windmill" action of your arms—thus unbalancing both *uke* and projecting them down onto the mat.

More complex examples of defense against multiple attacks launched simultaneously by more than two *uke,* are also practiced in aikido *dojo,* following substantially the same dynamic and technical rules of defense as those applicable to two attackers; always based, of course, upon those fundamental principles of inner centralization, extension, leading control, and sphericity, without which any technique, any strategy of defense would be extremely difficult if not impossible, to perform successfully.

Free Style (**Randori**)

One of the highest levels of practical proficiency on the mat is evidenced in aikido by the smooth, powerful, and controlled neutralization of an unexpected attack through free-style defense, or *randori*—a method of practice which has gained in importance in contrast to the period during which the techniques of aikido (as well as those of many other martial arts) were performed predominantly in a formal, ritualized manner *(kata)*.

In free style you will face the most demanding test of your harmonization/ integration of mind and body in the practice of aikido—at least on the mat. As two, three, or four men close in upon you, as you evade, as you lead their extension (their dynamic commitment to an attack) into an *aiki* throw, you will inevitably display the degree of development you have achieved in this art.

Before attempting free style, the regular practice of the individual aikido techniques, as well as the companion disciplines of breathing, meditation, etc., should have brought you to a certain level of proficiency. But with free style you will enter a more demanding and expanded dimension of this art of coordination, and only with time and practice will individual movements and techniques which have been programmed into your psyche separately, be unified and integrated as a whole into your responsive personality, blending and flowing in a typical aikido manner, entirely consistent with the principles of the art—both technical and ethical.

In free style, your *uke* will attack you, and you will be required to neutralize these attacks with a technique as strategically appropriate to the circumstances as possible. At this stage, the calm independence of your mind, your relaxed yet accurate perceptions, the feeling of constant centralization and the dynamic continuity of your extension, i.e., the outpouring of centralized energy should be so blended and fused as to result in that condition of serene and impenetrable control. The ancient masters of the martial arts often defined this as "no-mind" (borrowing the concept from the Buddhist School of Zen), meaning a condition of centralized perfection wherein the mind is at peace, aware of everything in general, but not hypnotized by any one thing in particular. In this state the body is said to function on such a high level of unconscious, yet smoothly controlled responsiveness that you will appear to have achieved the unification, in practice, of both the power of centralized stability (immanent) and that of active, dynamic, and transcendent motion (stillness in motion).

This type of free-style defense against multiple attack may often involve as many as six or more *uke* (depending upon the size of the mat and the number of available *uke*). Strange as it may seem, however, the strategic efficiency of any attack will decrease in proportion to the increase in the number of *uke,* since they will tend to get in one another's way, and—to a certain extent—neutralize one another.

The most difficult attack to control and, consequently, the most effective type of multiple attack appears to be one launched by four men against a lone man, because such an attack allows each man enough room to maneuver and to launch his individual attack.

In the sequence which follows, a multiple attack launched by four *uke* is neutralized statically by the employment of spinning techniques within a certain sphere of action. The general impression derived from this form of defensive strategy is one of dynamic convergence along a circular, centripetal pattern, transformed into an equally circular, but centrifugal one. And the result of such a final extension in every case will bring one of your *uke* across the pattern of convergence of the others or directly into them, through projections you will recognize from the basic techniques. Immobilizations are very seldom used in free style since their rather complicated mechanisms of subjugation, when concentrated upon a single attacker, will tend to slow down or even interrupt the flow of your defensive strategy. But their use upon occasion is not absolutely excluded (as illustrated by the use of immobilization no. 3 in the second example) not only to neutralize one man's attack, but actually to scatter all the others.

Finally, the training in free style—and the practice of aikido as a whole—reaches a summit of perfection and plastic beauty in the neutralization of a multiple attack achieved through "pure" motion of evasion, centralization, and extension, with hardly any recourse to particular techniques.

Here we enter the dimension of "pure" leading—exquisitely refined and total—as you move back and forth describing circular patterns in space, place, and time. A Western observer of Master Uyeshiba's demonstration of this kind of aikido practice said that the *sensei* seemed to have entered a different continuum. But, of course, that is at Master Uyeshiba's level.

FIRST EXAMPLE

SECOND EXAMPLE

CHAPTER **X**

Conclusion

In this book, which we have qualified as an illustrated introduction, there has been a necessary concentration upon the practice of the art, i.e., the theory of attack (that attack which will trigger your defensive strategy); the Inner Factors (centralization, extension, leading control, and sphericity); the Outer Factors, subdivided into physical factors (the components of a supple, healthy, responsive body) and functional factors (posture, motion of preparation, and the techniques of neutralization in the form of basic immobilizations, projections, and combinations). Even the brief survey just concluded of the advanced practice was necessarily focused upon the various movements, the forms, and the style of performance to be developed.

However, this external practical aspect of aikido and the forms which its practice assumes are not the only points of reference to be adopted. For, if you should become hypnotized by the techniques, or if you should be captivated solely by their grace and fluidity as performed by advanced practitioners of the art, you might with diligent practice become an accomplished performer, but your very concentration upon the technical aspect of aikido could result in an imitation of mere forms, gestures, and actions. You would lack the necessary deeper understanding of their substance, of their significance, of the essentially ethical motivations which should always be the ultimate justification, the final *raison d'être* of this art of coordination, from its most introductory levels to the most advanced spheres of its practice.

Strong and effective concentration upon technique, after all, is a tendency shared by many practitioners of many different martial arts and breathtakingly fluid movements are found in almost every sport worthy of note, not only in aikido.

Moreover (and this may come as a surprise to some people already practicing the art), not even the Inner Factors of aikido—the intriguing centralization in the lower abdomen *(hara)*, and the extension of centralized energy *(ki)*—should be considered the unique factors which set aikido apart from other martial arts. Both the *hara* and *ki* have long been considered (especially by the ancient masters of martial arts) to be devices or instruments which should be used, just as you would use the Outer Factors (strategies,

359

posture, motion, technique, etc.) to achieve a higher purpose transcending them all—a purpose linked to the most communally important spheres of man's existence; i.e., to the ethics, the norms ruling his conduct, his actions.

Both the *hara* and *ki*, then, are not concepts discovered suddenly or employed solely by the practitioners of aikido although—as is generally admitted —no other modern martial art seems to stress the importance of these factors to the extent found in aikido.

The fame of many martial schools of *aiki-jutsu* was based upon the skillful employment of these factors in their strategies of combat but, to varying degrees, all of the most reputable martial art schools, armed *(kyudo, yari-jutsu, kenjutsu,* and kendo, etc.), and unarmed *(sumo, yawara,* jujutsu, judo, kempo, karate, etc.), have both known and used them as the hidden pillars of various strategies, usually at their highest and most esoteric levels.

Therefore, a student of aikido who concentrates solely upon *hara* and *ki* will not differ substantially from the technical specialist who is hypnotized by technique. The only difference—as has been noted—will be that the former will become much more powerful than the latter. Many aikido *dojo* have more than one of these powerful men whose feats of undeniable prowess can amaze even the most blasé spectator—to the extent that these spectacular performers are regarded with considerable awe, and sometimes undiscriminating admiration.

That great unforeseen evils could be the result of unethical use of the power *(ki)* originating from a fully developed *hara* was a fact well known to many of the ancient masters of martial arts. Those masters left stern warnings to their disciples not to reveal these "secrets of the art" to those who would use them for base purposes. Today, however, there is often confusion between "strong" or powerful *ki* and "good" or ethically employed *ki*. As a man may be physically powerful and use this strength to intimidate other men, so also a man may have "strong" *ki* and use it to harm others or to profit himself at their expense.

While this distinction was often made by the ancient masters, there is a seemingly prevailing tendency today to think that "strong" *automatically* means "good." This is just not true. The power itself is generic. As such, it can be used for good or evil. It must be directed and employed by a mature personality with obvious and positive results if it is to be qualified as good.

If, therefore, the Outer Factors (or techniques) will not be the main term of orientation; if the Inner Factors of centralization and extension do not explain the uniqueness of aikido—what is it that sets this art apart? What gives aikido its unmistakable identity and qualifies it as a superior method of integration and development?

The answer is to be found in Master Uyeshiba's "Memoirs."* It is the

---

* *Aikido* by Kisshomaru Uyeshiba

ethical message which he, as a man of deep religious conviction, concerned with the improvement of the human condition, as well as an exceptional martial art master, has embodied in the practical method he called aikido.

It is the ultimate motivation of the art, the striving to bring order where there is disorder, to integrate where there is separation, to reconcile where there is strife, which marks aikido as a unique and distinctive martial art.

Unfortunately, we cannot undertake a survey in depth of these "remote" ethics in this brief conclusion to our introduction to the art. The subject of ethics in general and of the particular ethics of Master Uyeshiba's aikido is a thorny and complex one—the latter involving the spiritual dimensions of Asiatic culture from the Japanese form of Shinto to the continental doctrines of Buddhism, Taoism, and Confucianism in their original or adapted forms, individually and in combination, or rather as fused by and within Japanese culture.

Even Master Uyeshiba, quoted in a martial arts magazine,* seems to find it difficult to communicate his ethical message clearly. Perhaps it is because the "phenomenic" aspect of his art, the practice itself, is so hypnotizing and so visually impressive, his techniques so beautiful and the extension of his centralized energy so powerful that many students cannot see beyond this dazzling "how" to the elusive "why" which lies just beyond the screen of those superbly energized movements. This subject, however, is being dealt with by the authors in other works presently in preparation.

In synthesis, we may say that the ethics of aikido stress living and behaving well at every moment, in whatever circumstances a man may find himself. If the harmony of existence is broken—as it so often is—the aikido student should seek to restore harmony and, moreover, to improve upon it creatively and positively. He should strive to conduct himself well, avoiding all those excesses, whatever their nature, which might disturb that centralized equilibrium, that integrated balance of mind/body, of the self and the other(s)—without which "harmony" is an empty word.

The state or attitude of balance should be particularly evident in that dramatic action which may involve him in combat with his fellow man. For is there anything more indicative of disorder than combat? And, is there any other form of action which can be so easily qualified as "good" or "bad" provided there are alternate ways of dealing with the problems of combat—one of which defends but destroys, while the other defends and saves?

Aikido is a discipline, a "way" of integration, of harmony, of coordination which provides practical means whereby a student of the art can work toward achieving that harmony. In every action, in every strategy, in every technique of aikido, the practitioner will be confronted with two ways of resolving the problems of conflict, of separation, of disorder. He may—if he

---

* *Black Belt Magazine*, Vol. IV, No. 4, April 1966, p. 53

wishes—neutralize his attacker, either totally or partially. Obviously, the techniques—if so applied—can be lethal.

However, the aikido student may and should concentrate upon the neutralization of the attacker's *action,* without seriously injuring the attacker himself. And all of the techniques in the aikido repertoire can be applied with ease and efficiency to achieve that aim.

Of these two possible methods of applying his techniques, Master Uyeshiba has continually emphasized the second. Only through the neutralization of an aggressive action, rather than the aggressor himself, can harmony of existence be restored and improved upon through that reconciliation which is impossible if one or the other of the individuals involved is seriously injured or actually destroyed.

Whereas in many martial arts—armed and unarmed, ancient and modern —there is really very little choice, since the techniques themselves and the methods by which they are employed all work toward and are intended to injure if not actually destroy an attacker, in aikido the student is given the freedom and the responsibility of choice. He will always be able to defend himself efficiently but he can do it either by harming another human being in the process, or (although, admittedly, this requires greater skill as well as an ethical intention) he can achieve that same self-defense by leading his attacker's dangerous action into a potentially harmless Circuit of Neutralization.

A choice is possible, actually unavoidable in aikido. If the student has accepted and is in agreement with the underlying principles of the art (restoration, reconciliation, harmony), he will endeavor to act in accordance with these principles by trying to apply the techniques as means of neutralizing aggressions, not aggressors. Thus he achieves simultaneously the dual purpose of self-defense and restoration of that tenuous, living balance threatened by another man's temporary moral unbalance. And, in so doing, he will not create the conditions for another or different type of disorder, or of decentralization through the destruction or harming of another element, another subject of the same vital order who because of a momentary aberration may have disrupted the flow, the creative interaction of that order.

In this book then, we have tried to give at least an indication of what aikido is and—at its higher levels—what it can be. As an art of self-defense with roots in the ancient martial arts of Japan, it is an intriguing and practically effective method for preserving your integrity and your person against any unjustified attack—moreover in an ethical manner. Of course to become really proficient in any art takes time and application to the practice of its various techniques and disciplines. This is the rule whatever your field of endeavor, and it should surprise only those who seek "instant *satori,*" refusing to look behind the curtain of appearances, of the moment, to see the patience and application, the ofttimes unrecognized years of toil which provide the groundwork and foundation for any real accomplishment.

However, it is as a discipline of coordination that aikido has perhaps its widest field of application. In this dimension, the emphasis upon integration of mind and body, upon unity within the self, is expanded to include unity with a partner, with fellow men, and then that final flowering of unity of man and men with their universe. In this dimension, aikido moves from the particular and specialized to the general and universal.

The improved physical/mental health, the deeper understanding and awareness of the problems facing every man, the essential unity and identification of all men, their integration with and necessity to one another, as well as a sense of "belonging" to their times and their world—this is the potential that the theory and practice of the art of aikido can offer all men, wherever they may be.

Glossary

ai	the principle of harmony and integration
aikido	a modern discipline of harmony between opposites on a universal scale
aikijutsu	an ancient technique of combat based upon the principle of coordination between the attack and the defense
aiki otoshi	projection no. 5
aiki taiso	the basic exercises of aikido
ashi	leg or foot
ayumi ashi	alternated step
bo	stave, *jo*
bojutsu	the technique of the stave
bo kata	a formal exercise with the stave
bu	an ideogram related to the military dimension; used in compounds such as *bushi*
Buddhism	the doctrine of enlightenment propounded by the Indian philosopher Gautama Siddharta (563–483 B.C.)
bujutsu	the arts of the warrior
bushi	warrior
Bushido	the code of honor of the *bushi*
chudan	natural hand position, a central position
Confucianism	the moral doctrine of right conduct, extremely social in content, propounded by the Chinese scholar and philosopher Confucius (551–479 B.C.)
dan	a rank
do	the method, or " way," a discipline and philosophy with both moral and spiritual connotations
dojo	a training hall where the martial arts are practiced; in Zen monasteries, the hall of spiritual exercises, meditation, and concentration
gaku	calligraphy or motto hung on *dojo* walls
gedan	a low hand position
gi	the regular uniform, normally white, used in most schools of martial arts; in aikido it is worn under the *hakama*
gokyo	immobilization no. 5
goshi	the lateral pelvis; hips (see also *koshi*)

365

hakama	a divided skirt worn over the *gi*
hammi (hanmi)	guard; stance
happo undo	basic exercise no. 9
hara	the Centre of existence, abdominal and otherwise
haragei	the art of developing the *hara*
hidari	left
iaijutsu	an ancient method of combat centered upon the perfection of the initial movement of the sword
ikkyo; ikkajo	immobilization no. 1
irimi	an entering motion
irimi nage	a name given in general to projection no. 1, and in particular, to projection no. 2
jo	stave
jobajutsu	the technique of military horsemanship
jodan	a high hand position
jo kata	see *bo kata*
joseki	upper side of the mat, opposite *shimoza*
joza	another name for *kamiza* or the upper seat of the mat
ju	the principle of suppleness, adaption, and also nonresistance
judo	the "way of suppleness," a discipline of development devised from the ancient jujutsu technique and Budo ethics by Count Jigoro Kano, 1860–1938
kamae (gamae)	posture
kamiza	upper seat on the mat, opposite *shimoza*
kaiten	round; wheel
kaiten nage	projection no. 3
karate	a method of combat employing the whole anatomy as a weapon of combat, centered mainly upon the use of hands for percussion (*kara*, empty; *te*, hand), and introduced in Japan by Funakoshi Gichin 1869–1957
kata	a formal exercise consisting of a series of slow and stylistically uniform movements
katana	the Japanese sword
kata tori	a shoulder hold; attack no. 5
katate tori	a one-hand hold on one side, attack no. 1; or a one-hand hold on the opposite side, attack no. 2
katate tori ryote mochi	a two-hand hold on one hand, attack no. 3; or a two-hand hold on two hands, attack no. 4
kempo	an ancient martial art related to Chinese boxing (Shaolin) and karate
ki	centralized, coordinated energy considered as the energy of life itself
kogusoku	an ancient method of combat mentioned in connection with *kumiuchi* and *sumo* in the oldest records of the martial arts
koho tento undo or *koho ukemi undo*	basic exercise no. 19
koshi (goshi)	the lateral pelvis; hips

koshi nage	projection no. 4
koshi mawari	an ancient method of combat
kote gaeshi	immobilization no. 7
kote mawashi ho	immobilization no. 2
kokyu	total body-extension
kokyu dosa	special exercise of extension
kokyu ho undo	basic exercise no. 10
kokyu nage	a name given to projection no. 1, and in general to all other projections
kumiuchi	an ancient method of combat
kyu	a rank below *dan*
kyudo	the "way of the bow and arrow," the Japanese art of archery
ma-ai	basic distance
mandala	the spherical symbol of completeness and integrative balance derived from Indian metaphsics; the "wheel of life"
Mifune, Kyuzo	a great judo instructor, 1883–1965
migi	right
mune-tsuki	low blow to abdomen
Miyamoto Musashi	a famous swordsman who lived in the seventeenth century and made the style of fencing with two swords the basis of his own school of martial arts
nafudakake	the name board in a *dojo*
nage	the student who is attacked by *uke*, and who employs aikido strategy of defense to neutralize that attack
naginata	a curved spear once used by Japanese monks and samurai; also, the art of using it
nikyo; nikajo	immobilization no. 2
ninjutsu	the technique of *ninja*, the Japanese "commando" and super-spy
one point	a denomination for *hara*, the Centre made famous in aikido doctrine by Koichi Tohei, Chief Instructor of Hombu Dojo in Tokyo
Pa-kua	Chinese boxing method
Pericles	an Athenian general and statesman who died in 429 B.C.
ritsurei	standing salutation
ryu	school (as schools of the martial arts)
samurai	military retainer—feudal period
sankakutai	the geometrical figure of stability and potential motion adopted in aikido and other martial arts, with the feet in a triangular position
sankyo; sankajo	immobilization no. 3
satori	a Buddhist concept: enlightenment, or the moment of intense, total realization
sayu undo	basic exercise no. 13
seiza	sitting posture
Shaolin	ancient Chinese boxing reputed by most authors to be the forefather of karate and other arts of percussion

shiho nage	immobilization no. 6
shimoseki	lower side on the mat opposite *joseki*
shimoza	lower seat on the mat opposite *kamiza*
Shinto	the "way of the gods"; a national religion of Japan based on the cult of ancestors
shintai	straight motion
shizentai	basic, natural posture
shomen uchi	straight blow to the head; attack no. 13
sumi otoshi	projection no. 10
sumo	traditional Japanese wrestling
Suzuki, Daisetsu	famous author and scholar belonging to the School of Zen Buddhism
tachi oyogi	the martial art of swimming while in armor
tai sabaki	a circular motion
taiso	a basic exercise of aikido
taiyoku	a spherical symbol of completeness and integrative balance of Chinese derivation
Takuan	a famous abbot of the Zen School who wrote extensively on the mental aspects of his discipline considered as relevant in everyday living and in the martial arts (1573–1645)
tambo	the art of using the short stick
tantojutsu	the technique of knife-throwing
tao	the supreme essence of reality and existence (Chinese)
Taoism	the doctrine of total integration in the order of existence propounded by Lao Tzu
Tao Te Ching	Chinese classic book of Taoism
tatami	the mat on which a martial art is practiced
tedori	an ancient method of combat
tegatana	the outer edge of the hand when used as the blade of a sword
tegiki	an ancient method of combat
tekubi joho kosa undo	basic exercise no. 12
tekubi kosa undo	basic exercise no. 11
tekubi shindo	basic exercise no. 3
tenchi nage	projection no. 9
tenkan	a circular motion; "turning" in a spin
tsugi ashi	the follow-up step
ude furi undo	basic exercise no. 15
uke	the student who attacks *nage* and becomes the recipient of his opponent's strategy of aikido defense
ukemi	rolls and somersaults
UPA	Unified Power of Attack
UPD	Unified Power of Defense; also, defensive *ki*
ushiro kata tori	attack no. 9
ushiro kubi shime	attack no. 10
ushiro hiji tori	attack no. 8
ushiro tekubi tori	attack no. 7 and basic exercise no. 17

ushiro tori	attacks nos. 11 and 12
ushiro tori undo	basic exercise no. 16
wa	an ancient Japanese term for harmony, accord, and coordination
wajutsu	the technique of coordination
yari	straight spear
yarijutsu	the technique of using the straight spear
yawara	an ancient method of combat based on the principle of accord *(wa);* some authors believe it to represent the first matrix of the principle of harmony *(ai)* and the principle of suppleness *(ju)*
Yoga	a discipline of mental and physical development traced from early Indian metaphysics
yokomen uchi	a circular blow to the side of the head; attack no. 14
yonkyo	immobilization no. 4
zarei	a ceremonial bow from the sitting position
zazen	meditation posture and exercise employed in the School of Zen Buddhism, and in other disciplines as well
Zen	the intuitive discipline of enlightenment related to the Buddhist doctrine; called *Dhyana* in India, *Ch'an* in China

Selected Bibliography

I   **ON THE HISTORICAL AND PHILOSOPHICAL FOUNDATIONS OF AIKIDO**
Anesaki, Masaharu: *History of Japanese Religion,* Tokyo, 1963
Brinkley, Captain F.: *Japan,* Boston, 1902
Ch'u Chai and Winberg Chai (trans. and ed.): *The Humanist Way in Ancient China: Essential Works of Confucius,* New York, 1965
Creel, H. C.: *Chinese Thought—From Confucius to Mao-Tse-Tung,* Chicago, 1953
Coomaraswamy, Ananda K.: *Buddha and the Gospel of Buddhism,* London, 1916
Demoulin, Heinrich: *A History of Zen Buddhism,* New York, 1963
Hearn, Lafcadio: *Japan—An Attempt at Interpretation,* Tokyo, 1962
Herbert, Jean: *Introduction A' L'Asie,* Paris, 1960
Humphreys, Christmas: *The Wisdom of Buddhism,* London, 1960
Nitobe, Inazo: *Japan,* London, 1931
Lin, Yutang (trans. and ed.): *The Wisdom of Lao-Tse,* New York, 1948
Nakamura, Hajime: *Ways of Thinking of Eastern People: India-China-Tibet-Japan,* Honolulu, Hawaii, 1964
Northrop, F. S. C.: *The Meeting of the East and West,* New York, 1967
Reischauer, Edwin O.: *Japan—Past and Present,* New York, 1964
Sansom, George: *A History of Japan,* Stanford, California, 1958
Suzuki, Daisetsu T.: *Zen and Japanese Culture,* New York, 1960
Tsunoda, Ryusaku (comp.): *Sources of Japanese Tradition,* New York, 1958

II   **ON THE ESOTERIC FACTORS OF AIKIDO**
Conze, Edward: *Buddhist Meditation,* London, 1956
Humphreys, Christmas: *Concentration and Meditation,* London, 1959
Lasserre, Robert: *Etranges Pouvoirs,* Toulouse, 1960
Tohei, Koichi: *Aikido in Daily Life,* Tokyo, 1966
Von Durckeim, Karlfried Graf: *Hara-centre Vital de L'Homme,* Paris, 1964
——————: *The Japanese Cult of Tranquillity,* London, 1960

III   **ON THE STRATEGY AND TECHNIQUES OF AIKIDO**
Abe, Tadashi and Jean Zin: *L'Aikido.* Vols. I and II, Paris, 1958
Tohei, Koichi: *Aikido—The Arts of Self-defense,* Tokyo, 1961
——————: *This is Aikido,* Tokyo, 1966
Uyeshiba, Kisshomaru: *Aikido,* Tokyo, 1963

Index

abdominal: concept of, 69; breathing exercise, 107–9

advanced practice, 323

aggression; *see* attack

aikido: definition, 17; ethical purposes, 33, 359–63; practical purposes, 19, 26, 27

attack: importance of, 46; factors of, 47, 49–58; power of, 58–60; theory of, 48–60

attacking techniques, 56–58

balance, 76, 145–47

basic exercises: applications, 121–42; purposes of, 119–20

basic techniques: of attack, 55–58; of neutralization, 159–60

blows: in attack, 57; in defense (feint), 168

bow: ceremonial, 43; standing, 41

breath control, 107

breathing, special exercise, 107–9

calisthenics, 114

centralization: of thought, 18; objective, 70–71, 78–79; principle of, 69; subjective, 70–71, 73

centralized energy; see *ki*

Centre, 19, 21, 23; definition of, 69; of gravity, 23

choking techniques, in attack, 56–57

circuits of neutralization, 78, 83, 96–98, 100–3

classes, 41–44

club attacks, defense against, 338–39

combinations: in attack, 57; in defense, 318–22

concentration of strength, 80–85; special exercises for, 107–12

control, 20; principle of leading, 87–93

convergence of aggression, 54–55

coordination: aikido as, 17, 26; aggressive,

58–60; basic exercise of, 119–42; defensive, 79

dan, 35–36

defense: characteristics of, 65; concept of, 20; ethics of, 33–34; factors of, 47, 61

Deguchi, Wanisaburo, 29

direction: of the attack, 54; of the defense, 89, 93, 96–99

discipline of coordination, 17

distance, 145, 147–48

dynamic factors: of the attack, 47, 53–55; of the defense, 47, 144, 149

dynamic momentum, 53, 97

dynamic sphere, 100–3

dynamic spiral, 98

energy, 21–24, 79–86, 93, 107, 111–12, 119–21, 165, 323, 354, 359–60

ethics, 20, 33–34, 86, 361–62

etiquette, 41–44

exercises: basic, 119; formal *(kata),* 340–41; preliminary, 114; special, 103; stave, 336–40

extension: concept of, 23; principle of, 79–87; sitting exercise of, 109–11

falling, 139

force, 89

formal exercise, 340

foundations, 29–33

free style practice, 354–55; applications, 356–58

functional factors: of the attack, 47; of the defense, 47, 61, 143

fusion: of mind and body, 22; special exercises for, 103–12

gentleness, 77

373

grasping, 89, 163
guards; *see* stance
harmony, 17, 34, 361
hierarchy, 35
hip action, 77
holding techniques: of the attack, 56; of the defense; *see also* immobilizations

immobilizations: applications, 166–223; definition of, 165; classification of, 160, 165–66
inner energy; *see ki*
inner factors: of the attack, 47–48, 58; of the defense, 30, 47, 61, 62–69
intrinsic energy; *see ki*
injury: avoidance of, 19–20; caution against, 163–64

ki, 18–20, 79–87; definition of, 81; types of 84–85
killing, 20, 33
kneeling aikido: motion of, 324–25, 334–35; techniques of, 326–33
kyu, 35–36

leading control, principle of, 87–93
Leggett, T.P., 77
limbering-up exercises, 114

main sources of aikido, 30–33
major techniques of aikido; *see* immobilizations, projections, and combinations
martial arts: armed, 31; schools of, 33; unarmed, 32
mat: in the dojo, 40–41; practice on the; *see* kneeling aikido
meditation, 34; special exercise of, 107
mental energy, 17–18; extension of, 23, 81–87
Mitsujo Fujimoto, 29
morality of aikido; *see* ethics
motion: in attack, 53–55; in defense, 143–53; purposes of, 154–57
motivations: immediate or practical, 19–20, 26; remote or ethical, 33–34, 361–63
muscular strength, 80

Nakai, Masakatsu, 29
natural posture, 145
non-resistance, principle of, 89

organization of aikido, 35

outer factors: of the attack, 47–48; of the defense, 30, 61

pain, objective of, 51
partner practice, 160–64
physical factors: of the attack, 49–52; of the defense, 61
physical injury, theory of, 49–52
physical pain, 49, 51
physical preparation, 113–14
posture: basic, 41, 145–47; exercise of, 104; of defense, 145; sitting, 105; standing, 104
power: of attack, 58–60; of defense, 80–81
practice: basic, 45, 47; advanced, 323
practice hall, 40
preliminary exercises, 114–19
principles of aikido, 69
process of defense: factors, 62, 66; normal and abnormal, 65–66; factors of, 62, 66
projections: applications, 224–322; definition, 224; classification, 160, 165–66
promotion, 37–38

ranking system, 35–38
reaction, 62–67
relaxation, 77
relaxed atmosphere, 27
rolling, 139

safety, 163–64
Sakuma Shozan, 45
salutation: ceremonial, 43–44; standing, 41
self-defense, 17, 19–20, 26, 34
semi-spirals of neutralization, 98
sitting: extension, 109–11; position, 42; posture, 105; practice, 324–35
sliding; *see* stepping
stages of the process: of attack, 53–55; of defense, 143–45
somersaults, 139–42
speed: of the attack, 53; of defense, 93
sphericity, 19; principle of, 93–95
spirals of neutralization, 98
spirit, 17
sport, aikido as, 26
stances, 148
standing posture, exercise of, 104; stave exercises, 336–40
stepping: alternated, 151, combination, 153; follow-up, 151; pivot, 152; spin, 152–53
stillness, special exercise of, 106–7
strategy of neutralization, 24

strength, 81, 89
suppleness, 114
Suzuki, Daisetz(u), 75

Takeda, Sakaku, 29
Takuan, 75
technical factors: of the attack, 47, 55; of the defense, 47, 143
techniques of neutralization: advanced, 323; against armed attacks, 342–49; against multiple attack, 350-53; against unarmed attacks, 166–322; basic, 159; classification, 160; definition, 159

tension, 77
tests: for promotion, 37–38; for special exercises, 111–12
Tohei, Koichi, 23, 67, 69, 82, 91, 92
Tojawa, Tokusaburo, 29

unarmed attacks, 55
unbendable arm, 23, 82–83
unified power of the attack, 87–88
uniform, 39
unity of mind and body, 22
Uyeshiba, Morihei, 29–30, 33, 35, 81, 360–62

Also by Oscar Ratti and Adele Westbrook

Secrets of the Samurai:
The Martial Arts of Feudal Japan

❖ ❖ ❖

"Highly recommended." –*Library Journal*
"The only work of its kind." –*The San Diego Union*

Secrets of the Samurai is the definitive study of the martial arts of feudal Japan, and explains in detail the weapons, techniques, strategies, and principles of combat that made the Japanese warrior a formidable foe. Beginning with a panoramic survey of the tumultuous early struggles of warlords contending for political ascendancy, the work outlines the relentless progression of the military class toward absolute power and is lavishly illustrated with line drawings and charts. In addition to illustrating actual methods of combat, Ratti and Westbrook discuss the crucial training methods necessary to develop a warrior's inner power and to concentrate all of his energies into a single force. *Secrets of the Samurai* is the essential text for anyone with an interest in Japanese combat techniques, weaponry, or military tradition.

❖

ISBN 0-8048-1684-0